FETISH

The Ambassadors, Hans Holbein. Courtesy of The National Gallery, London.

Fetish

An Erotics of Culture

Henry Krips

CORNELL UNIVERSITY PRESS

ITHACA, NEW YORK

First published 1999 by Cornell University Press
First printing, Cornell Paperbacks, 1999

Printed in the United States of America

Library of Congress Cataloging-in-Publication Data

Krips, Henry.
Fetish : an erotics of culture / Henry Krips.
p.   cm.
Includes bibliographical references.
ISBN 0-8014-3542-0 (hardcover : alk. paper).—ISBN 0-8014-8537-1
(pbk. : alk. paper)
1. Social sciences and psychoanalysis.   2. Psychoanalysis and
culture.   3. Fetishism (Sexual behavior)   4. Gaze—Psychological
aspects.   I. Title.
BF175.4.S65K75   1999
306.7—dc21   99-22831

Cloth printing   10 9 8 7 6 5 4 3 2 1

Paperback printing   10 9 8 7 6 5 4 3 2 1

FOR MY PARENTS,
HENRY AND LUISE

Contents

Preface ix

Introduction: Fetish and the Gaze 1

I
INTRODUCING LACAN

1 The Song Not the Singer: Signifier, *Objet a*, Fetish 15

2 Body and Text: The Roots of the Unconscious 33

II
FETISH

3 A Slave to Desire: Defetishizing the Colonial Subject 45

4 Fetish and the Native Subject 57

III
SOCIALIZING THE PSYCHIC:
FROM INTERPELLATION TO GAZE

5 Interpellation, Antagonism, Repetition 73

6 The Ambassador's Body: Unscreening the Gaze 97

7   The Vice of the Virtual Witness   119

8   Seeing Texts   133

IV
INTERPASSIVITY AND THE POSTMODERN

9   Interpassivity and the Knowing Wink:
     Mystery Science Theater 3000   153

10   Crash and Subversion   171

     Appendix: The Oedipus Connection   185

     Bibliography   193

     Index   197

Preface

My introduction to social theory came through reading and teaching Althusser, Derrida, Foucault, and Lacan. This group of authors, situated on the break between what seemed to be a moribund structuralism (associated with Lévi-Strauss, Mauss, and Durkheim) and a new, intellectually vigorous poststructuralism, promised new concepts of the text and subjectivity. The works of these writers also hinted at the possibility of a new politics, one that bypassed the doctrinaire and formulaic certainties of traditional left-wing critique.

The intellectual project that I, like many others, took from this experience was a fascination with the constitution of the subject, specifically with the relation between the subject and that which, in an older vocabulary, was called the social setting. Lacan, in particular, became a key figure in this project, since it was clear that, through his reading of Freud, a substantive break had taken place from earlier structuralist and Marxist conceptions of the subject as a *ficelle*, a placeholder in a social structure. The Althusserian problematic of interpellation, specifically in its Lacanian reworking by Screen theory, and later by feminist critics, was a key site at which this project took shape. The problematic of interpellation also became a key point of transition at which the "serious" work of social theory intersected with what, on occasions, seemed to be lighter issues in cultural studies, film theory, and communication.

The book that follows has been written at this particular conjuncture. Its framing concern is with the intersection of the social and the individual, or, in theoretical terms, with the interface between Freud and Marx in their Lacanian and Althusserian reformulations. Two concepts provide key points of focus for my investigation: the fetish and the gaze. The strategic advantage of these concepts is that each has been theorized from two sides, as it were—from within a social theoretic framework (I have in mind Foucault's work on the panopticon, and the Marxist conception of commodity fetishism) as well as from a psychoanalytic perspective (Freud's work on the fetish and Lacan's on the gaze).

Some of the material in this book has appeared elsewhere. Parts of Chapter 4 overlap with an article, "Fetish and the Native Subject," which appeared in *Boundary 2* (Krips 1996); a much simplified version of Chapter 5 appeared as "Interpellation, Antagonism and Repetition" in *Rethinking Marxism* (Krips 1994b); and there is some slight overlap between Chapter 7 and "Ideology, Rhetoric and Boyle's New Experiments," which appeared in *Science in Context* (Krips 1994a). An earlier version of Chapter 6 appears as a chapter of *At the Intersection*, edited by Tom Rosteck, published by Guilford Press. I am indebted to the publishers for permission to reprint extracts.

In this work, which has taken far longer to complete than I could ever have imagined, I have been aided immeasurably by colleagues, friends, students, and casual acquaintances who shared my interests. My introduction into social theory was eased through the intellectual generosity and rigor of a friend and colleague, Geoff Sharp, with whom I taught social theory at the University of Melbourne for several years. The material on Lacan, centered in Chapters 1 and 2, but also pervading the book as a whole, has benefited greatly from discussion with Marie-Luise Angerer, Valerie Krips, Renata Salecl, Susan Schwartz and Slavoj Zizek, as well as Patrizia Lombardo and John Beverley, with whom I had the great pleasure of teaching Lacan at the University of Pittsburgh. Jonathan Arac and Ronald Judy generously read and commented upon the material on *Beloved* and about Homi Bhabha. The discussions of the gaze (Chapters 6, 7, and 8) and postmodernism (Chapters 9 and 10) have grown out of work undertaken at the University of Pittsburgh over the last few years, but also in Austria. I am grateful to the Internationales Forschungszentrum Kulturwissenschaften for enabling this work, as well as to my Austrian friends and colleagues, especially Marie-Luise Angerer, Lutz Musner, and Daniela Tugendhat, for much support and vigorous intellectual exchanges. Bernie Kendler, my editor at Cornell, has been amazingly supportive throughout this project; and I would also like to thank John LeRoy, Caroline Lurie, Nancy Zafris, and my son, Henry Krips, for contributing to the final work. Undoubtedly, however, the main influence upon this book, every page of which bears her imprint, is Valerie Krips. I am grateful to her in more ways than I can say.

FETISH

Introduction: Fetish and the Gaze

The American critic Jeffrey Masson, writing in the British *Guardian* newspaper on March 29, 1997, asks how "crazy" were the thirty-nine members of Heaven's Gate, the Californian millennial cult whose members had performed a ritual mass suicide a few days previously. He answers his own question: "It is in the nature of a cult to have enemies. This paranoia gives an edge to everyday existence: you can never tell when you will be seized by dark and evil forces, so be on the alert." He then generalizes these remarks to encompass not only what he calls "California fruitcake" but also J. R. R. Tolkien, under whose spell, Masson confesses, he had fallen: "The British know this well [the attraction of paranoid universes] from the extraordinary popularity of Tolkien's *Lord of the Rings*. It is just such a universe that Tolkien creates. . . . I was already a little bit alarmed just by reading it. I saw the appeal, I felt it, I gave in to it (the way some people give in to the music of Wagner). I could sense certain fascistic tendencies underneath the writing, a kind of overt anti-semitism."

In these comments Masson goes beyond identifying a group's behavior as symptoms of a collective psychic disorder. He also hints at the possibility of mass political and psychic disturbances—paranoia, fascism, anti-semitism—emanating from apparently innocent cultural artifacts such as *The Hobbit* and (perhaps less innocently) the *Ring* cycle. In an unintended irony, Masson repeats the trope of "dark and evil forces" which he criticizes in the pronouncements of the Heaven's Gate cult. Indeed, the irony

1

is doubled: Masson, arch-critic of Freud, employs Freudian concepts such as paranoia on a flimsier basis than Freud ever countenanced.

The feminist legal critic Catherine MacKinnon, arguing from within a psychological rather than a Freudian framework, claims that reading pornography has a brutalizing effect upon the male psyche. Porn, she claims, functions as "primitive conditioning, with pictures and words as sexual stimuli. . . . It makes them [men] want to [rape]; when they believe they can, when they feel they can get away with it, they do" (MacKinnon 1993, 16, 19). She continues: "The message of these materials, and there is one . . . is 'get her.' . . . This message is addressed directly to the penis, delivered through an erection and taken out on women in the real world" (21). According to MacKinnon, arguing from within a behaviorist model of the psyche, porn directly reflects male psychic reality by helping to create it. In a nutshell, pornography conditions men to sexual violence.[1] Like her associate Masson, MacKinnon sees the cultural as a source of widespread, perverse psychic effects.

Claims that cultural forms are causally linked to psychic structures are also advanced in contexts less hostile to Freud. In a recent book, *Fetishism and Curiosity*, the feminist film critic Laura Mulvey tells us that her focus will be upon "the way that feminist theory has constructed collective fantasy into a 'symptomology' through an analysis of popular culture, particularly the cinema. . . . Erotic images disavow those aspects of society's sexuality that are hidden and disturbing. In this sense, the obvious discourse of sexuality appears as symptoms, literally, in the case of cinema, screening its repressions" (Mulvey 1996, xiii–xiv). And the Lacanian critic Joan Copjec also proposes a link between cultural form and psychic structure. Among Chinese men, she claims, fetishism takes on a cultural dimension. For example, the disavowal associated with it finds form not in words but rather in the culture of binding women's feet. Thus the split or divided form of a cultural object, the woman's folded foot, directly reflects the split psychic structure of the men who revere it: "If the Chinese man mutilates the woman's foot *and* reveres it, it is the foot that wears the mark of this division, not the Chinese man" (Copjec 1978, 111).

Homi Bhabha, the postcolonial theorist, also invokes the trope of reflection as a means of describing relations between the cultural and psychic domains. In particular, he explains the internal dissonances of antebellum Southern discourse about slaves, specifically slave literature, by

---

1. The psychic reality MacKinnon countenances is pruned back to verifiable psychological mechanisms and structures, such as conditioning, beliefs, attitudes, behavioral dispositions, and so on, rather than the lusher Freudian psycho-scape implied by Masson's remarks in the *Guardian*.

proposing that its structure reflects the fetishistic form of master-slave relations. In his influential essay "The Other Question," for example, he
points to "contradictions and heterogeneity" surrounding racial stereotypes and argues for a "functional link" between such stereotypes and the
fixation of the fetish: "For fetishism is always a 'play' or vacillation between the archaic affirmation of wholeness/similarity—in Freud's terms:
'All men have penises'; in ours 'All men have the same skin/race/cul-
ture'—and the anxiety associated with lack and difference—again, for
Freud 'Some men do not have penises'; for us 'Some do not have the same
skin/race/culture'" (Bhabha 1994, 74, 82).

In this book, I explore such suggestions that cultural practices are the effects—and indeed symptoms—of psychic disorders. I also examine the
converse claim that cultural artifacts, whether books by Tolkien, music by
Wagner, pornography, or the films of David Lynch, may take on a constitutive role in psychically structuring their audiences (although without
necessarily imprinting or "conditioning" them as MacKinnon says). This
project involves considerable intellectual and political risk. As Masson's
diagnosis of the Heaven's Gate cult (sight unseen) and his speedy demoli-
tion of Tolkien indicate, claims that psychic structures mirror cultural
forms are open to abuse; they provide a cheap way of pathologizing marginal groups and activities. Freud himself, as I indicate in the next section,
issues a stern warning to interpretations that link psychic and cultural
realms.

Nevertheless, the project of linking the psychic and the cultural is worth-
while. It promises rewards: a new cultural politics that not only breaks
with the socialization model characteristic of older style Marxism but also
rejects more traditional idealist approaches. In this context the notions of
fetishism and the gaze are of central importance. But the way they have
been theorized assigns them an essentially conservative function. Screen
theory, one of the most influential theories of visual culture of the last
thirty years, takes the gaze as a mechanism for the transmission and reproduction of ideological effects. And, because it involves taking pleasure
from serving the Other's desire, fetishism (in its Freudian sense) has also
been taken as an exclusively conservative psychic formation.[2]

In this book I argue against Screen theory's concept of the gaze as a
mechanism for producing ideology. Instead, I present the gaze as ideologically constituted in its own right, an object to which ideological meanings
attach via chains of unconscious associations (Chapters 5 and 6). I also
counter the traditional picture of fetishism as an inherently conservative

2. In Chapter 4 I provide an illustration of fetishism operating in a conservative mode, a
point to which I return in Chapter 10.

psychic formation (Chapters 9 and 10). For example, in the course of analyzing David Cronenberg's film *Crash*, I demonstrate how a fetishistic scopic regime undermines the ideological forms of Hollywood domestic realism by exposing its effects upon the viewer. I also show how fetishism plays a subversive role in reversing the tendency to "abstraction" (in the sense of the erasure of difference), which is so characteristic of modernization (Sharp 1985). In particular, I show how *Crash* inducts viewers into a fetishistic scopic regime which drives a wedge between the human eye, with which viewers engage the filmic image, and the inhuman mechanical eye of the camera, which watches on their behalf. Thus, in a direct physical way, the film's fetishistic visual economy undermines the material processes of modernization as well as metaphysical theories of vision that collapse human seeing and mechanical techniques of signal transmission/scanning into a single abstract category of "vision." Briefly, in *Crash*, fetishism takes on a subversive role by undermining not only the ideological forms of Hollywood realism but also the modernizing processes of abstraction through which differences, specifically the difference between human and nonhuman, are erased.

Psychocultural Connections and Their Vicissitudes

In *Totem and Taboo* (1913), Freud points out that although cultural practices, such as religion and art, may resemble neurotic behavior, they are ontogenetically quite different. Neurotic behavior, he argues, is the result of "sexual instincts," which are "essentially the private affair of each individual," whereas cultural practices, such as religion and art, are driven by "social instincts" and involve "collective effort" (Freud 1989, 73–74). Consequently, actions that would be symptoms of sexual disorder, were they performed on an individual basis, may not be so when performed collectively as part of a cultural practice. A soldier's cold-blooded killing on the battlefield does not indicate a psychotic or sadistic pathology. Or, as Freud makes the point, collective behavior resulting from a social taboo may resemble the elaborate avoidance and cleansing rituals practiced by an obsessive, but at the level of psychic structure there is a world of difference between taboo and obsession: "A warning must be issued at this point. The similarity between taboo and obsessional sickness may be no more than a matter of externals; it may apply only to the *forms* in which they are manifested [the behavioral symptoms] and not extend to their essential character [psychic structure]. . . . It would be obviously hasty and unprofitable to infer the existence of any internal relationship from such points of agreement as these" (Freud 1989, 26).

In general terms, Freud's point is that what appears at first sight to be a collective symptom, indicative of a mass psychic disorder, may merely be ritualized conduct or have other less alarming psychic or nonpsychic causes. Indeed, on second glance, the possibility that the members of a large and diverse population have a uniform psychopathological profile, a view embodied in common national stereotypes—"the obsessive German," "the hysterical Frenchman," "the paranoid Albanian," and so on—seems totally implausible, not to mention politically regressive. The intellectual rationale behind such stereotyping is often a crude kind of "cultural dopism," which depicts popular cultural artifacts, such as pornography or advertising, as power points from which ways of being and acting, even psychic structures, disseminate into the populace. Such ideas (often associated with Adorno's work on mass culture) have been effectively discredited by recent media scholars who, influenced by Michel Foucault, Michel de Certeau, and others, have argued that resistance plays an important role in popular reactions to contemporary media (see Fiske 1987, chap. 5). The notorious attempt by Nazi science to develop personality profiles for national or large-scale social groups—Gypsies, Aryans, Jews, homosexuals, and so on—has also played a role in discrediting notions of collective psychic profiles. The American anthropologists Ruth Benedict and Margaret Mead attempted a similar project with equally dismal results (Heald and Deluz 1994).

Even Masson seems to concede that individuals may resist national psychological profiles when, in his *Guardian* article, he allows that, thanks to a certain "innate scepticism (of cults and, I am delighted to say, of psychoanalysis)," the English have by and large resisted the seductive invitations to paranoia and fascism that, he claims, are incipient in Tolkien's work. Nevertheless, the spell exerted by the idea of national stereotypes is evident in Masson's reference to an English "innate scepticism." Masson appeals to one national characteristic—skepticism—to break up another—fascism. Indeed, his whole article is permeated with nationalistic stereotyping, right down to the final comment, "I really do love the British."

Arguments against linking the cultural and psychic realms also seem apposite in criticizing MacKinnon's claim that there exists a direct causal connection between pornography and a psychic characteristic of its male consumers, namely sexual aggression. At a theoretical level, her argument fails to take into account Freud's point that identification with a phantasy figure flows readily across gender lines. For example, in the Dora case, Freud argues that Dora's behavior manifests an unconscious desire for Frau K., her father's lover and suitor's wife. For Freud her desire does not indicate any sexual instability. Instead, through an identification with her father's desire, it signals an unconscious paternal identification. In other words, for Freud the significant aspect of Dora's phantasy is not the sexual content of the desire but rather the paternal position from which she engages with it. By parity of reasoning, it follows that quite "normal" male readers of porn may identify with the position of woman victim rather than male aggressor, in which case their aggressive tendencies cannot be reinforced in the simplistic way that MacKinnon suggests.[3]

In short, as Laura Kipnis points out, neither the biology nor gender of readers of *Hustler* magazine determines the form of their identification with its pornographic materials, let alone forces them into a common psychic response (Kipnis 1996, 196). In the same way, one may argue, gender-swapping phantasy games played by Net users do not indicate their gender instability. On the contrary, one might turn the argument around and conclude that the preponderance of biological males among Net users suggests that even when playing at being a woman, they are engaging in a "boys' game."

The empirical and theoretical arguments so far seem to militate against any project to establish connections between the psychic and cultural domains. This conclusion is premature, however. Instead, the lesson to be learned is that if Freudian concepts such as paranoia and hysteria are to be used in the social and cultural domains, then careful attention must be paid to their conditions of application as well as scope. In particular, the psychic effects produced by a cultural artifact may be highly localized rather than general in the way that Masson and MacKinnon suggest.

Such localization of psychic effects is evident in the case of Gustave Flaubert's obsessive relation with his novel *Madame Bovary* (discussed in Chapter 8). In cases such as these, we must surrender Durkheim's influential conception that cultural objects are resonance points at which a whole society (a "primal horde") expresses and produces a collective identity for its members. On the contrary, it will emerge that particular users of a cultural object may adapt it to suit their own peculiar strategic and psychic ends.

In other cases, such as Hans Holbein's painting *The Ambassadors* (which I discuss in Chapter 6), I argue that on occasions psychic and ideological struc-

---

3. MacKinnon attempts to bolster her argument by claiming that porn, unlike other kinds of writing, blurs the boundary between representation and reality. Porn really *is* violence rather than merely its representation. By reading it, men are brutalized: habituated, conditioned, to violence. Thus their psyches are shaped along the lines of the pornographic images and words they read. However, without some independent argument for why porn as opposed to other forms of literature broaches the boundary between representation and reality, such claims amount to special pleading. In any case, the point remains that such conditioning of a man to violence may condition him to being a victim rather than an aggressor.

tures may become imbricated in such a way that a more widespread relation of reflection results. Even in this case, however, viewers' psychic profiles do not reflect the formal structure of the artifact in a uniform and transhistorical fashion. On the contrary, as I show in the Appendix, in my discussion of the Oedipus myth, only for very basic psychic structures will the relation between the psychic and the cultural assume an effectively universal dimension.

Socializing the Fetish

Because it has been theorized from a cultural as well as a psychic point of view, the fetish is a convenient site at which to begin an exploration of psychocultural connections. In his *Three Essays on the Theory of Sexuality*, Freud illustrates the fetish by means of a piece of fur, which, because it resembles pubic hair, may come to function as an adult's memorial to that moment when as a child he noticed his mother's lack of a penis and thus faced the possibility of his own castration: "The replacement of the [sexual] object by a fetish is determined by a symbolic connection of thought, of which the person concerned is usually not conscious. . . . No doubt the part played by fur as a fetish owes its origin to an association with the hair of the *mons veneris*. . . . Symbolism such as this is not always unrelated to sexual experiences in childhood" (Freud 1975, 21).

Freud emphasizes that such memorials to the moment of first contact with maternal lack are not necessarily veridical in content. Instead, they may point to a structure of lack that, although haunting the subject from birth, only later, and retrospectively, comes to assume a concrete form in connection with an imagined primal trauma, such as the first sight of the mother's genitals.[4] Of course, pieces of fur may not carry such meaning for everyone. When they do, however, this fact is signaled by the sort of unrealistic anxiety (an anxiety with no apparent appropriate object) that, according to Freud, gathers at the site of any such repetition (*Wiederholung*) of the primal scene.[5]

The function of the fetish is as much that of a screen as a memorial. That is, it stands in the place of that which cannot be remembered directly. It substitutes for that which is and must remain repressed (*verdrängt*). As

4. Arguably the whole notion of childhood innocence is an aspect of such retrospectively installed narratives of childhood trauma.
5. See Laplanche and Pontalis 1974, 36, 379, for a discussion of Freud's distinction between realistic and unrealistic anxiety. I return to this question in detail in Chapter 8.

such, the fetish is also a site of disavowal (*Verleugnung*), and specifically of contradiction: we know that fur is not pubic hair, *but even so*, in a way that is never clearly specified, we know that it is:

> In cases of *fetishism* . . . the patient (who is almost always male) not recognizing the fact that females have no penis—a fact which is extremely undesirable to him since it is a proof of the possibility of his being castrated . . . disavows his own sense-perception which showed him that the female genitals lack a penis. . . . The disavowed perception does not, however, remain entirely without influence. He takes hold of something else instead—a part of the body or some other object—and assigns it the role of the penis he cannot do without. It is usually something that he in fact saw at the moment at which he saw the female genitals. (Freud 1969, 59–60)

This traditional conception of the fetish strongly implicates Freud's theory of castration and thus accords a privileged place to the penis in the constitution of the human psychic economy. By distinguishing the penis from the phallus, Lacan's reworking of the Freudian architectonic promises to avoid such privileging. In particular, Lacan allows that whereas interest in the penis is historically and culturally contingent, something which he calls "the phallus" enjoys an omnihistorical significance. He defines the phallus as the signifier of lack in the Other, where the place of the Other (which may be occupied by the mother, a policeman, or any other authority figure) is the externally projected position from which the subject looks for an answer to the question of his or her own desire. According to Lacan, the subject projects this question in the form "*Che vuoi?*" "What do you [the Other] want?"—a question that, as the subject traverses his or her phantasy, takes on a new form: "What does he [the Other] want of me?" (Lacan 1977, 312).[6]

Lacan thus differs from the overtly patriarchal Freud, for whom confrontation with the possibility of loss or absence of the penis functions as a key moment in the accession to subjectivity.[7] Lacan, by contrast, argues that the accession to subjectivity involves introducing the subject into an economy of lack defined in relation to the phallus. In patriarchal societies,

6. In this context, the choice of the name "phallus" is unfortunate, since it carries with it penile connotations that open Lacan unnecessarily to accusations of phallocentrism. Admittedly certain of Lacan's remarks encourage such accusations, specifically his (questionable) claim that, because of its capacity for turgidity, the penis is uniquely favored as a phallic organ—see Lacan 1977, 319–320.

7. According to Freud, the child glimpsing the mother's genitals experiences it as her lack of a penis.

such as our own, the penis happens to occupy the position of the phallus, but this coincidence should not blind us to the fact that in the final analysis the phallus is defined in terms of a psychic economy of lack rather than the topological accidents of the male anatomy.

The Lacanian reworking of the Freudian architectonic (which I discuss further in Chapter 2) enables a reconceptualization of the fetish. Lacan distinguishes between the object that a subject desires—the "object of desire"—and another object that he designates the "*objet a.*" The *objet a* has a dual function. It is not only the object-cause of desire but also the object of the drive, that is, the object around which the subject turns in order to derive pleasure. The relation between the *objet a,* the desiring subject, and the object of desire resembles (I argue in Chapter 1) the relation between the chaperone, the suitor, and the beloved. By functioning as a site at which the suitor exercises his or her skills in order to get access to the object of desire, the chaperone covertly provides him with an opportunity for gaining pleasure (perhaps his only pleasure). Although the chaperone is not herself an object of desire, by standing in the way of what the suitor wants she becomes part of a structure that sustains, that is, causes, his desire. In short, like the *objet a,* she is covertly the object-cause of desire and a source of pleasure, without herself being desired.

I argue that the fetish is a special instance of the *objet a,* one for which repression is breached to the extent that the subject more or less clearly recognizes the real source of his pleasure, and thus enters an economy of disavowal. In this way, the fetish is reconceived in a way that divorces it from its specifically Freudian meaning as a memorial to the mother's lack of a penis.

The problem, then, is how to transpose the Lacanian conception of the fetish, which is geared to individual psychic structures, into the social arena. Althusser's notion of interpellation assists in this endeavor (Chapter 5). Althusser is concerned with the question of how the social constitutes individuals as subjects. Individuals, he argues, become subjects in response to being addressed, or "interpellated," by what he calls Ideological State Apparatuses. But he is less than fully helpful about how interpellation discharges its constitutive role; for instance, he makes no mention of the creation of desire. I argue that the Freudian notion of repetition (*Wiederholung*) helps to provide an answer here. By addressing subjects collectively and in incoherent terms, interpellation functions as a site of what Freud calls repetition, that is, a site where subjects repeat their own primal lack, projected as an incoherence within the terms in which they are interpellated. From a Lacanian perspective I argue that, as repetitions of the primal scene, interpellations become sites of anxiety, and thus sites for the production of the desire with which subjects respond to the question posed by their own lack: "Who am I—what do I want?" The question of whether such desire is fetishistic devolves, then, upon the issue of whether the corresponding *objet a* is also an object of disavowal.

I consider whether the concept of the fetish can be successfully transposed to the social domain in a range of cases. In particular, I criticize Bhabha's analysis of fetishism among black slave cultures (Chapter 3). In other cases, however, fetishism takes on a collective dimension: the Hopi Katcina dance and Ojibwa totemic identifications, I argue, are associated with fetishistic structures of desire; and the Oedipus myth operated as one element in a fetishistic structure of desire centered upon relations between a Greek (male) citizen, his wife, and the *eromenos*, a young male lover (Chapter 4).

Café Life and the Gaze

Because the gaze, like the fetish, has been theorized from both a cultural and a psychic point of view, especially by film theorists associated with the journal *Screen*, it too is a convenient site at which to situate an exploration of psychocultural connections. What Lacan calls the gaze is akin to what Roland Barthes calls the *"punctum."* Barthes develops this concept in the context of a distinction between the "true photograph" and the myriad banal images that circulate in the media. The surfaces of these banal images are covered in their entirety by visual elements to which meaning adheres by courtesy of highly conventionalized cultural codes. Such elements, which constitute the *"studium,"* evoke at most a polite interest or prurient "half-desire" (Barthes 1993, 26–28, 42–43). A "true" photograph by contrast, one that makes its viewers "pensive" (38), is distinguished by a *punctum*, which breaks up the tedium of the *studium*. The *punctum* is a detail or spot that arrests the viewer's eye, or, as Barthes says, "pricks" it. Refusing conformity with any creative logic, the *punctum* is a point of real violence, which in its sheer contingency, oddity, or even uncanniness violates the familiar codes of the *studium* (40, 41, 51).[8]

The *punctum* challenges the viewer, who feels himself under scrutiny, challenged to make sense of what is seen. As Barthes points out, the paradoxical nature of the *punctum* spills over onto the viewer, who is left without a sense of how he or she is seen. Thus the experience takes on the paradoxical dimensions of being looked at but knowing no one is looking.

---

8. At such points the picture does violence to the viewer even when the object it represents is not violent at all. Thus pictures with *punctums* constitute reversals of newspaper representations of violence, which do no violence at all despite their horrific content.

Barthes illustrates this phenomenon with a story taken from life: "The other day, in a cafe, a young boy came in alone, glanced around the room, and occasionally his eyes rested on me; I then had the certainty that he was *looking at* me without however being sure that he was *seeing* me; an inconceivable distortion: how can we look without seeing?" (111).

The *punctum* is closely related to what Lacan calls the gaze, which he illustrates with the story of an experience at sea. A fisherman, Petit-Jean, "pointed out to me something floating on the surface of the waves. It was a small can, a sardine can. It floated there in the sun, a witness to the canning industry, which we, in fact, were supposed to supply. It glittered in the sun. And Petit-Jean said to me —*You see that can? Do you see it? Well, it doesn't see you!* . . . I was not terribly amused at hearing myself addressed in this humorous, ironical way" (Lacan 1981, 95–96). Thus the gaze, like the *punctum*, is a distortion precipitating the viewer into looking back at himself or herself, into interrogating what is seen, "doubling reality" and "making it vacillate" (Barthes 1993, 41).

Walter Benjamin also offers a representative anecdote which points to the phenomenon of the gaze: "Looking at someone carries the implicit expectation that our look will be returned by the object of our gaze. When this expectation is met (which, in the case of thought processes, can apply equally to the eye of the mind and to a glance pure and simple), there is an experience of the aura to the fullest extent" (Benjamin 1973, 147). In Benjamin's terms, then, the tin can in Lacan's story takes on an "auratic" quality. Lacan's failure to see Petit-Jean's joke indicates that the tin can is a site not only of aura, however, but also of that which Benjamin opposes to the auratic, namely the raw shock of the lived, manifested as signs of anxiety. In short, as Terry Eagleton suggests, the Lacanian concept of the gaze links the elements of aura and shock, which Benjamin opposes (Eagleton 1981, 35, 38–39).

Barthes associates the *punctum* with striking visual elements in photographs, such as the strapped pumps worn on the feet of a slave girl (Barthes 1993, 43), but also with unusual "life" situations, such as the searching glance that looked over and overlooked him sitting in a cafe. But he offers no unified mechanism to account for such disparate effects. The "true" photograph, he tells us, creates its effect by doing violence to conventional expectations (the *studium*), but it is not so easy to see how this same account would apply to the case of the young boy's look. A similar difficulty affects Lacan's conception of the gaze, which he applies indiscriminately to images, such as Holbein's painting *The Ambassadors*, as well as to "life" situations, such as the glittering tin can floating on the sea.

Some of Barthes's remarks suggest that the gaze is an almost objective structure, supervening upon purely formal elements of an image. But elsewhere, it seems, Barthes intends the gaze as a private phenomenon, a relation between a particular viewer and an image. For instance, he allows that the photo of his mother may exert a spell for him but for no one else. This ambiguity between objectivity and subjectivity points to a further difficulty, which enables a return to my central question: How can a subjective psychoanalytic conception, like the gaze, account for the public, objective effects of images? How is it possible to bridge the gap between individual psychic responses and the communal effects of cultural artifacts?

I suggest answers to these question through the study of a series of examples; these include not only images—Holbein's painting *The Ambassadors* (Chapter 6), the television show *Mystery Science Theater 3000* (Chapter 9), and Cronenberg's film *Crash* (Chapter 10)—but also written texts which have an impact upon the visual imagination of the reader— Flaubert's *Madame Bovary* and Boyle's scientific experimental manual *New Experiments Physico-Chemical* (Chapters 7 and 8). My concern in studying these cases is not to expose Freudian themes in the contents of the various texts; rather, I employ psychoanalytic theory as a resource for illuminating and explaining constitutive effects.

I

INTRODUCING LACAN

1

The Song Not the Singer:
Signifier, *Objet a*, Fetish

In his collection of essays *Écrits,* Lacan describes a game in which a
group of children sing a nursery rhyme, "The dog goes miaow, the cat
goes woof-woof" (Lacan 1977, 303–304). To talk literally of the children's
aim or even intention in this context is inappropriate, since, as I argue in
my discussion of the *Fort-Da* game later in this chapter, such games pre-
date, indeed contribute to, the emergence of structures of desire and in-
tentionality. Nevertheless, from the point of view of their actions, it *appears* retrospectively as if the children intentionally made a mistake, that
is, sent out a wrong signal, and in that restricted sense it may be said that
they practice, or, more correctly, will have been practicing, a deception.

But who is the audience upon whom the deception is practiced? Lacan
remarks in a related context: "The child . . . does not address the other, if
one uses here the theoretical discourse derived from the function of the *I*
and the *you*. But there must be others there—they don't speak to a particular person, they just speak, if you'll pardon the expression, *à la cantonade*," where the phrase *"à la cantonade"* means "to no one in particular,
to the company at large" (Lacan 1981, 208; Lacan is, of course, punning
upon his own name here). In other words, each child sings for him or herself, or, more correctly, for a self-projection onto the other children who
are present, a projection that depends upon the fact that the children are
able to hear themselves singing. Thus, it appears, each child deceives him

15

or herself. The proof is that a child continues playing the game even when no one else is listening.[1]

The children's squeals of delight when they hear their mistake indicates that they recognize the self-deception. Nevertheless, they repeat it over and over again in order, it seems, to reexperience the pleasure of spotting their mistake. In that sense, then, the deception is doubled. That is, seeing through one deception is instrumental in falling for another.

The words of the song function not merely as signals (what Lacan refers to as "signs") but rather as signifiers, separable from the particular meanings they carry. Specifically, by systematically switching word order in a way that literally makes no-sense/nonsense, the children display a practical knowledge that words are elements in a signifying system governed by rules of substitution and combination, and that, by breaking the rules, word sense is lost. The children may not know this consciously, but the game shows that at a practical level they know it nonetheless: "The child, by disconnecting the animal (dog) from its cry ('woof-woof'), suddenly raises the sign to the function of the signifier" (Lacan 1977, 304). In Lacan's later terminology, the game may be said to embody a recognition of the sign's "dyadic" nature (Lacan 1981, 236). The Lacanian name for the signifier "woof-woof," which, through the double deception enacted in the game, comes to stand in the place of another signifier "miaow," is the Freudian term *"Vorstellungsrepräsentanz"* (representative of a representation).[2]

Is the structure of double deception sufficient to establish the signifier in its full status as a linguistic signifier, an element in what Lacan calls "Speech"? A certain ambiguity attends Lacan's pronouncements on this issue. He draws a distinction between a form of deception that animals practice, namely, "the pretence to be found in physical combat or sexual display" (Lacan 1977, 305), and a form of double deception that only humans undertake: "But an animal does not pretend to pretend. He does not make false tracks whose deception lies in the fact that they will be taken as false, while being in fact true ones, ones, that is, that indicate his true trail" (305). To be specific, human quarry, unlike animals, may cover their footprints on a path so carelessly that a hunter will "see through" the apparent dissimulation, and so presume that the quarry has gone down a second path. The hunter is then deceived by the quarry taking the first

1. In the terms that I foreshadowed in the Introduction, for each child the other children occupy the place of the Other, and may indeed be seen as stimuli for setting such a structure in place. I return to this issue below.
2. In the next chapter I present a more refined version of Lacan's concept of the *Vorstellungsrepräsentanz*.

path. This is double deception in exactly the sense in which I am using it as a deception that paradoxically depends upon the deceived seeing through another deception. The children's game involves a similar structure but with the added twist that the one against whom the deception is practiced is the same as the one who deceives.

Lacan's position seems to be, then, that from a structural point of view, the distinction between Speech and signaling coincides with that between double deception and the simpler deception involved in sexual display. In particular, Speech must be "capable of lying" in the special sense of lying by telling the truth. That is, Speech must be capable of the double deception of telling the truth as if it were a lie, thus deceiving the listener into taking what is said as a lie when in fact it is the truth. (Irony involves a similar structure of "intentional lying.") The famous Freudian joke that Lacan often quotes, "Why are you telling me that you are going to Cracow and not to Lemberg, when you're really going to Cracow?" illustrates such deception (Žižek 1989, 197; Lacan 1981, 139).

But Lacan also advances a second position in connection with the relation between Speech and pretense: "It is clear that speech begins only with the passage from 'pretence' to the order of the signifier, and that the signifier requires another locus—the locus of the Other, the Other witness, the witness Other than any of the partners—for the Speech that it supports to be capable of lying, that is to say, of presenting itself as Truth" (Lacan 1977, 305). Here, it seems, Lacan requires that Speech, and thus the order of signifiers, requires something more than pretense: a distinctively linguistic and specifically semantic dimension, that of Truth.

Despite their apparent difference, these two positions on the relation of Speech to pretense are identical. Lacan defines Truth not in terms of a formal system of semantics, or as correspondence with reality, but rather in terms of the existence of the Other, an ideal witness who transcends the particularities of intersubjective relations (who is, as he says, "Other than any of the partners"), and who exists as a sort of standard against which deception is judged. In other words, a subject sets in place a position from which to judge his or her own signaling performances: "Is it a lie? That is, is it deception? If not then (by definition) it is the Truth." Lacan's name for the position from which a subject judges whether he or she lies is "the Other." As Lacan says, "it is from somewhere *other* than the Reality that it concerns that Truth derives its guarantee: it is from Speech" (1981, 305–306, emphasis added to highlight Lacan's pun on "other").

Understood in this way, the function of the Other can be glossed in terms of the structure of double deception. That is, at least for the purposes Lacan has in mind in this argument, the Other can be construed as no more than the externally projected position from which a subject is able to implement certain judgments concerning the deceptiveness of his or her own activities. In short, the Other can be understood as a certain judgmental function, set in place retrospectively, by which subjects assess their own past performances as deceptive and, on that basis, are able to undertake a double deception.

On this conception, there is no question of the Other having special access to the Truth, construed as correspondence with Reality. Instead, the Other is a repository of knowledge, the place of the one who knows, understood simply as the point from which subjects expect to hear whether or not they have lied. In short, the Other is nothing more than the function of such an expectation. The signifier, then, is nothing more than the signal as it operates under the sign of the function of the Other: in other words, as it operates in the context of Speech understood as a structure of double deception.

Lacan also uses the term "symbolic order" to refer to what he calls "Speech." The substantive point that he makes by this variation in nomenclature is that a symbol is a sort of substitute, something that stands in the place of something else which is absent, but which we know is not the same as what it replaces. In standing for this something else, however, the symbol makes the other thing present after all, present "symbolically," as we say. Thus, even as we see through one deception, that is, know that the symbol differs from that which it symbolizes, we are caught in a second deception, in which what is absent somehow becomes present through its symbol. Thus what we call symbolic systems, whether linguistic or not, operate with the same structure of double deception that characterize Speech.

The *Objet a*

The signifier as *Vorstellungsrepräsentanz* also makes an appearance in another children's pastime, the *Fort-Da* game, where it takes on an additional dimension as what Lacan calls the *objet a*—the *objet petit autre* (small-*o* other object). Individuals, Lacan tells us, begin life lacking unity with their world and themselves, a lack (*manque*) manifested in the erratic presence of their providers. This lack is not so much a matter of the caregiver's absence but rather of the subject's failure of self-sufficiency, a dependence upon others that continues to be a source of anxiety even when the infant is safely in the arms of its provider (Lacan 1981, 63).

Lacan here takes up a suggestion made by Freud: for the young child in arms, the conception of an unconscious wish and inhibiting danger amounts to a sense of its own lack due to "a *growing tension due to need*, against which it is helpless," or "stimulation ris[ing] to an unpleasurable height without its being possible to be mastered psychically or discharged." This feeling of lack or helplessness, Freud claims, arises from and replicates the birth trauma (Freud 1993, 294). He goes on to say: "It is this factor, then, which is the real essence of the 'danger.'"[3]

Children express this lack/danger by demanding the return of an object, such as the breast. But no object is ever equal to the lack in question since, even when the object demanded returns, the child's dependence continues. Thus, by entering the path of demand, children effectively place themselves beyond the possibility of overcoming lack. Nevertheless, those who demand do not go uncompensated. They are able to distract themselves from their recurrent lack by activities that, as Lacan says, "go some way to satisfying the pleasure principle" (Lacan 1981, 62).

Such activities are apparent in children's earliest behavior, such as the *Fort-Da* game which Freud observes his grandson playing. The child repeatedly throws away and then retrieves a cotton-reel tied to the end of a piece of string: "For the game of the cotton-reel is the subject's answer to what the mother's absence has created on the frontier of his domain—the edge of his cradle—namely a *ditch*, around which one can only play at jumping" (62). As in the singing game, this activity involves a self-deception: the cotton-reel substitutes for the mother in the way that the signifier "miaow" substitutes for "woof" in the singing game. The reel is not a satisfactory substitute, however. It is, as Lacan says, "not the mother reduced to a little ball" (62). Nevertheless, the child is trapped into continuing the game by the pleasure it affords, a pleasure that evolves from seeing through the deception. The pleasure at issue here does not come from seeing through the deception as such, that is, does not point to some sort of primal epistemophilia. Instead, I argue later in this chapter, it arises from a combination of seeing together with seeing through what one has seen, and thus seeing oneself seeing.

In short, the substitution of cotton-reel for mother implemented in the course of the *Fort-Da* affords a certain quota of satisfaction without being totally satisfactory. This form of substitution is the child's best chance in a situation where it must lose something. In short, the game is the only interesting (that is pleasurable) "answer" to the gap created by his mother's absence. And so he must play: knowing that the cotton-reel is not the mother, he is nonetheless forced (a forced choice) to pretend that it is. Thus the child's deception is doubled, reinstituted, despite—indeed, be-

---

3. Lacan's famous/infamous notion of *jouissance* may be seen as a reworking of the Freudian notion of inhibition and instinctual wish as lack.

cause of—the pleasure that comes from seeing through it the first time around.

In virtue of the game's comings and goings and the mother's recurrent absences, the cotton-reel and the mother are both embedded in structures of alternating presences and absences. Thus the cotton-reel resembles the mother at a structural level. That is, the reel and the mother occupy homologous positions within networks of alternating presences and absences. The cotton-reel also substitutes for the mother in the sense of taking her place in the child's field of attention. In short, the cotton-reel substitutes for the mother on the basis of a structural resemblance. Thus, in an extended sense, the cotton-reel may be said to be in a metaphoric relation to the mother. In other words, in an extended sense, the cotton-reel may be said to take on the role of a signifier substituting for another signifier: the mother.

As in the case of metaphoric substitutions in general, the vehicle (cotton-reel) is palpably not the equivalent of the tenor (mother). Instead, there is a gap between the two, a gap that, in the case of linguistic metaphors, creatively shifts the meaning of the tenor in the direction of the vehicle. In the case of the *Fort-Da* game, this gap is productive of pleasure, pleasure which, I argued, fuels the game and thus sustains the substitution, despite the palpable gap separating substitute from substituted.

By virtue of his efforts in sustaining the game, the child displays a practical recognition that the cotton-reel, like the signifier "woof-woof," is a material object that can be lifted clear of its immediate context and relocated. Thus the cotton-reel takes on the structure of a *Vorstellungsrepräsentanz:* a signifier that the subject recognizes as dyadic. One might equally claim, however, as Lacan does, that it is the game as a whole rather than the cotton-reel which functions as a signifier. That is, by its similarity of form the game substitutes for the mother's comings and goings: "The activity as a whole symbolizes repetition. . . . It is the game itself that is the *Repräsentanz* of the *Vorstellung*" (62–63). The ambiguity concerning the identity of the signifier—whether it is the game as a whole or merely one of its parts, the cotton-reel—is harmless, an aspect of a more general ambiguity with respect to the boundary between signifiers and their contexts.

In the context of discussing the *Fort-Da* game, Lacan introduces a new category of objects, the *objet a*, of which the cotton-reel is an instance. The mother's breast, according to Lacan, is the paradigmatic and originary *objet a*. After the child has been weaned, this object is "lost" not only because, like the cotton-reel, it takes on a more or less separate existence but also because the child's access to it is proscribed. It thus comes to symbolize and embody the child's originary and never to be overcome state of lack due to its historical dependence upon others. To be specific, it retrospectively takes on a phantasmatic, purely functional identity as an endlessly satisfying cornucopia:

> It [the *objet a*] is precisely what is subtracted from the living being . . . it is of this that all the forms of the *objet a* . . . are the representatives, the equivalents. The *objets a* are merely its representatives, its figures. The breast—as equivocal, as an element characteristic of the mamiferous organization—certainly represents that part of himself that the individual loses at birth, and which may serve to symbolize the most profound lost object. I could make the same kind of reference for all the other objects. (Lacan 1981, 198)

Lacan argues that a certain lack of ontological consistency is essential to an object's role as *objet a*. Like the mother's breast, the object must be haunted by a specter, a phantasmagoric reminder of the originary lack from which the concrete *objet a* distracts the subject, and for which it functions as a tangible monument: "an ungraspable organ, this organ that we can only circumvent, in short this false organ" (196). This phantasmatic underside of the *objet a* does not echo a missing object in the way that a photo echoes things past. Instead the phantasm is a reification created by the simultaneous concealment and resurgence, in short repression, of the subject's originary lack, a lack that, I argued above, is a function of the subject's continuing dependence upon others.

In this respect, then, the *objet a* bears a structural similarity to the "commodity": it is not only a concrete object but also a ghostly value, a false essence carried by the concrete object and constituted through the processes of exchange. In sum, from a tropological perspective the *objet a* is not merely a metaphor, that is, a substitute for a specific other object. Rather, it is a catachresis, a substitute for an object constituted retrospectively through the act of substitution. To be specific, in putting itself forward as a substitute, the *objet a* creates the false impression that there was something—an original lacking object, for instance, the mythical endlessly overflowing maternal breast—for which it acts as a substitute (Chaitin 1996, 89–92).[4]

---

4. For a nice discussion of catachresis in the different but tantalizingly similar context of commodity fetishism, see Keenan 1993, 182–183. Lacan refused to permit the translator of *Seminar XI* to provide a formal definition of the *objet a* in the glossary of terms, instead "leaving the reader to develop an appreciation of the concept in the course of [its] use" (Lacan 1981, 282).

Desire

In the course of the *Fort-Da* game, Lacan tells us, the mother's "outline" is transformed, "made up of the brush-strokes and gouaches of desire" (Lacan 1981, 63). Desire thus manifests itself as the relation which is established between the subject and an object of need when the subject's attention is redirected to an-other object, namely, the *objet a*. In particular, by substituting the cotton-reel for his mother, the child falls from needing her into desiring. Or, to put matters more bluntly, desire is what happens to need when its object is traded for something more accessible but less satisfying.

The representative anecdote of the *Fort-Da* game displays a key feature of the relation of desire to the *objet a*. The *objet a* in the specific guise of the cotton-reel is not itself desired. That is, the child is clear that it wants its mother, not the cotton-reel. This is not to say that the *objet a* is totally free of desire. On the contrary, desire always plays around its edges: "You then say, as Freud observed, *I love mutton stew* . . . [but] [y]ou're not sure you desire it. Take the experience of the beautiful butcher's wife. She loves caviar, but she doesn't want any. That's why she desires it. You see, the object of desire is the cause of desire, and this object [the *objet a*] that is the cause of desire is the object of the drive—that is to say, the object around which the drive turns" (Lacan 1981, 243). Nevertheless, even when the *objet a* is desired, its function does not depend upon this fact. As Lacan makes the point, "The function of the *objet a* . . . is never found in the position of being the aim of desire" (186).

The *Fort-Da* game illustrates that the cotton-reel, as the *objet a*, not only is undesired but also, by distracting the child from trying to get his mother, blocks or defers access to what he really wants. This account of the emergence of desire repudiates the commonsense "humanist" view that distraction is a matter of offering the child one thing it wants in exchange for another. The cotton-reel is not a distraction in this sense because it is not itself an object of desire. In any case, the mother for which the cotton-reel is a sort of substitute becomes desirable only *after* the *Fort-Da* game is set in place. Although not itself desired, however, the cotton-reel is a key element in setting a scene within which the subject's desire unfolds, and in that sense it functions as an object-cause of desire. Thus the *objet a* takes on a paradoxical dual role in relation to desire, as both its cause and its impediment.

In order for desire to fulfill its characteristic adult function of motivating action, subjects must be under the misapprehension that pleasure arises from pursuing desire. They must fail to recognize what children know at a practical level: the real source of their pleasure lies in engaging with rather than avoiding the *objet a*.[5] Such failure of recognition is an aspect of what Lacan following Freud calls "repression" (*Verdrängung*) and is a constitutive element of the unconscious (a topic to which I return in more detail in the next chapter).

This does not mean that repression is always successful. On the contrary, from a Freudian perspective, there must be breaches or slippages, what Freud calls "returns of the repressed": parapraxes, unintended puns, and so on, by which subjects betray their knowledge that the real origins of their pleasure lie with the *objet a*. "Normal" (that is nonfetishistic) subjects do not systematically avow this knowledge. Instead, they accord it sporadic practical recognition by displays of excessive care or anxiety in approaching the *objet a*. By contrast, in the case of fetishistic structures of desire that I discuss later in this chapter, such knowledge takes on a systematic, practical character as a phantasy, perhaps even emerging into consciousness. In that respect, we may think of fetishism as a form of regression—not a return to childish innocence, but rather a resurfacing of knowledge repressed in the transition to adulthood.

The chaperone illustrates the structure of the *objet a*. Often represented as an aged female relative, she is not paradigmatically an object of desire but instead stands in the way of what the suitor wants: the beloved. Nevertheless, the chaperone is covertly instrumental in producing a certain quotient of pleasure for the suitor. This arises not from the attainment of desire or even the contemplation of such attainment but rather from engaging with the chaperone, in particular from successfully allaying her suspicions and evading her scrutiny. That is, as in the *Fort-Da* game, she is the object around which the subject moves to produce pleasure, the cause of desire rather than its object.

Thus far, my account of the formation of desire has been pre-Oedipal. At the Oedipal stage, access to the mother is forbidden, a proscription reinforced by a threat of danger (castration, for example), which distracts the little man from what he wants. As a result, the idea (*Vorstellung*) of the mother is "decathected" or "repressed," so that at the level of consciousness it is unclear how much and in what respect he wants her. Does he merely crave her attention, want her close presence, or desire access to her body in some more intimate respect of which he is only dimly aware?

5. This does not imply that pleasure never comes from getting what one wants. On the contrary, the child takes pleasure from the breast which it also desires. In this case, however, pleasure comes from the desired object only because it is also an object of need. The question of producing pleasure will be addressed in more detail below.

Under these circumstances, the decathected desire or, as Freud calls it, the "unconscious wish" (*unbewusster Wunsch*) for the mother persists at a conscious level but in disguised form, as a series of affective attachments to other objects connected to the mother by chains of associations of the kind connecting her to the cotton-reel. Lacan takes such disguised resurfacings of unconscious desire as the result of an intrinsic instability of desire, that is, its continuing tendency to displace onto new objects. By such displacements, he says, subjects avoid or at least manage to distract themselves from facing the always and already recurring trauma of their own lack.[6]

Freud's own life provides an illustration of such displacement. During his summer holidays one year he journeyed by carriage from Ragusa to Herzegovina. He fell into conversation with his traveling companions about "the various peculiarities of the Turks living there, as I had heard them described years before by a friend and colleague who had lived among them for many years as a doctor." For reasons which only become apparent later, Freud found himself unable to relay a further story, namely, that "upon encountering sexual disturbances" the Turks "fall into utter despair" (Weber 1992, 91–92, quoting Freud 1953–73, 3:290–291, 6:3). The conversation then drifted to Italian art, and Freud strongly recommended the frescoes at Orvieto cathedral. Again he found himself strangely restrained in his conversation, unable to recall the name of their painter, Signorelli.

In his rereading of this episode from Freud's life, Lacan suggests that an unconscious desire betrays its presence in Freud's lapse of memory in connection with the painter's name, a lapse which we may retrospectively identify with the earlier failure to tell the story of the Turks' attitude to failures of sexual performance. The desire in question is Freud's secret concern with his own impotence, the unmanning of the master, the *Seigneur*, a desire which, Lacan argues, manifests in disguised form as a forgetting of the name "Signorelli."

But this claim makes sense only if the path connecting the desire to the forgetful behavior operates at the level of signifiers rather than the objects to which they refer. That is, nothing links forgetting the name "Signorelli" to the question of Freud's impotence other than the accident that erasing the name is a rebus for Freud's own unmanning. This connection is established in virtue of Freud's status as master—*Seigneur*—but also through

---

6. According to Lacan, such avoidances also belong to the Freudian phenomenon of repression. In this respect, then, the repressed, that is, the unconscious, emerges not as some deep, dark, hidden reservoir of facts and urges but rather as a systematic oversight structuring subjects' practices, a point to which I return in the next chapter.

the "accident" that the first three letters of "Signorelli" coincide with the first three of "Sigmund." In short, as Lacan makes the point, "a desire . . . [is] situate[d] in the denuded metonymy of [this] discourse . . . where the subject [in this case Freud himself] surprises himself in some unexpected way" (Lacan 1981, 28).

Pleasure

Freud proposes two mechanisms for producing pleasure. The first, cathexis, involves stabilizing a subject's libidinal energies by anchoring or "fixing" them to a particular object of need. The fixing is not a physical act of attachment but rather a fixing of attention to an idea (*Vorstellung*) of the object.[7] For instance, a child derives pleasure by fixing libidinal energies to a particular idea of the mother's breast.

The other mechanism Freud proposes is the drive (*Trieb*).[8] Each drive is associated with an imbricated pair of needs; the scopic drive, for example, with the need to see (voyeurism) and be seen (exhibitionism): "What the voyeur is looking for and finds is merely a shadow, a shadow behind the curtain. . . . If also the structure of the drive appears, it is really complete only in its return form [namely] in exhibitionism" (Lacan 1981, 182–183).[9] The drive produces pleasure by stabilizing the libidinal flux associated with such paired needs, neither of which fully fixes upon its object: "'Pleasure' obeys the law of homeostasis that Freud evokes in *Beyond the Pleasure Principle*, whereby through discharge the psyche seeks the lowest possible tension" (281). How is such stabilization or "homeostasis" achieved?

Discussing the scopic drive, Lacan introduces a new kind of object, "the lure." Operating in its "natural function," the lure is exemplified by animals who, casting off their skin, create a double, a visual simulation, which deceives their enemies. Humans are deceived in a more complex way: "the human subject . . . is not, unlike the animal, entirely caught up in this imaginary capture" (107).[10] Instead, and here Lacan repeats a

---

7. See Laplanche and Pontalis 1974, 62–65, 162–164, for useful discussions of the vagaries of the Freudian notion of fixing and cathexis.

8. Lacan's term for the drive, *pulsion*, is a translation for Freud's term *Trieb*, which is mistranslated in the Standard Edition of Freud as "instinct." On this point of mistranslation see Laplanche and Pontalis 1974, 214–215.

9. Lacan discusses the scopic drive and its connection to such circular movements of seeing and being seen in Lacan 1981, 181–184. See too 165–168 for a general discussion of the connection between the drive and the production of pleasure.

10. See also Lacan 1981, 102, 104, 111, 186; see as well my remarks on the signifier earlier in this chapter.

theme from his earlier work in *Écrits* that I discussed above, humans are deceived through simulacra—or "lures"—which work in a paradoxical way by permitting viewers to see through them. For instance, in Plato's story, Parrhasios wins a painting competition by tricking his competitor Zeuxis with a painting of a veil: "Zeuxis has the advantage of having made grapes that attracted the birds [the lure in its natural function]. . . . Parrhasios triumphs over him for having painted on the wall a veil, a veil so lifelike that Zeuxis, turning towards him said, *Well, and now show us what you have painted behind it*" (103). Zeuxis, unlike the birds, is not deceived into thinking the painting depicts something real, since, in saying "show us what you have painted," he recognizes that the veil's image is merely a painting. Nonetheless, despite seeing through the deception, indeed because he sees through it, he is trapped by the image since, in asking what is painted behind the veil, he mistakenly infers: veils conceal, therefore something must be painted behind the painted veil. His mistake, an instance of what I am calling double deception, is characteristic of the deceptions created by *trompe l'oeil*—deceptions sustained even as, indeed because, they are seen through. In short, Parrhasios wins the prize by creating a lure fit for humans, while Zeuxis produces a lure which, operating in its "natural function," is strictly for the birds.

A mask hanging on a wall functions similarly to Parrhasios's painting. The simulated eye sockets are, as viewers well understand, not eyes at all; no one is looking from behind the mask. Nevertheless, in the same way that the painting of the veil seems to conceal something in a fictional place painted behind it, a scrutiny seems to emerge from a fictional location behind the mask: "Man, in effect, knows how to play with the mask" (107). The mask's eyeless eyes, doubly deceptive, thus function as a lure.[11]

But how, in allowing viewers to see through it, does the lure trap viewers? The mechanism of entrapment, Lacan tells us, depends upon the pleasure created in seeing through what has been seen: "What is it that attracts and satisfies us in *trompe l'oeil*? When is it that it captures our attention and delights us? At the moment when, by a mere shift of our gaze, we are able to realize that the representation does not move with the gaze and that it is merely *trompe l'oeil*?" (112). The pleasure produced is not an intellectual satisfaction at uncovering a deception. That is, Lacan is not hinting at a primal form of epistemophilia. On the contrary, the viewer knows all along he is being deceived. Instead it depends upon the workings of the

---

11. In the case of works of *trompe l'oeil* the deception concerns the object rather than its relation to the subject, that is, the subject is deceived about the reality corresponding to the appearance. In the case of the mask, a certain ambiguity obtains: is the subject deceived about the mask itself—about whether it constitutes a real face—or does the deception concern the more general question of whether someone is looking from behind the mask?

scopic drive. As they see through the first level deception, viewers look back at what they have seen, thus scrutinizing themselves, and specifically their own role as viewers. Thus they place themselves and what they see on display. That is, even as they recognize that the eyes that they see are *trompe l'oeil*—a masquerade—viewers feel themselves to be the object of a "look" coming from the object's vicinity. In this way the raw materials of the scopic drive are brought together, namely, voyeuristic and exhibitionistic libidinal thrusts (*poussées*) arising from the twinned needs to see and be seen, neither of which is fully satisfied. For instance, the eyeholes of an empty mask provide an evasive target for the those who need to see. We look at the holes but also behind them for the absent eyes that look back at us, and the scrutiny from the direction of the mask takes on an ambiguous quality: we feel under scrutiny but know we are not: "What the voyeur is looking for and finds is merely a shadow, a shadow behind the curtain" (182–183). The pleasure which emerges, the delight at viewing the *trompe l'oeil*, proves that such a drive structure has successfully locked into place.

Lacan's name for structural distortions of the visual field, those that are not only seen but are also the source of a look turned back upon the viewer, is "the gaze." A gaze in this sense is created by the visual semblance of a viewer behind the mask's eyeholes as well as the simulation of a scene behind Parrhasios's painting of the veil. In short, the gaze is a pseudo-object, masquerading as something objective when it is merely a structural effect of the visual field, a hollow or absence around which the scopic drive is constructed. By contrast, the mask, like the painting on the wall, is a concrete object, a lure, that sustains the gaze as a structural element in the field of its effects. As Lacan puts it, the mask is "that beyond which there is the gaze" (107). According to Lacan, all drives are structured in this way, as responses to a twinned pair of needs. The responses circle a pseudo-object, the "object of the drive," which in turn is screened by a concrete object—in the case of the scopic drive, called "the lure" (170–180).

The question arises, then, how the drive, as the structure through which pleasure emerges, connects with desire. Lacan answers by advancing a bold hypothesis identifying the *objet a* in its role as object-cause of desire with the object at the center of the drive. This identity is well illustrated in the case of the *Fort-Da* game, for which, as I explained above, the cotton-reel functions as *objet a* in its role as object-cause of desire. We saw that the game involves a double deception. The first deception takes the form of an identity or, more accurately, a relation of metaphoric substitution between mother and cotton-reel, which is based upon a shared relational structure: both cotton-reel and mother leave and return to the child. The child is well aware of the deception. Nevertheless, because of the pleasure the game affords, he continues to play, thus allowing the deception to retain a grip.

The mechanism at work here, I claim, is the scopic drive, for which the distortion of the visual field created by the sudden reappearances and disappearances of the cotton-reel functions as the gaze. To be specific, the *Fort-Da* game, through its structure of double deception, is homologous to *trompe l'oeil*, and thus a site for the operation of the scopic drive.

Thus the cotton-reel fulfills a dual role: it is the *objet a* qua object-cause of desire, and it is, like the mask, a lure supporting the gaze, a pseudo-object at the center of the scopic drive. The phantasm, "the false organ" that, I argued earlier, haunts the *objet a* as a reminder of the subject's originary lack, may then be identified as the gaze. As Lacan (1981, 243) puts the point, "This object that is the cause of desire [the *objet a*] is the object of the drive." He repeats this identification in the specific context of the scopic drive: "Is it not clear that the gaze intervenes here only in as much as . . . the subject . . . who feels himself surprised [is] the subject sustaining himself in a function of desire?" (85). And he then reasserts it in the context of the oral drive, for which the breast functions as an archetypical *objet a:* "To this breast in its function as object, *objet a* cause of desire, in the sense that I understand the term—we must give a function that will explain its place in the satisfaction of the drive" (168).[12] In what follows, and except where I need to do otherwise, I shall follow Lacan in reading the term "*objet a*" fairly elastically, to cover not only the lure but also the *objet a* proper, as well as the object at the center of the drive. In particular, the gaze may be taken as an instance of an *objet a*.

Fetishism

In this section I argue that Lacan's account of the *objet a* as both object of the drive and object-cause of desire provides a way of understanding the phenomenon of fetishism. A chaperone, I have argued, may take on the characteristics of an *objet a*. Although not herself desired by the suitor, she is nonetheless the cause of his desire as well as the center of the evasive activities through which he produces his pleasure. In some cases the suitor may become overattentive to the chaperone, so scrupulous about satisfying the letter of her demand for restraint that it is as if he puts her desire before his own or, what comes to the same thing, appears to be afraid of

12. See also Lacan 1981, 179–180.

getting what he wants. In Lacanian terms such a subject "gives up on his own desire" and instead dedicates himself "perversely" (as we say) to abetting the *objet a* in its function as impediment to desire. Such giving up is a matter of foregoing the pursuit of desire rather than eliminating desire or (as it may seem) displacing it onto the chaperone. That is, the suitor continues to desire his beloved but systematically gives up her pursuit in order to return to the fascinating business of evading the chaperone.

The sacrifice is not without its compensations since the suitor's engagement with the *objet a* yields a return of pleasure by stabilizing his libido. Under such a regime, the *objet a* takes on the role of what Freud calls "the fetish." Conceived in this way, fetishism is not a matter of a socially unacceptable or unusual desire but rather a paradoxical refusal to follow up on one's desire.

This conception of the fetish, as a special sort of *objet a* that attracts the attention normally reserved for the object of desire, fits well with recent work suggesting that fetishism is no less a feature of women's psychic structure than men's (see Apter 1993; Gamman and Makinen 1994). But how can this conception be linked to the more traditional Freudian approach discussed in the Introduction, which defines fetishism in terms of the disavowal of an object (the "fetish") that functions as a substitute for the mother's missing penis?[13]

The fetishistic suitor *knows*, indeed sees, that the chaperone is only an old woman with no real power to stop him getting what he wants. This knowledge plays the role of what Freud in his classical treatment of fetishism calls avowal. But even so, and for reasons which often remain conveniently obscure, the suitor recognizes that the chaperone is important. That is why he lavishes such attention on her. This contradictory recognition, which constitutes the fetishistic disavowal, may not be a matter of explicit belief, may indeed be vigorously denied. Instead, it is a matter of a phantasy scenario that structures the suitor's behavior, taking on the dimensions of a symptom which, as Freud tells us, is always a coded message.

When the "normal" (that is nonperverse) subject confronts the chaperone, by contrast, the disavowal impacts behavior only at the level of slips punctuating his practices—strange hesitations, blushes, and so on—as if he found her attractive. Apart from such slips, he keeps as far away from the *objet a* as he can without giving up on what he wants. Thus for both the

---

13. Dylan Evans, following Lacan, identifies perversion as a general clinical structure connected with disavowal. Fetishism, then, falls under this concept as a special case of perversion in which a fetish object functions as a symbolic substitute for the mother's missing phallus (Evans 1996, 138–139). I do not need to make such fine distinctions here, and will refer to perversion and fetishism interchangeably.

fetishist and normal subject the situation is unequivocal at the level of consciousness: "she's only an old woman; if only we could get rid of her, what fun we would have." But for the fetishist, this knowledge is betrayed by a contrary knowledge encoded into the phantasies structuring his behavior.

In situations of fetishism there is no need for repression, that is, no need to defer the otherwise dangerous knowledge that satisfaction derives not from acquiring what one desires but rather from engaging with the *objet a*, the chaperone, for example. Consequently, such knowledge rises easily into consciousness although, as Copjec points out, it is rare for the revelation to be total: "It is important to recall Freud's several warnings against possible misunderstandings: the construction of the fetish does not itself reveal, except in certain 'very subtle' cases, the subject's simultaneous affirmation and denial of loss" (Copjec 1994, 113). Instead, the knowledge surfaces in veiled form, as a recognition that contrary to perception, the fetish is important in some sense never made totally clear. Such knowledge is expressed in the characteristic split form of what Freud calls disavowal: "I *know* that, but *even so* . . ."[14]

The other feature emphasized by traditional Freudian accounts of fetishism is an associative connection between the mother's missing penis and the fetish. This connection is clear in specific instances of fetishism, but it can also be established on general theoretical grounds by deriving a connection between the *objet a*, of which the fetish is an instance, and the mother's lack—not specifically her lack of a penis but rather her lack in a more general sense. The derivation is relatively straightforward in the case of the *Fort-Da* game.

The cotton-reel is joined to Freud's grandson by a piece of string. But the game drives a wedge between the child and his toy, thus consigning the latter to the position of missing part. Through this process of "self-mutilation," the child creates a new lack, his own lack of bodily integrity (Lacan 1981, 62). Because the game only goes *"some way* to satisfying the pleasure principle" (62, my emphasis) the child is subjected to a second lack, constituted by the gap between the satisfaction he gets from the game and the (purely imaginary) state of total satisfaction which is and continues to be his aim (*Ziel*). These two lacks are structurally equivalent in virtue of sharing the same position in the child's causal history: both emerge as aspects of his response to the problem of failure to get satisfaction.[15]

14. Freud originally conceived disavowal simply as "the subject's refusal to recognize the reality of a traumatic perception" in the specific context of psychosis; but it came to take on a more extended meaning in his work as a contradictory belief concerning the existence of an object of unrealistic anxiety (Laplanche and Pontalis 1974, 118–120).
15. The equivalence here is a matter of a shared metonymic relation with a prior common cause. As Freud has shown us, psychic equivalences are grounded in such relations.

Because it emerges as a response or, as Lacan says, an "answer" to orig-inal lack, the double lack created by the *Fort-Da* game is an exchange for the child's original lack due to his dependence upon others for the satis-faction of his needs. In short:

Subject's original lack = Lack of *objet a* = Continuing lack of satisfaction

This series of equivalences can be extended to include the mother's lack. That is, the subject's lack implies that the mother is also a site of lack since, insofar as she cannot give satisfaction, she too must be lacking. This equivalence depends, of course, upon the contingent fact that it is the child's mother, as the source of his needs, whom he misses. Thus:

Mother's lack = Subject's original lack

Therefore we arrive at a chain of identities:

Mother's lack = Subject's original lack = Continuing lack of satisfaction = Lack of *objet a*

from which it follows that

Mother's lack = Lack of *objet a*

Thus the proposition that the *objet a* is important—that its lack is a catas-trophe—is equivalent to that qualified denial of the mother's lack which Freud designated by the term "disavowal."

Similar equivalences can be derived for all the *objets a* introduced by Lacan (the breast, the turd, the gaze, the voice, and so on), since in all cases the *objet a* provides a focus around which diversions from the sub-ject's continuing lack are organized. In this way, then, the fetish, as a spe-cial sort of *objet a*, takes on the role of substitute for maternal lack. This role for the fetish is not one of its essential characteristics, however; it de-pends instead upon a culturally and historically contingent fact, namely, the role of the mother as caregiver in the early life of the child.

This redefinition of fetishism and reconceptualization of the relation be-tween pleasure and desire have consequences that extend well beyond the arena of Freud scholarship. According to a tradition going back to Aris-totle, human actions are defective—irrational or incontinent—if they are not directed to achieving what their agents desire. The phenomenon of fetishism provides an exception to this Aristotelian principle of action.

Fetishists are "irrational" in the sense of not pursuing their desires. Instead, they attend perversely (as we say) to something else, the fetish, which thereby functions as an impediment, a delaying mechanism, with respect to the attainment of their desire. So, for example, they may rivet their attention upon an item of clothing or a bodily part instead of pursuing that which they continue to desire, from a safe distance as it were: the consummation of sexual relations with the beloved.

Nevertheless, as I have argued, their actions, specifically their engagement with the fetish, produce pleasure, and in that respect may be seen as "properly motivated," that is, "done for good reason." This combination of "irrationality" with "done for good reason" suggests new possibilities for the relation between human subjects and their objects.

2

Body and Text:
The Roots of the Unconscious

If psychoanalysis is to be constituted as the science of the unconscious, one must set out from the notion that the unconscious is structured like a language. . . .

At a time that I hope we have now put behind us, it was objected that in giving dominance to structure I was neglecting the dynamics so evident in our experience. It was even said that I went so far as to ignore the principle affirmed in Freudian doctrine that this dynamics is, in its essence, through and through, sexual.

Jacques Lacan, The Four Fundamental Concepts of Pychoanalysis

Lacan's name is associated famously with the view that "the uncon-scious is structured like a language" (Lacan 1981, 203). But Lacan's lin-guistic and specifically structuralist conception of the unconscious has been the target of much criticism. In particular, orthodox Freudians have accused him of promoting linguistic aspects of the unconscious at the ex-pense of its sexual nature. Lacan has shown himself quite sensitive to such criticism. He agrees that "the reality of the unconscious is sexual re-ality. . . . At every opportunity, Freud defended this formula, if I may say so, with tooth and claw"; and then acknowledges that "in advancing this proposition [the sexual nature of the unconscious] I find myself in a prob-lematic position—for what have I taught about the unconscious? The un-conscious is constituted by the effects of speech. . . . The unconscious is structured like a language" (149–150).

In this chapter I argue that, provided the embodied, material nature of speech is taken into account—speech as *parole* rather than *langue*—a con-ception of the unconscious as linguistically structured can be reconciled with the notion that it is sexual in nature. I start by unfolding some of the many ways in which one may read Lacan's deceptively fertile aphorism "The unconscious is structured like a language." For argument's sake I restrict the terms "signifiers" and "Speech" in this chapter to their conventional meanings, as essentially linguistic in nature, rather than using them in the somewhat broader sense introduced in the previous chapter.

The Unconscious Is Structured Like a Language

According to Freud, the unconscious consists of intertwining chains of associations formed by the primary processes of condensation and displacement. These processes, Roman Jakobson argues, are structurally identical with the linguistic tropes of metaphor and metonymy. From this it follows trivially that "the unconscious is structured like a language" (Lacan 1981, 149, 203). Lacan's aphorism can also be understood less trivially, however: the slips, bodily symptoms and dream images that offer a royal road into the unconscious, as Freud maintained, operate as signifiers or, indeed, as rebuses that despite their visual form depend upon language for discharging their symbolic function. As Lacan makes the point more generally:

> The unconscious is that chapter of my history that is marked by a blank or occupied by a falsehood: it is the censored chapter. But the truth can be rediscovered; usually it has been written down elsewhere. Namely:
> —in monuments: this is my body . . . in which the hysterical symptoms reveals the structure of a language. (Lacan 1977, 50)[1]

Lacan also indicates, and here a third sense of his aphorism emerges, that the unconscious is manifested, indeed constituted, by certain "effects of speech," not only Freudian parapraxes ("the frontiers where slips of the tongue and witticisms, in their collusion, become confused," 299) but also the split between the subject of *énonciation* (the one who speaks) and the subject of *énoncé* (the fictional figure in terms of which a speaker speaks about himself or herself). This split, Mikhail Bahktin argues, is a consequence of the impossibility of a speech act referring to itself. Either the act asserts that it is already completed, in which case it falsely claims the termination of something which, ex hypothesi, is still ongoing; or it asserts that it is incomplete, in which case, when completed, it will be guilty of false modesty, that is, of denying its own achievement. Speech, it seems, always arrives too early or too late at the scene of its own production. To be specific, a temporal gap ex-

---

1. He lists these other locations: "in semantic evolution . . . the stock of words," "in my style of life and . . . character," "in traditions . . . which bear my history," "in the distortions necessitated by linking of the adulterated chapters to the chapters surrounding it."

ists between the moment of speaking and the operation of the referential apparatus by which speech refers to itself, a gap which, in turn, creates a split between the subject of *énoncé* and its intended referent, the subject of *énonciation*. As Tzvetan Todorov puts it, "If I tell (orally or in writing) an event that I have just lived, in so far as I *am telling* (orally or in writing) this event, I find myself already outside the time-space where the event occurred. To identify oneself absolutely with oneself, to identify one's 'I' with the 'I' that I tell is as impossible as to lift oneself up by one's hair" (Todorov 1984, 52).[2]

The process of speaking distracts the speaker from this split. Speech creates the illusion that the referent of the spoken "I" refers to the one who speaks, thus protecting speakers from recognizing the limping quality of their own utterances. This convenient illusion is not merely a matter of suppressing from immediate consciousness the split between the subject of *énonciation* and the subject of *énoncé* but rather of overlooking it at the level of discursive practice. That is, at issue is a certain practical lack of attention to the split rather than a failure to recognize or "know" it at the level of consciousness.[3] According to Lacan, such overlooking is a constitutive moment in the formation of the unconscious:

> Once the structure of language has been recognized in the unconscious, what sort of subject can we recognize for it?
>
> We can try, with methodological rigour, to set out from the strictly linguistic definition of the I as signifier, in which there is nothing but the "shifter" or indicative, which, in the subject of the statement [*énoncé*], designates the subject in the sense that he is now speaking.
>
> That is to say, it designates the subject of the enunciation. (Lacan 1977, 298)

Thus far I have followed the strand of argument in the early Lacan (of *Écrits*), which demonstrates that the unconscious is an "effect of speech" (149). But in his later work, specifically *Seminar XI*, Lacan may be seen as reversing the ontological priority of speech over the unconscious, by arguing that the constitution of the unconscious in dream work creates a split in the subject similar to that between the subject of *énoncé* and *énonciation*. Thus, rather than speech preceding and providing a constitutive basis for the unconscious, the latter precedes and sets in place a structure subsequently realized in the unfolding of the spoken word—what Saussure calls *parole*. In other

---

2. As Lacan makes the point, the "me" *(moi)* that signifies the subject of *énoncé* "designates the subject of the enunciation but does not signify it" (Lacan 1977, 298).

3. As with Louis Althusser's conception of ideology, the "knowledge" referred to is not so much a matter of ideas in the head as of representations structuring practices—see my discussion of Althusser in Chapter 5.

words, the structure of the unconscious lays the groundwork for language rather than the other way around. I turn to this argument in the next section.

Dreaming the Unconscious

In *The Interpretation of Dreams* (1965, 547–550), Freud recounts an incident in which a father, sleeping in the room next door to his dead child, is shocked by a noise. He wakes up with a start, whereupon he discovers that a candle has overturned in the next room, and that the old man whom he had charged with watching over the dead child has fallen asleep. The father subsequently reports having dreamed that the infant stood by the bed where the father was sleeping, took him by the arm, and said: *"Vater, siehst du denn nicht das ich verbrenne?"* (Father, don't you see that I am burning?).

In the context of discussing this dream, Lacan recounts another: "The other day, I was awoken from a short nap by a knocking at my door just before I actually awoke. With this impatient knocking I had already formed a dream, a dream that manifested to me something other than this knocking. And when I awake, it is in so far as I reconstitute my entire representation around this knocking—this perception" (Lacan 1981, 56). Lacan clarifies this last point by adding that when he awakes, "I know that I am there, at what time I went to sleep, and why I went to sleep. When the knocking occurs, not in my perception, but in my consciousness, it is because my consciousness reconstitutes itself around this representation—that I know that I am waking up, that I am *knocked up*" (56).

In Lacan's dream, as in the one recounted by Freud, a man is woken by a perception invading his sleep. By imposing the forms of consciousness upon this perception after he awakes, the dreamer retrospectively symbolizes what disturbed him. At the same time he formulates his own identity as one who, having woken, retrospectively recognizes what woke him.

Lacan then poses the following question: "Here I must question myself as to what I am at that moment—at the moment, so immediately before and so separate, which is that in which I began to dream under the effect of the knocking which is, to all appearances, what woke me" (56). What is Lacan signaling by this strange question concerning the identity of the dreamer—"What am I at that moment?"—at that liminal moment when I am still asleep but on the threshold of waking? And what is Lacan telling us by juxtaposing an account of this structurally similar but symbolically impoverished dream next to Freud's?

Lacan is making the point that what is important in dreams is not so much their manifest or latent content as their abstract *form:* that the dream's content, including the dreamer's perception, is inserted retrospectively into his consciousness after he wakes. What does Lacan mean by "consciousness" here? As he uses the term, it refers to something that differentiates waking from dreaming. It cannot, then, refer simply to awareness or even perception, since in dreams no less than in waking we are aware of, indeed perceive, aspects of reality, for example, the knocking that the father noticed during his dream of the burning child. Instead, by "consciousness" Lacan means a particular set of symbolic forms in terms of which, after waking, the one who was dreaming comes to characterize the reality he perceives, including the remembered knocking that, having impinged upon his perceptual field even as he slept, woke him.[4]

In this context, the unconscious is exemplified by the way the knocking is perceived at the moment when it occupies the center stage of the dream, as a literally indescribable source of dread that, while retaining the semblance of a message, breaks the boundaries of the symbolic forms in terms of which the sleeper represents his waking experiences. In this guise, the noise that disturbs the sleeper constitutes an intrusion of what Lacan calls the Real: a site of anxiety where the symbolic order breaks down. This disturbance incites Lacan, "interpellates him," as Althusser would say, to restore order by finding a sense to the noise, which, by a catachretic substitution of meaning for non-meaning, reworks the knocking into something sensible. The sleeping Lacan effects this transformation by waking up and retrospectively identifying the terrifying aspect of the noise as "just a dream." As he puts it, when he is awake "the knocking occurs not in my perception [as it did in the dream], but in my consciousness. . . . It is because my consciousness reconstitutes itself around this representation . . . that I know that I am waking up" (56).

This reconstitution involves not only a reworking of reality to fit the symbolic order but also a splitting between two "I's": the "I" who, while dreaming, hears the original meaningless noise as a disturbance of the symbolic landscape, and another "I" who, after waking, retrospectively perceives, *knows,* what is going on: "I [the second I] know that I [the first I] am . . . *knocked up*" (56). At the liminal moment of waking the disjuncture between these two "I's" breaks into the open, thus leading Lacan to ask, "What am I at that moment?"

A similar mechanism is at work in speech. When parapraxes, unintended puns, and so on break up the pattern of speech to the point where they indicate what Freud calls "unrealistic anxiety" (an anxiety with no apparently appropriate object) speakers are led to reassess their own words for some-

---

4. In Lacan's dream, this reality was aural in nature, a knocking, as was the noise of the overturning candle in the dream of the burning child recounted by Freud. In the context of establishing what Lacan means by "consciousness," it is germane to take note of his complaint that Freud never returned to the problem of consciousness (Lacan 1981, 57).

thing more that they might be saying, for something they have missed. This veiled excess of meaning defamiliarizes speech, filling it with resonances that, like the anonymous, free-floating "acousmatic" voice of a film sound-track (the mother's voice in Hitchcock's *Psycho*) seem to come from a somewhere else which is nowhere (Žižek 1996, 92). Speakers are thus trans-formed into listeners to their "own" alienated utterances, and correspond-ingly a wedge is driven between the "I" producing the speech and the "I" reflexively listening to what is being said. Such distortions of speech, which cause speakers to listen to their own utterances coming back from else-where, fall under the heading of what Lacan calls "the Voice."

It is true, of course, that speakers quickly seal off these moments of insta-bility in their speech, retrospectively passing them off as accidents. Never-theless, the structural similarity with dreams remains, since in Freud's ac-count of the dream of the burning child the father too engages in a sealing off, erasing the waking moments of disorientation in his sense of self and the world. To be specific, almost as soon as he wakes, the father comes to a retrospective (mis)understanding that the noise disturbing his dream was merely the result of a candle overturning in the next room. Thus the uncon-scious, which is constructed around an assortment of such troubling little pieces of reality located outside the symbolic order, displays a structure of splitting similar to that manifested in speech. Here, then, we see another sense in which "the unconscious is structured like a language."

The Sexual Unconscious

In its material form as clusterings of liminal objects crossing the oral and aural orifices of the body, speech constitutes the raw material of what Lacan calls the invocatory drive. This drive forms when libidinal impulses or cathexes associated with the subject's twinned needs (*Bedürfnisse*) to speak and be spoken to circulate a distortion in the vocal field, such as the burning child's cry in the father's dream. These imbricated speakings and listenings, such as the father retelling his dream while reworking his per-ception of the noise that disturbed his sleep, have the effect of stabilizing the libidinal flux, thus producing pleasure in accord with the Freudian pleasure principle (Lacan 1981, 281). Such pleasure, according to Lacan, is always sexual in nature: "For the moment, I am not fucking, I am talking to you. Well! I can have exactly the same satisfaction as if I were fucking. That's what it means. Indeed, it raises the question of whether in fact I am not fucking at this moment" (165–166).[5]

---

5. In this context it is important to point out that the book in which this passage appears is a written transcript of oral performances.

The pleasure produced by the invocatory drive distracts subjects from, and thus in a practical sense leads them to forget, not only the split between the subject of *énonciation* and the subject of *énoncé* but also a more basic, indeed originary, gap created by the subjects' lack of self-sufficiency—their dependence upon others for satisfying their needs: "The variation [telling and being told] makes one forget the aim of the significance, by transforming its act into a game, and giving it certain outlets that go some way towards satisfying the pleasure principle. . . . The game . . . is the subject's answer to what the mother's absence has created on the frontier of his domain—the edge of his cradle—namely a *ditch* around which one can only play at jumping" (62).[6] According to Lacan, such forgetting corresponds to what Freud calls repression (*Verdrängung*) and thus institutes the function of the unconscious. Insofar as the distracting pleasure that enables this forgetting is sexual in nature, so too is the resultant unconscious.

This conception of the unconscious differs from that advanced in my earlier discussion of the dream of the burning child, where I identified it with the troubling "little pieces of reality" such as the dream presentation of the knocking that woke Lacan. The present reconceptualization of the unconscious focuses upon its effects rather than its causes, upon the domesticated leftovers of repression rather than the chaotic, anxiety-provoking materials which call for repression.

Lacan's account of the origins of the unconscious can be generalized by proposing that, in all instances, repression, and thus the unconscious, result from pleasurable distractions created by what he calls the "partial drives" (invocatory, scopic, oral, anal, sadomasochistic). Insofar as all these drives are sexual in nature, so too is the unconscious: "Everything . . . [that] assumes sexual value, passes from the *Erhaltungstrieb*, from preservation, to the *Sexualtrieb*, only in terms of the appropriation . . . its seizure, by one of the partial drives" (191).[7]

Freud's argument for the sexual nature of the unconscious runs along somewhat different lines. Like Lacan, he introduces the function of the unconscious through repression. Unlike Lacan, however, he explains repression in terms of the "Law of the Father," a prohibition that takes the

6. These remarks are advanced in the context of a discussion of a parent reading to a child but also of the *Fort-Da* game, where, one can argue, the scopic rather than invocatory drive is operative.

7. See also Lacan 1981, 177. Lacan calls these drives "partial" in the sense that each, although sexual in nature, is "partial with regard to the biological finality of sexuality" (Lacan 1981, 177). According to Lacan, there is no sexual drive as such (189). Instead, activities are sexualized, libidinally invested, in relation to one of the "partial drives." It is important to keep in mind here that Lacan distinguishes sexual from gender relations. That is, for Lacan the sexual is a matter of the drive, whereas gender is a higher order structure involving the subject's relation to desire.

form of an explicit threat directed against an erotically charged wish. For instance, little Hans's desire to "coax with" [caress] his mother is inhibited—"repressed"—by a threat, in this case maternal, to "cut off his widdler" (Freud 1990, 167–305). Thus, for Freud (as indeed for the earlier Lacan of *Seminar IV*) the sexual nature of the unconscious is parasitic upon the sexual nature of repressed materials, such as little Hans's wish, which retrospectively, that is, after repression, take an unconscious form.

The later Lacan (of *Seminar XI*), by contrast, does not assign an originary role to prohibition in establishing repression. Instead, even when the mother is its agent, as in the case of little Hans, the Law of the Father, like the father himself, arrives too late on the scene, after all the hard work of repression has been done: "when the Legislator (he who claims to lay down the Law) presents himself to fill the gap, he does so as an imposter" (Lacan 1977, 311). Thus the paternal contribution is a purely formal prohibition that sets the seal on repression by mystifying and concealing its origins: "It is not the Law itself that bars the subject's access to *jouissance*— rather it creates out of an almost natural barrier a barred subject" (319).

Lacan deals rather carefully with the matter of his differences from Freud concerning the origins of repression. He indicates that Freud or at least Freudians have taken the sexualization of the child too far (Lacan 1981, 176–177). In particular, he suggests that, rather than sexuality functioning as a source of effects from the earliest moments of a subject's existence, its importance is established retrospectively: "The legibility of sex in the interpretation of the unconscious mechanisms is always retroactive. . . . Infantile sexuality is not a wandering block of ice snatched from the great ice-bank of adult sexuality" (176).

The connections Lacan proposes between the unconscious, language, and the sexual are evident in his account of the dream of the burning child. He argues that the terrifying "little pieces of reality" that erupt into dreams—the knocking, the noise of the candle overturning, the smell of burning, and so on—all suggest the idea of another, unspeakable reality— *die Idee einer anderer Lokalität* (56)—the memory of which has been lost, and for which the "little pieces of reality" seemingly function as traces. Such traces constitute what Lacan, following Freud, calls *Vorstellungsrepräsentanzen*, representatives for representations: representations that substitute for, stand in the place of, other representations that are missing because what they represent is unrepresentable. Rather than being some *urverdrängt* primal scene too horrible to relate, the "unrepresentable" in this context is a void created by the absence of any object that would fill the subject's originary lack. The cause of this void is *not* the subject's lacking a particular object, such as the mother's breast, but rather his or her dependence upon others for the satisfaction of basic needs.

Although the void concealed by the *Vorstellungsrepräsentanz* contains no objects, it is not totally empty but instead, according to Lacan, constitutes the site of an "other reality hidden behind the lack of that which takes the place of representation" (60). That other reality is the drive. Lacan clarifies this point in connection with his subsequent discussion of the *Fort-Da* game (62), where he argues that it is the pleasure produced by the drive that, by distracting the subject, "takes the place of representation."

The drive at issue in Lacan's discussion of the dream of the burning child is, of course, the invocatory drive. That is, the noise of the candle overturning takes on resonances of the terrible cry through which the father addresses himself on behalf of his child lost beyond the grave— *"Vater, siehst du denn nicht das ich verbrenne?"*—and from which he can flee only by bursting into wakefulness. As Lacan claims, we do not dream in order to escape reality; rather we wake in order to escape the Real, which is Lacan's name for the order of anxiety provoking disruptions to the symbolic order typified by the child's cry (58).[8]

The noise and the cry in combination take on the ambiguous dimensions of the Voice around which the invocatory drive forms as the father moves to and fro in two dimensions (Lacan 1981, 60): in and out of the dream, but also between audition and uttering, attempting to evade the cry that hounds him in his dreams but also ventriloquizing his dead child, an act that he repeats in censored form after waking. The pleasure produced in this way is sexual in nature because it is an effect of a drive (177).

In this context, then, the origins of the unconscious are located in the distractions created by the invocatory drive as it turns around the terrifying cry haunting the dreamer's sleep. This same drive structure sets in train a splitting of the subject as he vacillates between the "I" who speaks and the "me" who listens to what is said, a splitting that is forgotten as the subject moves into fully wakened speech.

Thus the covert operations of the drive explain not only the irreducibly sexual nature of the unconscious but also its linguistic structuring, specifically its implication in a splitting of the subject that parallels the split between subject of *énonciation* and subject of *énoncé*. In short, the tension noted by Lacan between linguistic and sexual approaches to the unconscious is resolved in Freud's theory of the drive.

8. See also Žižek 1989, 45. The Real may take either of two forms: either an unsymbolizable point of excess, that which Freud associates with *das Ding,* or a residue, a leftover from the process of symbolization, a piece of white noise from which all categorizable sounds have been sifted.

II

FETISH

3

A Slave to Desire:
Defetishizing the Colonial Subject

Sometimes I woke up, and found her bending over me. At other times, she whispered in my ear, as though it were her husband who was speaking to me, and listened to hear what I would answer. If she startled me, on such occasion, she would glide stealthily away; and the next morning she would tell me I had been talking in my sleep, and ask who I was talking to. At last, I began to fear for my life.

Harriet Jacobs, Incidents in the Life of a Slave Girl

In his influential essay "The Other Question," Homi Bhabha points to "contradictions and heterogeneity" surrounding racial stereotypes: "The black is both savage (cannibal) and yet the most obedient and dignified of servants (the bearer of food); he is the embodiment of rampant sexuality and yet innocent as a child; he is mystical, primitive, simpleminded and yet the most worldly and accomplished liar, and manipulator of social forces" (Bhabha 1994, 82). Bhabha argues for a "functional link" between such stereotypes and the disavowal of castration, which Freud takes as characteristic of fetishism: "For fetishism is always a 'play' or vacillation between the archaic affirmation of wholeness/similarity—in Freud's terms: 'All men have penises'; in ours 'All men have the same skin/race/culture'—and the anxiety associated with lack and difference—again, for Freud 'Some men do not have penises'; for us 'Some do not have the same skin/race/culture.'" (74) This argument, which characterizes fetishism in terms of a discursively constituted, anxiety-ridden point of contradiction, is the key to legitimating Bhabha's projection of fetishism onto whole colonial populations. Specifically, it authorizes a reading of the vacillations about the black body/slave displayed in Southern ante-bellum discourse as symptoms of a collective fetishistic structure of desire.

In a later essay, "Of Mimicry and Man: The Ambivalence of Colonial Discourse," Bhabha argues for an apparently different link between racial stereotypes and structures of mimicry, a link that, he argues, applies to the colonial subjects of British India no less than to the slave population of the Carolinas:

> The effect of mimicry on the authority of colonial discourse is profound and disturbing. For in "normalizing" the colonial state or subject, the dream of post-Enlightenment civility alienates its own language. . . . The ambivalence which thus informs this strategy is discernible . . . in this double use of the word "slave": first simply, descriptively as the locus of a legitimate form of ownership, then as the trope for an intolerable, illegitimate exercise of power. What is articulated in that distance between the two uses is the absolute imagined difference between the "Colonial" State of Carolina and the Original state of Nature. (Bhabha 1994, 86)

The difference from his earlier argument turns out to be more rhetorical than substantial, however. By figuring the colonial subject as *"almost the same but not quite,"* mimicry shares the ambiguities and disavowals characteristic of fetishism (86).

Bhabha also looks for reflections of the structure of mimicry-fetishism in colonial slave literature as well as contemporary works like Toni Morrison's *Beloved:* "I want to link this *circulation* of the sign from the 1870s in the world of *Beloved,* to the circulation of other signs of violence in the 1850s and 60s in northern and central India" (199). And in closing his discussion of *Beloved* he refers to "the ambivalences and ambiguities" of the "unhomely world . . . enacted in the house of fiction . . . its sundering and splitting performed in the work of art" (18).[1]

In short, Bhabha seems to be claiming that in British India no less than the slave plantations of the deep South, master-slave discourses and popular literature are indicators, indeed symptoms, of a fetishistic structure of desire that marks black bodies and continues to circulate today in books like Morrison's *Beloved.* Bhabha admits to a certain "recklessness" in proposing a black desire that so readily slips across cultural and historical

---

1. He also writes, immediately before the quotation on page 18: "When the present tense of testimony loses its power to arrest, then the displacements of memory and the indirections of art offer us the image of our psychic survival." Thus, in terms of Bhabha's framework, colonial literature and *Beloved* take on interestingly different roles, although the apparent privileging of the latter is complicated by complex intertextual relations as well as by the ideological nature of literature—ideological even when most arresting. (Morrison indicates her indebtedness to nineteenth-century slave narratives in several interviews—see Taylor-Guthrie 1994, 29, 182, 257.)

divides. His recklessness serves a noble political cause, however. In locating a similarity in desire between different marginal groups, he claims to be laying the groundwork for a common collective resistance against colonial oppression: "I want to move from the tortured history of Abolitionism to the Indian Mutiny. My reckless historical connection is based not on a sense of contiguity of events, but on the temporality of repetition that constitutes those signs by which marginalized or insurgent subjects create a collective agency" (199).

I do not intend to question the propriety of Bhabha's liberatory political goals or question his claim that historical acts of psychic violence perpetrated upon black bodies left their mark in fetishistic forms of desire.[2] Instead, I propose alternative readings of the texts Bhabha considers, readings that reveal the alleged scenes of perverse desire as something less than pathological. Specifically, I argue that Harriet Jacobs's *Incidents in the Life of a Slave Girl* and Morrison's *Beloved* may be read in terms of quite "normal," that is, nonperverse, forms of desire.[3]

My point is not to reverse Bhabha's claim by suggesting that normal rather then perverse desires were endemic to colonial/slave societies. To draw such a conclusion would simply reproduce in reverse form Bhabha's mistake of reading psychic structure from literary representations. Rather, my point is that even if, for argument's sake, and despite all the attendant political risks of pathologizing the black slave, we concede Bhabha's assumption concerning the perverse nature of the slave's desire, then my readings of *Beloved* and the Jacobs's narrative fail to uncover such desire. In short, my readings provide counterexamples to Bhabha's claim that certain privileged literary texts reflect the psychic structures of the social conditions that produced them.

Mama's Baby

In the Jacobs's narrative the slave's body functions as a source of anxiety for the jealous mistress who is driven to make nightly visits in order

---

2. One might well object that his strategy of looking for a common representation of black desires, and thus erasing differences between and within such desires, is repressive rather than liberatory. Indeed, it is a highly dubious strategy in the cause of black liberation, since, as I showed in the Introduction, it lends itself all too readily to a politically regressive pathologizing of a marginal group.

3. Of course, such literary illustrations do not provide evidence that the connections in question were instantiated in the lives of real slaves. In the case of the Jacobs narrative, though, this issue is complicated, since the narrative can be taken as a form of self-narration or folk history rather than literature. See Jean Yellin's preface to the Jacobs story.

to check that her husband is not sleeping with his slave (see the quotation at the beginning of this chapter). This anxiety is "unrealistic" in Freud's sense that it is inappropriate to its object. The inappropriateness is not a matter of the mistress, Mrs. Flint, having no cause for her jealousy but rather of the lengths she goes to in acting it out. Such anxiety, according to Freud, is the result of an unconscious link to the primal scene of lack. In Lacan's words, it "introduces us, with the greatest possible accent of communicability, to the function of the lack or fault [*la fonction du manque*]" (Lacan's unpublished *Seminar X*, of 1962/63, quoted in Weber 1991, 153).[4]

In such traumatic situations, according to Lacan, desire emerges: "It should not be forgotten that . . . 'trauma' is only the reverse side of the process by which not only 'perceptions' but also 'desires' themselves are constituted." Specifically, as I argued in Chapter 1, desire is created at sites where the subject is assailed by unrealistic anxieties arising from failure to come to terms with the Other's desire: "The desire of the *Other* does not recognize me. . . . It challenges me [*me met en cause*], questioning me at the very root of *my own desire* [my emphasis]. . . . And it is because this entails a relation of antecedence, a temporal relation, that I can do nothing to break this hold other than to enter into it. It is this temporal dimension that is anxiety" (Lacan, quoted in Weber 1991, 155, 160).[5]

In what form does desire manifest in the scene of southern discomfort portrayed by Jacobs? Hortense Spillers suggests that the mistress's desire takes the form of sexual attraction to her slave's body: "a sexuality that is neuter-bound, in as much as it represents an open vulnerability to a gigantic sexualized repertoire that may be alternately expressed as male/female."

Spillers analyzes the bedroom scene described at the beginning of this chapter along these lines: "Suspecting that her husband, Dr. Flint, has sexual designs on the young Linda [Harriet Jacobs] . . . Mrs. Flint assumes the role of a perambulatory nightmare who visits the captive woman in the spirit of a veiled seduction. . . . The 'jealous mistress' here (but jealous for whom?) forms an analogy with the 'master' to the extent that male dominative modes give the male the material means to fully act out what the female might only wish" (Spillers 1987, 76–77). Spillers continues: "Neither could claim her body . . . as her own. . . . In the case of the

---

4. Note that according to Freud in *The Interpretation of Dreams*, anxiety is a response to the traumatic "perceptual loss" that inhibits the proper functioning of the pleasure principle, that is, prevents the maintenance of fixed cathexes (Weber 1991, 154, 160).

5. Lacan also says along the same lines: "Anxiety manifests itself clearly from the very beginning as relating—in a complex manner—to the desire of the *Other*. . . . The anxiety-producing function of the desire of the *Other* [is] tied to the fact that I do not know what object *o* I am for this desire" (Weber 1991, 161).

doctor's wife, *she* appears not to have wanted *her* body, but to desire to enter someone else's" (77). A variety of familiar desires are mentioned in the course of Spillers's analysis: the husband's carnal lust, the wife's "ecstasy of unchecked power," and the "fabric of dread and humiliation" constructed by the two women, projected differentially by each in terms of their local narratives of loss and desire.[6]

Spillers's proposal finds little independent support in the text. In particular, it has difficulty in explaining the mistress's behavior toward the sleeping slave, circling her persistently, whispering in her ear, then "gliding stealthily away" as she awakes. If there exists what Spillers calls a "gigantic sexualized repertoire" at work here, then it is, it seems, subject to a strong negative proscription or inhibition. In that case, however, guilt should be part of Mrs. Flint's response to her slave. But the text provides little evidence of this.

An alternative reading is that the slave's body is an impediment to the mistress's real desires. Mrs. Flint is intent on maintaining not only the dignity of her social position, as a married woman and the wife of a professional man, but also her appearances as a good wife: a skilled manager of the home, virtuous, and both honored and, by implication at least, desired by her husband. The text provides reasons for why she should be insecure about these matters. Mrs. Flint, we are told, was not herself "a very refined woman," "a second wife, many years the junior of her husband," who was a "professional man" much concerned with saving appearances (Jacobs 1987, 34, 33).[7] The fact that the real Dr. Flint's first marriage ended in a famous and acrimonious divorce case—which cited his first wife's drinking, addiction to laudanum, promiscuity, and general carelessness with household expenses—no doubt contributed to the second Mrs. Flint's insecurities.[8] These come to a head in a bitter confrontation during which the slave is made to reveal Dr. Flint's sexual advances to her: "As I went on with my account her color changed frequently, she wept, and sometimes groaned . . . but I was soon convinced that her emotions arose

---

6. Like Bhabha, Spillers offers her analysis not only as a reconstruction of a fictionalized character but also as an account of the psychic structure of real slaves, including the historical protagonist of the Jacobs narrative. Unlike Bhabha, however, Spillers interrogates the terms of her analysis by historicizing her theoretical framework: "This narrative scene from Brent's [Jacobs's] work, dictated to Lydia Maria Child, provides an instance of a repeated sequence, purportedly based on 'real' life. But the scene in question appears to so commingle its signals with the fictive, with casebook narratives from psychoanalysis, that we are certain that the narrator has her hands on an explosive moment of New-World/U.S. history that feminist investigation is beginning to unravel" (Spillers 1987, 76–77).

7. The historical figure Mary Horniblow, upon whom the figure of Mrs. Flint was based, was the daughter of an inn keeper (Jacobs 1987, 260–261).

8. See Jacobs 1987, 262 n. 1, 263 n. 8.

from anger and wounded pride. She felt that her marriage vows were des-
ecrated, her dignity insulted. . . . She pitied herself as a martyr" (33).

In this context, the slave's body seems to function for Mrs. Flint less as
an object of desire (Spillers) than as what Lacan calls the *objet a*, which, by
openly attracting her husband's attention, stands in the way of the re-
spectability and respect that Mrs. Flint wants: an impediment to her desire
rather than its object. In short, from Mrs. Flint's perspective, desire attaches to the slave's body indirectly—"clings to it," as Lacan says (Lacan
1981, 245).

The slave's body occupies this role not only because Dr. Flint wants her
but also because, in treating Linda Brent as a rival who needs to be
watched, Mrs. Flint inadvertently brings about the very thing she fears. To
be specific, Mrs. Flint leaves her own bed at night for the slave's bedroom,
where she can continue her scrutiny. By so doing, the slave comes between husband and wife, although not in exactly the way the wife fears.[9]

On this reading, a quite different explanation of Mrs. Flint's strange behavior emerges. According to Lacan, pleasure arises not from subjects getting what they want but rather from their engaging with the *objet a*. Thus
the mistress's endless returns to the scene of her rival's body do not manifest conflicted desire so much as the pursuit of pleasure. In short, the real
source of pleasure arises not from some repressed pansexual desire, as
Spillers suggests, but rather from circling the *objet a*.

Lacan also indicates that too close an approach to the *objet a* creates
loathing. By exposing the *objet a* and associated lure as the "piece of shit"
around which the subject's activities turn, the phantasy upon which both the
staging of desire and the production of pleasure depend is threatened (Lacan
1981, 268). Such loathing is apparent in Mrs. Flint's repeated hesitation to
touch the "black" skin and her precipitate flights from the slave's waking
body, *as if* such contacts threatened to expose her in the nakedness of forbidden desire. These withdrawals are not flights from the illicit; they are
means of preserving the phantasy of a rival for Dr. Flint's affections, which in
turn sets the scene in which she produces pleasure and enacts her real desire
to secure her marriage. Specifically, if she comes too close or stays too long,
she risks seeing through the "black" body, recognizing it as merely a slave
with no real claim on her husband's affections, and thus destroying the narrative underpinnings of her pleasurable nightly peregrinations.

Harriet Jacobs was quite fair skinned, as the photo on the cover of the
Yellin edition of her diary indicates and as she herself tell us. The contradiction between this empirical fact and the equally undeniable fact of her

9. Slavoj Žižek (1989, 64–69) argues that such wayward chains of causes are typical of the
workings of the *objet a*.

"blackness" does not detract from her role as *objet a*. On the contrary, it makes a close approach to her body even more dangerous, since it threatens to expose the arbitrary nature of the color bar upon which antebellum Southern society was based.

This reading does not preclude the possibility of fetishism. In order for Mrs. Flint's desire to be fetishistic in the strictly Freudian sense, however, an extra element is required, namely, a discourse of disavowal to the effect that "the slave doesn't want to sleep with my husband, *but even so* she is taking him from me." Mrs. Flint's utterances and behavior show no signs of such vacillations. On the contrary, against all the evidence, she seems totally convinced that Linda is open to her husband's ineffectual attempts at seduction and is equally determined to stop him. Obsession rather than perversion seems to be the structure of Mrs. Flint's psychic universe.

In sum, Jacobs's story provides evidence neither of fetishistic desire (as Bhabha claims) nor strange pansexual rites (Spillers's contention). Instead, the reader is presented with the spectacle of a wife going about the familiar business of milking what pleasure she can from the deferrals of the bedchamber. The peculiar mixture of pleasure and loathing displayed by the mistress toward the slave's body confirms its identity as the *objet a*, or, more correctly, its associated lure.

Beloved

Halle, the husband of Sethe, *Beloved's* protagonist, works on Sundays in order to purchase his mother's freedom. Sethe is attracted to him as much for this self-sacrifice as for the amazing strength of his love: "Maybe that was why she chose him. A twenty-year old man so in love with his mother that he gave up five years of Sabbaths just to see her sit down for a change was a serious recommendation" (Morrison 1987, 11). His mother, Baby Suggs, expresses similar amazement at her son's strength of desire, which she allows to move her north against her better judgment: "When Halle looked like it meant more to him that she go free than anything in the world, she let herself be taken 'cross the river. . . . Halle, who had never drawn one free breath, knew that there was nothing like it in this world. It scared her" (141).

In the light of Halle's example, Sethe's own desires are transformed. But under the benevolent paternalism of the Garner family, her desire for freedom, like Halle's, is bounded by the overarching restraints imposed by slavery and the system of indentured labor: "Gettin away was a money thing to us. Buy out. Running was nowhere on our minds"—a theme repeated elsewhere in the book: "The . . . girl he knew as Halle's girl was obedient (like Halle), shy (like Halle), and work-crazy (like Halle)" (197,

164). It is only when the schoolteacher takes over the home farm ("Sweet Home," as it is called) and sets his adolescent boys to suck dry her breasts that Sethe conceives a desire for freedom at all costs. Initially this manifests in a restrained and covert way as "the Plan," but her desire finds full expression when she reaches freedom, experienced as an exultant and selfish pleasure at successfully bringing her children to safety: "I did it. I got us all out. . . . Decided. And it came off like it was supposed to. We was here. Each and every one of my babies and me too. . . . It was a kind of selfishness I never knew nothing about before. It felt good" (162).

The pertinent changes in Sethe's desire take place not so much at the level of content or even affect but rather in the structure of subjectivity within which possibilities for enacting desire are defined. Paul D, Sethe's lover, describes the new Sethe in terms similar to those employed by Baby Suggs in describing her son's desire to free her, a desire so powerful that it brooked no interference from others: "This here Sethe was new . . . talked about love like any other women . . . but what she meant could cleave the bone. . . . This here new Sethe didn't know where the world stopped and she began. . . . It scared him" (165).

Much of the narrative of *Beloved* is structured by this theme of the terrifying power of desire. It is embodied in the figure of Beloved, the book's eponymous and mysterious protagonist: "But it was Beloved who made demands. Anything she wanted she got, and when Sethe ran out of things to give her, Beloved invented desire" (240). In a mysterious way that the book never clarifies, Beloved is related to the daughter whom Sethe killed out of love/desire, and thus is also the effect of desire. In short, she stands in a doubly metonymic relation to desire, as both its effect and cause. Thus her eventual banishment, the community's ritualized failure to incorporate her, signals a failure to come to terms with desire, a failure that structures and plays havoc with the lives of three generations of women: Baby Suggs, Sethe, and Sethe's other daughter, Denver.

In Lacanian terms, Beloved is the Real of desire, the *objet a:* not the desired itself but that which controls and flows from desire: inchoate, unspeakable, horrifying, overwhelming, that which always escapes the ordering of the symbolic, a presence surrounded in mystery. She appears in this role to a group of women who see her and her adopted family standing together on the porch of their house: "Well, they saw something . . . it was standing right next to Sethe. But from the way they describe it, don't seem like the girl I saw in there" (265), an apparition that comes to takes on almost legendary status—"Later, a little boy put it out how he . . . saw, cutting through the woods, a naked woman with fish for hair" (267). Such sightings are accompanied by a peculiar loss of memory on the part of those who participate in their telling: "Everybody knew what she was called, but nobody anywhere knew her name. Disremembered and unaccounted for, she cannot be lost because no one is looking for her. . . . It was not a story to pass along" (274). Beloved's unsocialized nature—her thoughts lack even the most rudimentary spatial and temporal structure—reinforces the indeterminacy surrounding the question of who or what she is: "All of it is now   it is always now . . . . I am always crouching   the man is on my face   his face is not mine his mouth smells sweet but his eyes are locked" (211).

The book incorporates a counterpoint to the theme of desire and its terrifying consequence: an ethic of self-denial which recommends loving small: "Being so in love with the look of the world, putting up with anything and everything, just to stay alive in a place where a moon he had no right to was nevertheless there. Loving small and in secret" (221), a theme repeated later in Sethe's self-description: "Nobody loved her and she wouldn't have liked it if they had, for she considered love a serious disability" (256). This austere ethic renders personal desire and its enactment problematic, even hubristic, an occasion for anxiety: "And it worked out fine, worked out just fine, until she got proud and let herself be overwhelmed by the sight of her daughter-in-law and Halle's children . . . and have a celebration of blackberries that put Christmas to shame. Now she stood in the garden smelling disapproval, feeling a dark and coming thing, and seeing high-topped shoes that she didn't like the look of at all. At all" (147).

Subjects, black ones at least, it seems, get their pleasure not from following their desire but rather, as in fetishism, from serving the other. As the Jacobs narrative puts it: "My mistress was so kind to me that I was always glad to do her bidding and proud to labor for her as much as my young years would permit. I would sit by her side for hours, sewing diligently, with a heart as free from care as that of any free born white child" (Jacobs 1987, 7). These lines are echoed in Morrison's evocation of the Sweet Home regime: "She wanted to love the work she did, to take the ugly out of it. . . . A few yellow flowers on the table, some myrtle tied around the handle of the flatiron holding the door open for a breeze calmed her, and when Mrs. Garner and she sat down to sort bristle, or make ink, she felt fine" (Morrison 1987, 22).

Much of the narrative tension in *Beloved* comes from an interweaving of such episodes of self-denial with the horrendous consequences of untrammeled desire. For instance, Sethe's "crime," the consequences of which continue to haunt her throughout the book, is presented as the result of indulging a love that is "too thick":

"Your love is too thick," he said . . . .
"Too thick?" . . . "Love is or it ain't. Thin love ain't love at all."

"Yeah. It didn't work, did it? Did it work?" he asked. . . . "Your boys gone you don't know where. One girl dead, the other won't leave the yard." (165)

At the end of the book, following Beloved's expulsion, a semblance of normalcy returns to the local Cincinnati community of blacks in the form of a chilling reassertion of the historically dominant ethic of self-denial: "Her smile, no longer the sneer he remembered, had welcome in it. . . . Paul D touched his cap. 'How you getting along?' 'Don't pay to complain'" (266). This final act in the story constitutes a sort of return, a "welcome back" to the false sweetness of Sweet Home. Denver's chilling "Don't pay to complain" repeats the quietism characteristic of the black slaves at the story's opening. Similarly, the relation between Denver (Sethe's daughter) and the Bodwins, who benevolently open a space in their town house for a new black servant, repeats the paternalistic relation between the Garners and Sethe. Education and the educated stand as a continuing and dangerous support of this ethic: a chain stretching from Jacobs's Dr. Flint, to Morrison's schoolteacher of Sweet Home, and Miss Bodwin's generous offer: "'She says I might go to Oberlin.' And he didn't say, 'Watch out. Watch out. Nothing in the world more dangerous than a white school teacher'" (266).

In the context of these retreats and returns to the ethic of self-denial, the white man and his congeries play the role of *objet a* (or associated lure), that which stands in the way of the black woman's desire both by impeding access to the place of desire (freedom) and by occupying it in her stead. The white man is also that around which, despite his lack of desirability, the black woman always turns. Beloved's horrifying description of "the men without skin [who] push them through with poles" (210), as well as Linda Brent's crude attempts at manipulating her white lover, Mr. Sands, for whom she displays a total lack of passion, position the white man not so much as an object of desire as a strange attractor around which black lives circulate: "Revenge, and calculations of interest, were added to flattered vanity and sincere gratitude for kindness. I knew nothing would enrage Dr. Flint so much as to know that I favored another; and it was something to triumph over my tyrant even in that small way. . . . I made a headlong plunge. Pity me, and pardon me, O virtuous reader . . . the painful and humiliating memory will haunt me to my dying day" (Jacobs 1987, 55–56).

Baby Suggs's final lament echoes this theme of the white man who, like the bad luck he brings, always returns: "those white things [who] have taken all I had or dreamed . . . and broke my heartstrings too. There is no bad luck in the world but whitefolks" (Morrison 1987, 89). For Sethe and Paul D, too, the white man as represented by Sweet Home constitutes the *objet a* (/lure): an object Sethe wants to desire "because she wanted to love the work she did, to take the ugly out of it" (22); Sweet Home as the some-time tender trap in which the white man holds them, and to which they seem condemned to return not merely in their memories and conceptions of home but also as a certain structure of servitude:

> "How come everybody runs off from Sweet Home can't stop talking about it? Look like if it was so sweet you would have stayed."
>
> "Girl, who you talking to?"
>
> Paul D laughed. "True, true. She's right, Sethe. It wasn't sweet and it sure wasn't home." He shook his head.
>
> "But it's what we were," said Sethe, "All together. Comes back whether we want it or not." She shivered a little. (13–14)[10]

In sum, the regime of desire open to the inhabitants of Sweet Home under the benevolent stewardship of the Garners or in the Cincinnati household of the Bodwins displays all the characteristics of fetishism: the attenuation of desire and agency as well as a more or less overt preoccupation with the white man as an *objet a* that, in functioning as a site of disavowal, takes on the trappings of the fetish.

Fetishism is not the only regime of desire envisaged by *Beloved*, however. By living extravagantly with desire, the book's various *ménages à deux*, Sethe–Denver, Paul D–Sethe, Denver–Beloved, Sethe–Beloved, all run the risk of transgressing the ethic of "loving small." In each case, the couples are disrupted by a third party who catalyzes the release of a destructive excess of desire. Paul D, for instance, muses sorrowfully upon the cataclysmic effect Beloved has upon his relation with Sethe, as he is moved "like a rag doll" from room to room, away from Sethe, toward the ultimate scene of his seduction in the cold room: "SHE MOVED HIM . . . Paul D didn't know how to stop it because it looked like he was moving himself" (114); "And then she [Beloved] moved him. Just when doubt, regret, and every single unasked question was packed away, long after he believed he had willed himself into being, at the very time and place he wanted to take root—she moved him. From room to room. Like a rag doll" (221).

Normal—that is, nonperverse—desire always and already returns, breaking up these fetishistic regimes of self-denial, whether it be through

---

10. Beloved and the white man thus occupy similar roles in relation to desire, namely, as *objets a*. Whereas the white man comprises the *objet a* in its guise as the gift which turns to shit even as it is exchanged (Lacan 1981, 268), Beloved comprises the *objet a* in its more ephemeral manifestation, as a hitch in the symbolic order around which activities circulate (Žižek 1989, 169–171).

the opportunities for earning freedom offered by Sweet Home or "free" waged labor in Cincinnati. In particular, repression overtakes the moment of avowal, leaving disavowal in sole possession of the field, "there is no bad luck in the world but whitefolks" (from Baby Suggs's last lament— 89). At the same time, the importance of the white man as the *objet a* disappears from view as he becomes the invisible framework for black lives rather than its all-seeing and ever visible pivot.

Thus, Bhabha's characterization of the slave's desire as fetishistic proves to be only half the story. A second "normal" regime of desire is present in both Morrison's and Jacobs's narratives, a regime which, despite its normality, is no less oppressive than the one forged by and around the white masks of Sweet Home. Morrison's *Beloved* may be read as an exploration of the interweaving of these two different regimes, an exploration that casts a deep shadow across the nostalgically invested Sweet Home and its modern reincarnation in the streets of Cincinnati. In this light, Baby Suggs's retrospective evaluation of her response to Sweet Home stands as a key moment in such an exploration: "In Lillian Garner's house, exempted from the field work that broke her hip and the exhaustion that drugged her mind; in Lillian Garner's house where nobody knocked her down (or up), she listened to the white woman humming at her work; watched her face light up when Mr. Garner came in and thought, It's better here, but I'm not. . . . It surprised and pleased her, but worried her too" (140).[11]

Thus, contrary to Bhabha's claim, the representations of desire in *Beloved*, as in Jacobs's narrative, fail to reflect ("enact" as Bhabha says) the split forms, the "ambivalences and ambiguities," of fetishistic desire, which Bhabha takes to be characteristic of slave/colonial regimes (Bhabha 1994, 18). On the contrary, the desires portrayed in these texts constitute a complex interweaving of fetishism with other "normal" forms of desire. If psychic structure is reflected in cultural forms, as Bhabha claims, then it is not in the straightforward way which he envisages.

11. This evaluation is echoed in Paul D's subsequent musings: "He wondered how much difference there really was. . . . Garner called and announced them men—but only on Sweet Home, and by his leave" (Morrison 1987, 220).

4

Fetish and the Native Subject

In the previous chapter, I criticized Bhabha's attempt to draw a connection between psychic structure and cultural form. In particular, I denied his thesis that the psychic splitting resulting from violences inflicted upon black bodies in slave/colonial societies was reflected in certain cultural artifacts. On the contrary, I argued, the texts Bhabha analyzed should be read in terms of an interweaving of "normal" (nonperverse) and other desires. In this chapter, I reverse the argument by presenting three cases in which the split form of a cultural artifact not only reflects but also partakes in a structure of disavowal characteristic of communal fetishism. The point against Bhabha, then, is not that relations of reflection between psychic structures and cultural forms do not exist, but rather that such connections should not be established in a question-begging way by reading psychic structure from what is simply assumed to be a "corresponding" cultural form. On the contrary, both cultural form and psychic structure should be independently established, so that the claim of a connection between them emerges as nontrivial and empirically confirmable.

The Hopi Son

In *Soleil Hopi*, Taleyseva, a chief of the North American Hopi Indians, narrates his childhood. Hopi ritual, we are told, included a ceremony during which certain masks, called *Katcina*, were worn by dancers. The

Hopi encouraged a belief among their offspring that the masked dancers were gods (also called *Katcina*). Young children were frightened into behaving themselves by being told that if they did not eat their porridge, go to sleep, stop crying, and so on, then the Katcina would come and eat them. At initiation, however, apparently to the great consternation of the young initiates, fathers and uncles of the clan revealed themselves as wearers of the masks, a revelation that threatened to destroy not only key elements in the children's cosmology but also the rationale for much of their learned behavior. As Taleyseva recounts the story of his own initiation: "I was greatly shocked: these weren't spirits. . . . I felt unhappy because all my life I had been told that the Katcina were gods. I was above all shocked and furious to see my clan uncles and fathers dancing as Katcina. But it was even worse to see my own father" (Mannoni 1964, 16).[1]

As they were exposed to the apparently devastating revelation, initiates were offered additional knowledge in mythological form: a recounting of *un autrefois*, a golden age, when the gods had danced openly among the people. The myth went on to claim that "in a mysterious way" the gods were still present on dance days: "You know that the *real* Katcina don't come to dance in the pueblos as they did in other times. They come only in an invisible fashion, and inhabit the masks during the dance days in a mysterious way" (16).

Commenting on this moment of revelation, Mannoni observes that "one sees there . . . the moment when belief, abandoning its imaginary form, enters the symbolic mode sufficiently to open out into [religious] faith, that is to say, onto commitment" (16–17). The operation of what Mannoni refers to here as the "symbolic" involves a form of double deception that I alluded to earlier in my discussion of the signifier in its role as *Vorstellungsrepräsentanz*.

The first level of deception practiced upon the children involves the masks functioning as false tokens of the gods' presence, thus concealing their absence. In the context of the initiation, the masquerade becomes more complex, however. It is admitted that the masks hide the absence of the gods, but the admission is made only in order to advance a second deception: that the absence is only an apparent one, since the gods are present invisibly (*de façon invisible*). Mannoni associates such deception with the operation of religious symbols, which signal the presence of the divine by the paradoxical device of admitting their own poverty as representations.

Michael Taussig remarks a similar structure of deception among the Selk'nam of Tierra del Fuego. During the initiation dance, known as the

---

1. All translations from Mannoni are mine.

Hainu, men wearing horned masks mime women-hating spirits. Taussig comments upon two quite different forms of "sacred violence" attached to this performance:

> On the one hand the women and children, forming the "audience," have to pretend—to mime—on pain of death that what they are witness to are real gods and not their kinsmen acting as gods. In this way the public secret essential to mystical authority is preserved.
>
> On the other hand is the violence associated with the demasking of the gods that the male initiates are forced to witness in the privacy of the men's house. Through the violence of demasking fused with laughter, the power of the mimetic faculty as a socially constitutive force is thereby transferred from the younger to the older men, the duped becomes one with the dupers, and . . . "the great secret" fortifies [the] "invisible state." (Taussig 1993, 85–86)

Thus not only the initiates but the audience too are involved in structures of double deception. That is, "knowing" that the masks are fakes, the audience see through one deception, but even so, indeed because of this, they must enter a second deception, that is, they must pretend that they have not seen through the first. The initiates are trapped in a similar structure, which, by its difference, marks their special status. Like their audience, prior to initiation they only pretended to believe in the masks. But then, in the secrecy of the men's hut, they must act as if they are shocked by the unmasking, that is, they must engage in a second deception. They must pretend that prior to initiation they had not seen through the earlier deception.

What separates the "knowing" initiates from the "ignorant" audience is not a matter of knowledge but rather of power relations and social arrangements, a matter of who is forced ("on pain of death") to pretend to whom. That is, from the outset, everyone knows that the dancers are their kinsmen. After the ceremony, however, the audience are forced to continue the pretense that the initiated have access to the "truth," whereas, at least among themselves, the initiated are able to drop the pretense. Their superior status resides, then, in the fact that they can speak the real truth—the cruel fact that there is no truth—while the uninitiated must continue to conspire in what they know to be a lie: that the truth exists. The fact that everyone knows all along that the "truth" in question is a lie makes the demonstration of power more effective rather than less.

The Katcina initiation ritual and the attendant revelation became a site at which a contradiction took shape: "*I know* that the dancers are my uncles and fathers, not spirits, *but even so* the Katcina are present when my uncles and fathers dance in the masks" (16). This contradiction takes the logical form of what Freud calls "disavowal" (*Verleugnung*): "I know that . . . but *even so* . . ." But can we claim, as Mannoni does, that Hopi engagement with the Katcina masks is one of disavowal in the full Freudian sense? More specifically, can we take the Katcina masks as fetish objects in Freud's sense? Or by doing so do we commit Bhabha's mistake of exporting psychoanalytic concepts into the cultural domain on the basis of overgeneralized structural homologies?

As I pointed out in Chapter 1, according to Freud fetishistic disavowal consists of two components: first, an "avowal" of the form "I know that," usually grounded in commonsense perception, which more or less directly asserts what has been repressed, such as the mother's missing penis or some other metaphoric transcription of her primal lack; second, the disavowal proper, expressed in the form "but even so," which by denying what has been avowed reinstates repression, for instance denying the mother's penis is missing through investing some other object, such as a knee or a piece of fur, as a substitute. Does the Hopi initiation ritual and its attendant revelation involve such a structure, in which the repressed surfaces in order to be disavowed?

In many Hollywood films the repressed is portrayed as a sort of unnamable and unmentionable thing (Freud's *das Ding*) that adults cannot bring readily to mind because of its associations with childhood experiences so horrifying that they are wiped from memory almost as soon as they happen (for example, sight of the mother's genitalia, an incident in the family romance, and so on). Only later, in adult life, does the repressed return in various sinister guises, brought to full consciousness by much painful and difficult psychoanalytic work of a hermeneutic kind.

Lacan turns this traditional portrayal of repression upside down by advocating a return to Freud's insight that subjects may without much difficulty bring to mind repressed memories, indeed do so without occasioning themselves much distress: "Freud made it quite clear that, although it was difficult for the subject to reproduce in dream the memory of the heavy bombing raid, for example, from which his neurosis derives—it does not seem, when he is awake, to bother him either way" (Lacan 1981, 51). The memory's "repressed" status, according to Lacan, resides not in the putative fact of its burial beyond immediate recall but rather in the phantasy structure of symptoms, including the various and varied hidden forms of return that punctuate a subject's life practices. The subconscious status of repressed memories pertains not to their content, which may be quite open to consciousness, but rather to their hidden connections with these practices (slips, symptoms, and so on). The phenomenon of disavowal illustrates precisely such a possibility, since it allows repressed knowledge to surface systematically and more or less openly.

In the context of the Hollywood portrayal of repression, it is tempting to interpret the moment during the Katcina ritual when the masked dancers are revealed to be the novices' uncles as representing a resurfacing or "return" of what has been repressed. Specifically, it is tempting to understand the revelation "I *know* that the dancers are my uncles and fathers, not spirits," as a brutal confrontation with the repressed or hidden knowledge that the gods are not there at all, a confrontation deflected at the last minute by the sophistic device of reconceiving the gods' presence as invisible or perhaps symbolic in some way: "*but even so* the Katcina are present when my uncles and fathers dance in the masks." The disavowal, in particular the (mis)representation of the gods' apparent absence as a sign of their invisible presence, emerges, then, as an attempt to reinstate repression in the wake of the return of what previously has been hidden. Since, according to Freud, the return of the repressed is always accompanied by anxiety, this view has the virtue of explaining, indeed predicting, the "consternation" (reconstrued as anxiety) that Taleyseva retrospectively associates with the initial revelation of the masked dancers' identities.

A Lacanian conception of repression suggests a quite different account. Repressed knowledge, I argued in Chapter 1, takes the form of affirming the importance of the *objet a*, which in turn functions as a stand-in, or metaphoric equivalent, for the subject's lack. In the case of the Hopi initiation, for reasons I discuss below, the *objet a* is the Katcina mask, and so the claim that the masks are vessels for the gods expresses the importance of the *objet a*. Thus the act of revealing that uncles rather than gods are inside the masks counts as the reinstatement of repression rather than its easing. The repressed knowledge at issue is not some deep truth too horrible to bear, but rather a simple claim with which everyone is familiar, namely, that the gods still dance in attendance upon the tribe. It is an open secret that this claim is false. Indeed, it is through this structure of open secrecy that repression is set in place. Here, then, repressed knowledge is upon everyone's lips, but everyone knows it to be a lie. By contrast, according to the Hollywood conception, the repressed is a horrible truth that is difficult to bring to light, but when it does emerge (with the help of an analyst) one is forced to acknowledge it by the sheer force of the insight it offers.

In short, the repressed nature of the knowledge that the gods are in the masks does not reside in its failure to enter consciousness. On the contrary, like the shell shock victim's memories of the bombing raid, it lies well to the forefront of awareness (Lacan 1981, 51). But neither does the repressed nature of the knowledge reside simply in the fact that, through a structure of open secrecy, subjects deny its truth. Instead, as I indicated above, its repressed nature lies in a subject's failure to realize the extent to which, even when knowing it to be untrue, it structures the subject's actions, specifically his or her symptoms. In Žižek's terms, repression is not simply a subject's failure to know but rather a failure to know what knowledge is being acted upon (Žižek 1989, 69).

As we have seen, however, belief in the gods' presence inside the masks is recuperated after the revelation; specifically, it returns in mythological form as a denial of what the initiates plainly see: *"but even so the Katcina are present when my uncles and fathers dance in the masks."* In terms of my analysis, such recuperation constitutes a "return of the repressed" at the level of consciousness. By surfacing more or less openly into consciousness instead of reappearing merely as slips, this return of the repressed constitutes a disavowal in the full Freudian sense. And a fortiori the contradiction between the revelation that the masks are empty and the subsequent mythological recuperation of the gods' presence functions as a disavowal.

The exact moment of disavowal is not easy to identify. Taleyseva recounts another, even earlier childhood incident in which he surprised his mother making the traditional gifts given by the masked Katcina to Hopi children: "The mothers . . . redeem their terrorized children [from the Katcina] by giving the Katcina meat; in exchange, the Katcina give the children maize balls, *piki,* which on this occasion are exceptionally colored red." "On one occasion," Taleyseva tells us, "I surprised my mother cooking the piki. When I saw that it was red, I was bowled over. That evening I couldn't eat, and when the Katcina distributed their gifts I didn't want them" (Mannoni 1964, 14–15). How can this story, which implies that Taleyseva knew the dancers were fakes long before his initiation, be reconciled with the apparently contradictory claim that the revelation of his uncles' role in the initiation ceremony came as *un grand choc?*

Freud argues that trauma attaches to an event not because it is horrible or shocking when it happens but rather because a subsequent pattern of symptoms retrospectively positions that event at their fictional origin. In particular, Taleyseva's traumatic memory of his initiation, *"J'ai eu un grand choc,"* is not significant as a veridical historical record of a shocking childhood experience, since if the episode with the *piki* is to be credited, he already knew well before his initiation that the dancers were not gods. Instead, the memory took on its traumatic quality retrospectively, as later anxieties (we don't know which) attached themselves to it. In short, by a process of rememorization the initiation took on the paradoxical status of a memorial to later events. It follows that, rather than arising at the moment of initiation, the structure of disavowal was instituted retrospectively, as an aspect of initiates' integration of their experiences into historical remembrances of their lives.

Unmasking the Katcina

Mannoni argues that Hopi initiation precipitated a structure of disavowal, a conclusion I qualified by emphasizing the retrospective nature of that process. A fine-grained analysis is needed in order to justify the further claim that the Katcina mask is the fetish object implicated in this structure.

Prior to initiation the Katcina mask was employed as a threat to make Hopi children behave themselves. It thus prevented them from getting what they really wanted. But also, like the cotton-reel in the *Fort-Da* game, it provided an object around which their activities circulated. The children carefully approached the masks on dance days, fascinated and terrified by the prospect of falling under their gaze, then with howls of mixed delight and horror quickly withdrew to a safe position of invisibility from which they could see without being seen, before venturing out again.

Such dovetailed activities of seeing and being seen, like the successive throwings away and retrievals of the *Fort-Da*, set in place the scopic drive, and along with it the creation of pleasure as well as anxiety. As in the *Fort-Da*, desire emerged from such activities, enabling the masks to take on the role of object-cause of desire: "From that time he [Taleyseva] took care to do what was good" (16–17). In the context of this process the Katcina mask, like the cotton-reel, played the role of lure, and thus a front for the gaze as an *objet a*.[2]

After the revelation and counterrevelation during initiation, the Katcina no longer functioned as threats, sources of divine retribution for misbehavior. Instead, as Taleyseva tell us, the young Hopi initiates behaved well out of a sense of responsibility rather than fear (16–17). Nevertheless, the Katcina masks continued to fill the role of lure screening the *objet a*. Such continuity was mandated by the fact that many of the "good" practices acquired in childhood survived into adulthood, practices that, since they were organized originally to selectively attract and avoid the attention of the Katcina, continued to carry the imprint of the masks at their center. By playing with the deception that the masks were gods—first undermining it (via the revelation) and then reinforcing it in qualified form

---

2. Not any such dovetailing of seeing and being seen results in a drive structure. On the contrary, it is the paradoxical combination of anxiety and pleasure associated with the children's relations with the Katcina which signals that a drive was at work in such situations.

(via the myth)—the initiation positioned the mask as a lure screening the gaze.

In Chapter 1, I argued that in becoming a site of disavowal, a lure is transformed into a fetish. The Katcina mask exemplifies such an object. The relevant disavowal takes the characteristic form noted by Copjec, "between the disavowal that produces the fetish object [the mask] and an avowal that allows subjects to do without it" (Copjec 1994, 113). Specifically, it takes the form of a contradiction between the assertion that the gods inhabit the masks in an invisible fashion and the observation that the masks are empty, a contradiction repeated at the level of Hopi practices as a tension between adult responsibility and childhood fear of the Katcina.

According to Freud, such contradictory structures are constitutive of perverse or, more correctly, fetishistic forms of subjectivity. The element of perversion resides not in the unusual or socially unacceptable nature of the object of desire but rather in the way that the structure indirectly brings to the surface the gap between the production of pleasure and the achievement of desire. That is, by deferring access to the object of desire and lingering with the corresponding lure in its role as fetish, the perverse subject shows that pleasure resides in engaging the fetish rather than the object of desire. In short, the fetishistic subject constitutes a novel type of subjectivity for which agency resides not (as it does for the normal subject) in trying to get what one wants, but rather in sticking with the impediment to desire.

Hunting the Fetish

The structure of fetishism is also evident in a case discussed by Claude Lévi-Strauss in his book *Totemism*. Among the Ojibwa and Algonquin the totem is an element in a system of norms restricting partners with whom individuals trade, eat, cohabit, and so on. In this way it acts as a systematic guide but also impediment to achieving desired alliances. It functions also as an object around which the transmission and reception of speech circulates. In particular, the totemic animal is "killed and eaten [only] with certain ritual precautions, viz., that permission had first to be asked of the animal, and apologies be made to it afterwards" (Lévi-Strauss 1963, 21).

The domain of ritual thus functions as an arena for exfoliating intellectual difficulties about the totem's status in the same way that Hopi practices act as an arena for working out difficulties concerning the status of the Katcina masks. What are we to make of such rituals? Are they merely "empty ritual," as we say, or do the Ojibwa literally think that the dead are listening, that the animal's spirit hears the apologies and retrospectively sanctions its own killing?

According to Lévi-Strauss, the Ojibwa are perfectly clear that an animal's totemic nature does not imply any special connection with the spirit world: "'It's only a name,' they said to the investigator" (21). Nevertheless, in Durkheimian terms, the totemic animal operates as a "sacred" object around which individuals' responses resonate with and reinforce each other. Because of this, although it appears as a perfectly ordinary object ("only a name"), in confronting it the Ojibwa act as if they were facing a far greater spectacle, that of society itself, as Durkheim puts it (Durkheim 1915, 322; Lukes 1975, 589).[3] The Ojibwa's apologies may be understood, then, as directed not to the hunted animal as such but rather to society as a whole in its specific manifestation as the totem.

Not only does the hunter address the animal/totem, but also the totem addresses or at least listens to the hunter through the medium of the totemic animal. I do not mean that the hunter is addressed in any literal sense or even in the Althusserian sense of "interpellated" (although it is true that the field of practices lying behind the totem "hail" the hunter in Althusser's sense). Instead, I mean that the animal/totem leads the hunter to enter into a dialogic situation if not into actual dialogue. Specifically, by falling to his arrows the animal causes the hunter to experience his ritual imprecations as heard, and even in a metaphoric sense "answered." Specifically, by going through a form of apology to the animal for killing it, he enacts a self-deception—namely, that the animal hears what he says when in fact, as we would say, he is only listening to himself.

Jean-Paul Sartre's story of looking through a keyhole, as retold by Lacan, makes a similar point.

> The gaze that surprises me and reduces me to shame . . . is not a seen gaze, but a gaze imagined by me in the field of the Other. . . . Far from speaking of the gaze as of something that concerns the organ of sight, he [Sartre] refers to the sound of rustling leaves, suddenly heard while out hunting, to a foot-step heard in the corridor . . . [a]t the moment when he has presented himself in the action of looking through a key hole. A gaze surprises him in the function of voyeur, disturbs him, overwhelms him and reduces him to a feeling of shame. (Lacan 1981, 84)

In this episode, an intrusion from outside the domain of the scopic, namely, the noise of a footfall, precipitates the voyeuristic Sartre into a sit-

3. Lévi-Strauss was keen to divorce himself from any connections between the religious and totemic orders. That is, for Lévi-Strauss, the religious has to do with the spirit world (which the Ojibwa designate as *manido*), which cuts across the totemic order of *ototeman* (Lévi-Strauss 1963, 18, 22). Because of the religious connotations of the term "sacred," Benjamin's terminology of the "auratic" is less misleading than Durkheim's.

uation in which he falls under the eye of an Other located ambiguously within his field of visibility. In the same way a kill at the end of the Ojibwa hunt constitutes an "answer" to the hunter's prayers, a sign that he has been heard. And as in the case of Sartre's story of peering through the keyhole, the unrealistic anxieties associated with the activity ("Have I performed the appropriate rituals correctly?" "Will the gods smile on me?" and so on) identify the hunter's interlocutor as located in the field of the Other.

Of course the hunter knows that the animal doesn't hear him when it is dead; and even while it is being hunted there is no question of dialogue between hunter and hunted. Nevertheless the self-deception of talking with the animal exerts a grip, proven by the hunter's experience of the slain animal as "an answer to his prayers," which, in turn, transforms his invocatory field into a site of a dialogical exchange with the Other. Such distortion of the vocal field constitutes an *objet a* for the invocatory drive, what Lacan calls the Voice, with the hunted animal playing the role of corresponding lure. The pleasures of the hunt and the associated anxieties confirm that in the framework of the hunt, the twinned activities of speaking and being spoken to have set in train such a drive structure.

Identifying the animal as a lure helps make more understandable the distinction between totem and guardian spirit upon which Lévi-Strauss dwells at some length. The Ojibwa, it seems, like to have a guardian spirit and work hard to get one, but do not to care much one way or the other about their totem. By contrast, a certain anxiety attends relations with the totem: desire relates to it tangentially rather than attaching directly: "At most there were reported hints of physical and moral distinctions [between totems]" (Lévi-Strauss 1963, 22). This is not to deny that it is important, indeed a matter of life or death, to identify with a totem; on the contrary, all the native's subsequent ritual practices take place within a framework constructed in terms of that object. The totem itself, however, appears to be peculiarly lacking as a site of desire. It is not so much an object of desire as a prop for it. These are exactly the characteristics of the lure, which is on the way to desire but is not itself desired.[4]

The totemic animal is also a site of disavowal, an intricate system of practical and cognitive contradictions that asserts as well as denies the im-

---

4. According to Lacan, metonymy is the trope associated with desire. Thus the suggestion that the distinction between the guardian spirit and totem corresponds to that between the lure and the object of desire fits well with Lévi-Strauss's claim that the guardian spirit is associated with causal (or religious) modes of thought, that is, with metonymy. It also fits with Lacan's view that the *objet a* is the first signifier, and thus associated with metaphor, the trope that, Lévi-Strauss notes, is associated with totemic relations since they depend upon an isomorphism between the set of totems and set of clans.

portance of the *objet a*. That is, on the one hand, Ojibwa and Algonquin practices and beliefs suggest a commitment to an affinity between the totemic animal and clan members. On the other, Ojibwa clan members protest that the totem is no more than a name, and the Algonquin take the matter of an affinity between clan members and their totems as a topic for jokes: "The Algonquin . . . [told] jokes such as 'My totem is the wolf, yours the pig. . . . Take care! Wolves eat pigs'" (Lévi-Strauss 1963, 22).

This discursive contradiction is echoed at a practical level. Specifically, it reappears as a conflict between the already noted ritual apologies to totemic animals before killing or eating them and a certain casualness concerning their extinction: "Although the caribou had completely disappeared from Southern Canada, this fact did not at all worry the members of the clan named after it" (21). The domain of practice thus functions as an arena for exfoliating intellectual difficulties about the totem's status, in the same way that Hopi practices acted as an arena for working out difficulties concerning the status of the Katcina masks.

Thus the totemic animal takes on the characteristics of a fetish. It is not only a lure screening a corresponding *objet a* but also a site of disavowal echoed at the level of practice. The fetishistic nature of the totem is confirmed by the peculiar lack of affect attending the disaster of the totemic animals disappearing from the hunting grounds. Such lack of affect is characteristic of engagement with the fetish because, although the fetish gets all the perverse subject's attention, it does not comprise his object of desire.[5]

In sum, a Lacanian approach explains aspects of Lévi-Strauss's ethnographic materials, specifically the Algonquin's jokes, which a purely structuralist approach marginalizes. It also indicates more generally how, despite their internal cognitive dissonances, fetishistic structures comprise a good strategy for traditional, strongly bounded societies. The Ojibwa deny the authority of the various hunting and eating rituals: "*I know* the totem is only a name." Nevertheless there is a strong incentive for attending to rituals—not because of the contradictory avowal that "*all the same* it is important to respect the rituals," but rather because of the pleasure produced by the structure of fetishism. Indeed, such pleasure may be the only one the fetishist gets, since his own desires are sacrificed on the altar of the Other. A similar situation, I argue in the next section, is evident in connection with Lévi-Strauss's discussion of the Oedipus myth.

5. This conclusion can also be justified along more orthodox Freudian lines. Since the totem is a fetish, its vanishing signals an end to pleasure, thus repeating the primal wound that Freud calls "trauma." Lack of affect is one characteristic reaction to such a catastrophe, a point that Lacan makes in the context of his discussion of Freud's case of the shell-shocked neurotic (Lacan 1981, 51).

Man, Wife, and Boy

According to Lévi-Strauss, the Oedipus myth functioned in the classical Greek context as a means of exploring a contradiction between a traditional or what Lévi-Strauss calls "theoretical" belief in autochthony (born of the earth) and an experientially grounded belief in sexual procreation as applied to the origins of man. The contradiction in question may be expressed in terms of the following disavowal: "*I know that* I am born of man and woman (experience tells me so), *but even so* (theory tells me) I am born of the earth." This contradiction was extended by classical Greek metaphors and rituals which, by associating woman/womb/birth with nature/soil/cultivation of plants, allowed the contradiction to be reframed as a disavowal concerning woman's lack of reproductive self-sufficiency: "*I know that* man is the product of intercourse between husband and wife, *but even so* he is born of earth-woman-wife alone."

According to Lévi-Strauss, the Oedipus myth provided a means of coping with this contradiction by showing it to be equivalent to a "real contradiction" negotiated in Greek social life between two marital strategies: endogamy (marrying in) and exogamy (marrying out) or, as Lévi-Strauss puts it, between overrating blood relations and undervaluing them:

> Although the problem [the contradiction between the two models for the origin of man] cannot be solved, the Oedipus myth provides a kind of logical tool which related the original problem—born from one or born from two?—to the derivative problem: born from different or born from same? By a correlation of this type, the overrating of blood relations is to the underrating of blood relations as the attempt to escape autochthony is to the impossibility to succeed in it. (Lévi-Strauss 1979, 216)[6]

Thus the myth implied that settling upon a marriage partner involved more than a private arrangement of who lives with whom: the origins of humanity (is man autochthonous or the result of sexual reproduction?) and his place in the universe were in the balance as well.

These imbricated cognitive and practical contradictions, I suggest, constituted a structure of disavowal for which the mother's lack, represented in this case by her lack of reproductive self-sufficiency, filled the role of fetish.[7] Whereas the Hopi initiation myth functioned exclusively as a site

6. I discuss this myth proof in more detail in the Appendix.
7. Lévi-Strauss presents no evidence that the structure of fetishism surrounding the Oedipus myth includes a traumatic childhood revelation that, like the unmasking of the

of avowal ("but even so the gods are in the masks"), the Oedipus myth staged both the disavowal ("but even so man comes from woman/earth alone") and the avowal ("woman is lacking/needs a man"). Indeed, the Oedipus myth went further by inflecting the resultant contradiction out of the domain of cosmological schemes into the domain of marital strategies.

In the case of fetishism staged within the Oedipus myth, as for fetishism generally, the object of desire must reside somewhere other than the fetish. In the classical as well as Hellenic Greek context it is not difficult to locate that object. A man's object of desire was the *eromenos*, the young male lover, relations with whom were in uneasy tension with the adult male's responsibility to the *oikos*, that is, the household and its attendant women embodied in the figure of the mother and wife. Michel Foucault argues that such tension was not the result of an opposition between homosexuality and heterosexuality, or even between love of boys and an ethic of marital fidelity (which in any case seems to have been a later Roman and specifically Christian development), but arose instead from a conception of the adult male as one who, loving the beautiful, whether male or female, also exhibited suitable moderation and self-control in his daily life:

> In so far as he was married . . . a man needed to restrict his pleasures . . . but being married in this case meant, above all, being the head of a family. . . . This is why reflection on marriage and the good behavior of husbands was regularly combined with reflection concerning the *oikos* (house and household). . . . For the wife, having sexual relations only with her husband was a consequence of the fact that she was under his control. For the husband, having sexual relations only with his wife was the most elegant way of exercising his control. This was not nearly so much the prefiguration of a symmetry that was to appear in the subsequent ethics, as it was the stylization of an actual dissymmetry. (Foucault 1987, 150–151.)

Thus a familiar pattern emerges: man's access to the object of his desire is blocked by or in tension with a need for sexual relations with his wife, which in turn functions as a practical embodiment of her lack expressed as a lack of reproductive self-sufficiency. In short, the fetish as an embodi-

---

Katcina among the Hopi, constitutes a real historical origin for the structure. As I indicated in connection with my earlier discussion of the Katcina ritual, there may be no such origin. Local stories asserting the contrary may be merely fictions, which take on significance purely retrospectively by the way in which they organize subjects' subsequent self-narratives. Instead, what matters is the imbricated structure of disavowal and perversion that, according to Freud, repeats the primal experience of separation from the mother.

ment of woman/mother's lack blocks man's access to the object of his desire. In this case, however, the structure emerges directly rather than
through covering over woman's lack with a lure and corresponding drive
object.

The fetish, I have argued, is a lure screening the *objet a* at the center of a
network of practices diverting subjects from attending to their desires. It
is also an object of disavowal, the site of a real contradiction ramifying
within the subject's discursive as well as nondiscursive practices. Lacan
explains how such fetishistic structures act as sites at which the usual
processes of repression are breached, thus leading to a perverse form of
subjectivity exposing the constitutive split at the heart of the subject. By
using the evidence provided by ritual and myth, I have argued that in
three cases, among the Hopi, the Ojibwa, and Hellenic Greeks, such psychic splitting of subjects is reflected at a social level.

III

SOCIALIZING THE PSYCHIC:
FROM INTERPELLATION TO GAZE

5

Interpellation, Antagonism, Repetition

Ideology interpellates individuals as subjects. . . . All ideology has the function
(which defines it) of "constituting" concrete individuals as subjects.
                                        Louis Althusser, Lenin and Philosophy

Ideology is not a dreamlike illusion that we build to escape insupportable reality;
in its basic dimension it is a phantasy construction which serves as a support for
our "reality" itself; an "illusion" which structures our effective, real social
relations and thereby masks some insupportable, real, impossible kernel (conceptu-
alized by Ernesto Laclau and Chantal Mouffe as "antagonism": a traumatic social
division which cannot be symbolized).
                                        Slavoj Žižek, The Sublime Object of Ideology

In the previous chapter I established the possibility of communal
fetishistic structures of desire. In this chapter, through an examination
of Althusser's theory of interpellation, I begin a discussion of the more
basic question of how social structures, and specifically ideological practices, shape psychic structures at a communal level. Althusser's theory, it
turns out, is overgeneralized in its approach to this question. He proposes
a mechanism by which, as he puts it, ideology affects "nine out of ten" of
the "right" individuals, but he fails to specify how and why the mechanism works in some cases but not others. By supplementing Althusser
with Lacan, I attempt to reduce but also come to terms with this lacuna
(lacana) in Althusser's theory.

Althusser's work, especially his famous ISA (Ideological State Apparatuses) essay, has proven decisive in introducing the issue of human subjectivity and its constitution into contemporary cultural studies (Althusser 1971). Both the Birmingham School and Screen theory have
adopted the concept articulated in the ISA essay that subjects are created
in response to a process of "interpellation." Althusser illustrates this concept by a piece of what he calls "theoretical theatre" (Althusser 1971, 163).
A policeman in the street shouts, "Hey, you there!" The hailed individual,

Althusser tells us, "will turn around. By this mere one-hundred-and-eighty-degree physical conversion, he becomes a subject. Why? Because he has recognized that the hail was 'really' addressed to him" (163).

The appropriation of the concept of interpellation by cultural studies, especially Screen theory, has been dogged by a persistent misreading. It has been and continues to be commonplace to take interpellation as a form of "discipline" (in Foucault's sense) or even "socialization" in something like a traditional Durkheimian sense: determining who individuals are by pressing them into already formed subject positions. Even Judith Butler, from whose reading of Althusser I borrow key elements, reproduces this misreading: "For the most part, it seems, Althusser believed that this social demand—one might call it a symbolic injunction—actually produced the kinds of subjects it named. He gives the example of the policeman on the street yelling 'Hey you there!', and concludes that this call importantly constitutes the one it addresses and cites. The scene is clearly a disciplinary one; the policeman's call is an effort to bring someone back into line" (Butler 1997, 95).

In this chapter I read Althusser differently. My key point will be that paradoxically the effectiveness of the call depends not upon the precision of the terms in which it addresses individuals but rather upon the gaps in what it says. Individuals conceal from themselves the existence of such gaps by piecing out the content of the call, thus constituting for themselves a picture of what the caller wants of or for them. Thus subjects conspire in their own subjection, or, as Althusser puts it, "subjects work by themselves" (Althusser 1971, 182). In short, interpellation leads its audience to actively construct a position by and for themselves.

Subjects are also led to misrecognize their active role in the production of such positions, thus preserving their sense that already before the call they were someone in the eyes of the caller. In particular, the positions that they make for themselves appear to preexist them, may even take on a "natural" inevitability, in the face of which resistance appears not only futile but also inappropriate.

Althusser also claims that interpellation leads subjects to relate to such positions in a way that they are misrecognized as "freely subjecting themselves." The misrecognition at issue here, he says, is not a matter of "false consciousness" in any straightforward sense. On the contrary, subjects really are free, free to be "bad subjects" and resist the imprecations of the call. This is not to say that subjects are self-fashioning agents, totally "free" to choose who they are. On the contrary, Althusser would claim, such a view is itself ideological, and must be rejected along with the opposing deterministic conception that subjects are merely the effects of socialization.

But if neither socialization nor individual choice power the constitutive workings of the call, what does? As Butler poses the question: "What leads to this reproduction? Clearly, it is not a mechanistic appropriation of norms, nor a voluntaristic appropriation. It is neither simple behaviorism nor a deliberate project" (Butler 1997, 119). Specifically, how does the call lead subjects not only to (re)produce themselves but also to misrecognize, indeed elide, their own active role in this (re)production? In this chapter, I shall turn to these questions in an extension and reworking of Althusser's hypothetical example of the policeman's call.

Althusser's position, as I have presented it, corresponds with Freud's view that the constitution of the subject involves both the formation of an ideal ego, that is, an idealized self-image, and an ego ideal, an externally projected standpoint from which the subject judges himself or herself in relation to that image. The ideal ego corresponds with the self-image in terms of which a subject is interpellated and, more specifically, with an idealized image that a subject has of himself as it is reflected back from the site of the Other. As Lacan puts it, the ideal ego is "the point at which he [the subject] desires to gratify himself in himself" (Lacan 1981, 257). The ego ideal, by contrast, corresponds with the position from which the subject judges himself in relation to his ideal ego, and thus the position from which "he will feel himself both satisfactory and loved" (or not, as the case may be) (257). In short, it is "the point [in the space of the Other] from which he looks at himself" (144).[1] Althusser goes beyond Freud, however, in arguing that subjects are constituted by "freely" taking up a position in relation to the gap between these two ego functions and, in particular, by "deciding" about what to do in relation to how they are supposed to be.

The question arises, of course, whether in going beyond Freud and exposing the ideological construction of the human subject as a self-motivating, free "agent" at the center of the little drama of his own ac-

---

1. For Lacan's account of the classical Freudian distinction between ideal ego and ego ideal, see Lacan 1981, 144, 257. See too Laplanche and Pontalis 1974 for an interesting genealogy of this distinction. Note that, according to Lacan, the construction of the ideal ego involves the ego ideal, which, in turn, of course, involves the ideal ego; in short, these two ego functions are reciprocally constitutive: "By clinging to the reference point of him who looks at him in the mirror [the parent in the position of ego ideal], the subject sees appearing, not his ego ideal, but his ideal ego, that point at which he desires to gratify himself in himself" (Lacan 1981, 257). The implication of the ego ideal in the ideal ego is a consequence of the point I made above: subjects complete their own self-image (ideal ego). This is possible only if, in constituting their self-image, subjects are already able to occupy a position, namely, the ego ideal, which, for strategic purposes, they locate outside of themselves. For Freud, by contrast, the ideal ego remained firmly connected to the imaginary order and the function of primary narcissism, and thus predates the ideal ego. Lacan's reworking of these Freudian concepts corresponds to an important shift in his work in the 1960s, when he took the Real rather than the Imaginary as the limit to the symbolic order and site of the pleasure principle, a point to which I return—see Žižek 1989, 131–133.

tions, Althusser's account of subjection is itself ideological. I shall return to this point when I discuss the more general question of the ideological status of Althusser's position.

Screening the Call

According to Althusser, the policeman's call, "Hey you there!" is structured in terms of two interlinked ideological representations: first, a historically specific ideology-in-particular which proposes a prior, original guilt on the part of the one, the "you there" whom it addresses; second, an omnihistorical ideology-in-general which, even when there are several who respond to the call, addresses each as a unique, individual subject—*the one* who is called: "It's *you*, it really is *you*!"—to which, in turning around, each of them replies in a concrete, "material" fashion: "It's me, it really is me!" (Althusser 1971, 161).

In classifying both of these representations as "ideological," Althusser implies that they not only address individuals but also are sources of constitutive effects. The question, then, is the nature and mechanism of such effects. What power is responsible for the amazing piece of rhetorical legerdemain whereby the many who pass by and hear the call ("nine times out of ten it is the right one," 163) experience themselves as uniquely, personally addressed, and (according to Althusser) however innocent they may have considered themselves to be, experience a presentiment, a thrill, of guilt? In short, how does the call bridge the gap between the one and the many, between the fictional addressee it poses for itself and the casual passersby who belong to its real-life audience?

This question may be given concrete form in the context of magazine advertisements. How is it that the photograph of a pair of eyes looking into the camera, coupled with the cheesy slogan "For the you who is really you," manage to make each viewer ("nine times out of ten it is the right one") feel that they have been not only personally addressed but also recognized in the innermost core of their being, despite being totally sure at an intellectual level that the advertisement knows nothing of who they are?

Althusser suggests a specular mechanism for this process of interpellation. First, the subject constructs an imaginative self-projection at the site of an external figure whom Althusser designates the "Subject"; second, the projection returns to the subject in the form of a recognition of himself as that figure. This process, Althusser suggests, is an analogue of the process of coming to recognize oneself in a mirror. He describes it in terms of what I call "the mirror thesis":

The duplicate mirror-structure of ideology ensures simultaneously:

1. the interpellation of individuals as subjects;
2. their subjection to the Subject;
3. the mutual recognition of subjects and Subject, the subjects' recognition of each other, and finally the subject's recognition of himself.
4. the absolute guarantee that everything really is so, and that on condition that the subjects recognize what they are and behave accordingly, everything will be all right: Amen—'*So be it*.' (Althusser 1971, 168–169)[2]

The mirror structure that Althusser evokes may involve direct physical resemblance, a possibility he illustrates using Christian ideology. Here the role of Subject is filled by God, in whose image, so the scripture tells us, man is made (167). This ideology—the specular relation between man and God—is materially embodied in the many images of the Holy family at the center of daily Christian life. Since, according to Althusser, ideology exists at the level of material practices rather than ideas, the fact that we know intellectually that these pictures are merely symbolic or allegorical is beside the point. What counts is not what we "believe" in our head but rather what we perform in our rituals—that we kneel down before the images, our eyes devouring them, and intone the words of worship, as if we saw our God before us.

In other cases, the relevant mirror structure may be less elaborate, comprising no more than the subject's recognition that the Subject recognizes him: "Yes, it's really me, he knows who I am, and I know him as one who knows me!" For example, although he may not admit it in so many words, the subject as citizen recognizes that the State knows how it really is with him, a practical knowledge that the State manifests in treating him in certain ways.[3] To be specific, the subject knows he is just a number, a knowledge that, it appears, is confirmed, "mirrored," as we might more properly say, by the impersonal way in which the State treats him, identifying him by his social security number, evaluating him according to the dollar amount of his salary, and so on.

What remains ambiguous, perhaps even concealed, in this situation is that the State's treatment of him, and its practical knowledge of his situa-

2. For a working out of this structure in a concrete case see Williamson 1978, 67.
3. In some cases, Althusser tells us, the Subject is a concrete individual—the king, for instance—in relation to whom the subject's whole being is shaped as a loyal subject. In other cases, the Subject is abstract or totally fictional—God, the State, and so on—reified as aspects of the representational schemata within which subjects frame answers to the calls made upon them (Althusser 1971, 169). In particular, in the case of interpellation by the policeman's shout the Subject is the abstract function of the Law embodied in the robust figure of its representative, the policeman.

tion, brings about the state of affairs in which the subject knows that he is just a number. This means that the Subject's appearance of independent knowledge, although persuasive, is only a mirage, one in which the subject conspires to his own advantage in order to give what he knows the appearance of independent and authoritative support.

In the subsequent appropriation of Althusser's work by cultural studies, I shall argue, the specular model of interpellation encapsulated in the mirror thesis has gained covert support from an illegitimate connection with Lacan's theory of a "mirror stage," during which children make "imaginary identifications" with images of themselves and their parents.[4] This connection between the work of Lacan and Althusser takes its cue from an unfortunate (although not altogether unintentional) homonymy between Lacan's term "imaginary" and the term "imaginary" used by Althusser as shorthand for the ideologically distorted nature of individuals' relations to their real conditions of existence ("Ideology is a representation of the *imaginary* relationship of individuals to their real conditions of existence," 153, my emphasis).[5]

Consider, for example, Judith Williamson's *Decoding Advertisements*, which typifies 1970s Screen theory approaches to the constitutive effects of images: "Lacan says that the ego is constituted, in its forms and energy, when the subject 'fastens himself to an image which alienates him from himself' so that the ego 'is forever irreducible to his lived identity.' Clearly

---

4. This theory was articulated as early as 1936, reworked in Lacan's 1949 paper "The Mirror Stage," and published in *Écrits*, chap. 1.

5. In the ISA essay, by contrast with Screen theory's appropriation of it, Althusser is careful to avoid articulating any connection between his own and Lacan's senses of the imaginary, although, given his close relation with Lacan, it would be disingenuous of him to claim that such a connection was not implicit in what he wrote. His refusal to enunciate the connection explicitly may be seen as growing out of his close (ultimately unhappy) relations with the French Communist Party, which in the 1960s vigorously denounced psychoanalytic ideas, specifically Lacan's, as "reactionary ideology"—see Althusser's letter of February 21, 1969, to the translator of his article for *New Left Review* (reprinted in *Lenin and Philosophy*) in which he discusses Lacan (Althusser 1971, 177).

The nearest Althusser comes to explicitly invoking Lacanian ideas in support of what I have called the mirror thesis is in the closing paragraphs of his article on Lacan, written five years before the ISA essay but redrafted as a companion piece to it, where he draws a parallel between, on the one hand, the Marxist thesis that "history . . . has no 'center' except in ideological misrecognition" and, on the other, Freud's discovery that "the human subject is de-centered, constituted by a structure which has no 'center' either, except in the imaginary misrecognition of the 'ego,' i.e. in the ideological formations in which it recognizes itself" (201). This parallel between the decentered subject and history's lack of center, he adds circumspectly, "has opened up one of the ways which may perhaps lead us some day to a better understanding of this *structure of misrecognition*, which is of particular concern for all investigations into ideology" (201).

this is very similar to the process of advertising, which offers us an image of ourselves that we may aspire to but never achieve" (Williamson 1978, 63–64, quoting Lacan 1971 on the mirror stage). Here Williamson explicitly presents the mechanism of interpellation as specular in nature, operating by a mechanism that is "very similar" if not identical to the Lacanian process of imaginary identification.[6]

In this chapter I argue against any such connection between Althusserian and Lacanian senses of the imaginary, between interpellation and the mirror stage. This, in turn, raises the question of whether the notion of interpellation can survive such drastic conceptual surgery. Can there be interpellation without mirrors? I answer this question by developing a model of interpellation which, instead of focusing upon the role of mirror identification, invokes Lacan's later view that the constitution of the subject involves confrontation with and concealment of what Lacan calls the Real.

The Imaginary

Althusser makes clear that what he calls the "imaginary" nature of a subject's ideological relations to the real conditions of existence has nothing to do with how those relations are imagined in the literal sense. Instead, their imaginary nature is a matter of "material effects," particularly the fact that they overlay and distort the "real conditions of existence," understood in the sense of the economic circumstances governing individuals' lives. For example, a teacher performs paid labor, churning out her students as workers, managers, investors, and so on, who despite her best intentions help to lubricate the cogs of capitalist production. These are the brutal, unflattering, "real" conditions of her existence as a paid functionary of the State. The ideological apparatus within which she works, the school, modifies or distorts these real conditions, turning them in what Althusser calls "an imaginary direction." She is, for example, encouraged to be loyal to the institution, dedicated to the cause of learning, and so on, all of which enable her activities to be integrated more productively into the system of production, contributing to its overall stability.

---

6. She does add, however, that the process of "imaginary identification" involved in ideology does not require a mirror image in any literal sense ("I prefer to use the idea of 'mirror phase' as a metaphor, a shorthand for all the social and external reflections of the self," 63). Nevertheless, as the quotation in the text makes clear, she takes mass-mediated images including advertising to operate according to processes that are "very similar" to the processes of imaginary identification manifested in the mirror stage.

The ideological—what Althusser's calls "imaginary"—nature of these relations to the institution in which she works is not simply a matter of the educational state apparatus placing a flattering gloss on her activities. On the contrary, teachers ("nine out of ten") really are dedicated and loyal. Instead, as Althusser indicates, it is a matter of the relations between pupil and teacher distorting the real conditions of their lives in a way that serves to reproduce the overall system of production.

Althusser also proposes that, at least in the capitalist era, such ideologies are set in place with the help of what he calls a *dispositif* (Althusser 1971, 157–158), an ideological device that positions subjects as having "freely" chosen to be who they are. By reaffirming those choices, subjects confirm not only their identity but also, as part of that identity, their ability to choose: "The individual *is interpellated as a (free) subject in order that he shall submit freely to the commandment of the Subject, i.e. in order that he shall (freely) accept his subjection*" (169).

Althusser does not take this ideological *dispositif* as merely an idea in the head, since for him ideology is always a matter of material effects (1971, 165–170). And, in fact, in most cases teachers really do chose to follow their profession, a "vocation" to which, it is said, they were called, and which they elected to follow. And even when it is a fiction, the story that an individual really chooses to be a teacher is not merely flattering self-deception, incidental to her pedagogic practices. On the contrary, it affects her actions in "real"—that is, "material"—ways, insofar as, at a practical level and on a daily basis, she takes responsibility not only for her students but also for the institution within which she works.

Althusser thus diverges from the traditional Marxist conception of ideology as "false consciousness" or "beautiful lies" that mystify and conceal the exploitative nature of the real conditions in which people live. Indeed, he explicitly criticizes this tradition on the grounds that, by analyzing ideology in idealist terms as a form of "consciousness," it fails to be materialist (149). Instead, he analyzes ideology in terms of materialist concepts such as "practices," "rituals," "apparatuses," and what he calls "representations"—by which he means not ideas in the head but rather "implicit beliefs," that is, propositional schema that structure human practices without necessarily emerging at the level of consciousness: "The 'ideas' or 'representations,' etc., which seem to make up ideology do not have an ideal (*idéale* or *idéelle*) or spiritual existence, but a material existence" (155). "Disappeared: the term *ideas*. . . . Appear: the terms: *practices, rituals, ideological apparatus*" (159).

It follows, then, that in Lacanian terminology what Althusser calls the "imaginary," namely, material distortions of the real conditions of existence, belong to the symbolic realm rather than the imaginary, that is, to the domain of symbolizable material realities rather than mental images. This conclusion directly contradicts the popular Screen theory gloss of Althusser, exemplified in the above quotation from Williamson, which proposes a convergence between the Althusserian and Lacanian senses of the imaginary. It also undermines the support that such a convergence would provide for the mirror thesis.

Althusser's transformation of the terms "imaginary" and "ideology" can be understood in the context of his broader theoretical practice. The term "ideology" brings with it meanings from an early "descriptive" stage of Marxism, exemplified by the "early Marx" of the 1844 manuscripts and the *German Ideology*, when Marx had not yet shed his ideological roots in Feuerbachian humanism. At that stage ideology was conceived as "beautiful lies" or, in traditional formulaic terms, as an imaginary representation (a false system of ideas) which misrepresents (mystifies by inverting) the real (true) conditions of existence.

This traditional formulation for ideology came up against a limit from within Marxism itself. Marx's materialism contradicted the idealist and purely "descriptive" terms in which this early formulation was framed. Following the lead of Marx's later work, Althusser reworked the definition of ideology in materialist terms. In particular, he redefined ideology in terms of a syntactic permutation of the traditional formula: as "a 'Representation' of the Imaginary Relationship of Individuals to their real Conditions of Existence" (Althusser 1971, 152).

This new definition incorporates two decisive shifts from the traditional formula. First, ideology is taken to be a representation of individuals' relations to their real conditions of existence rather than of the conditions themselves; second, the term "imaginary" is applied to the actual relations between individuals rather than, as in the traditional formula, to the representations of those relations. In short, ideology is not (as the early Marx contended) a set of ideas that are "imaginary" in the sense of creations of the imagination with no correspondence to reality, but rather a set of relations through which the real conditions of existence are modified.

Thus Althusser's theoretical transformation of the classical Marxist definition of ideology may be seen as dialectical, a sublation of a particular Marxist concept in response to its negation from within Marxism itself. Specifically, Althusser's redefinition of ideology preserves key terms of the classical formula, while purging it of idealist elements in favor of a purely material ontology. Thus Althusser's criticism of those who steer the question of ideology in the direction of "false consciousness" does not reflect a postmodern disinterest in or dismissal of issues of truth and falsity. Rather, his point is that an emphasis upon questions of truth or falsity in talking about ideology indicates an ideological commitment to an idealist ontology of propositions rather than to material practices (156).

Questioning the Mirror

In general terms, then, Althusser takes interpellation as a means of distorting the real conditions of existence so that they take the form of specular relations to a "unique, absolute *Other Subject*" who, despite the inherent diversity among subjects, manages to provide each of them with a mirror image of who he or she "really" is (178). In support of these claims. Althusser makes "it [ideology] speak" in a particular case in a way that we, his readers, will recognize its specular nature. We thus become our own authorities for his (Althusser's) analysis (165). He achieves this rhetorical sleight of hand by assembling a "fictional discourse" which, he claims, encapsulates what the Christian ideology says, "not only in Testaments, Theologians, Sermons but also in its practices, its rituals, its ceremonies and its sacraments. . . . God addresses himself to you through my voice. . . . It says this is who you are. . . . This is your place in the world! This is what you must do" (165–166). We are expected/persuaded to recognize this fictional discourse as structuring Christian religious practice, even though, as Althusser implicitly concedes, no one may ever say it in so many words.

Althusser's argument at this point masquerades as a form of empirical justification. But the justification is a sham, its persuasive effect having less to do with the structure of reader experiences than with the argument's interpellative form. Specifically, we, as readers, are called upon to recognize certain experiences as our own—"Yes, that's it, that's how it really is!"—which Althusser then "decipher[s] into theoretical language" on our behalf (168). In short, Althusser's text seeks to create the experience of specularity, of finding a mirror image of oneself in the figure of the Subject, as an ideological effect.

To be blunt, for all its pretensions to scientific, "theoretical" status, Althusser's description of interpellation as "specular" is couched in terminology, including idealist notions of visualization, which, in belonging to the level of "spontaneous description," are themselves ideological. In short, it seems that in the context of Althusser's argument for the mirror thesis, empiricism in the form of an appeal to experience functions, as it often does, as a bridgehead for ideology.

Since I am not assuming a "false consciousness" model of ideology, this does not mean that Althusser's account of interpellation is false. Rather, my point is that because it is not "scientifically" validated according to the accepted canons of scientific induction, there is a "real" (that is, scientific, not just logical) possibility that the experience of specularity is misleading. To be specific, like any pure sensory input, the experience of a specular relation provides a poor basis for justifying the mirror thesis which it appears to confirm.

Lack of proper justification is not the most serious threat to the mirror thesis, however. According to Althusser's discussion in his essay "On the Materialist Dialectic" (Althusser 1982, chap. 6) propositions acquire "scientific" status not through avoiding ideology (that, according to Althusser, is impossible) but rather through being embedded within a theoretical praxis that criticizes the ideological nature of their language. Such criticism is not merely a matter of ideas in the head but rather of practical recognition (*connaissance*) constituted by an (of necessity only partial) breaking with ideological language: "While speaking in ideology, and from within ideology we have to outline a discourse which tries to break with ideology, in order to dare to be the beginning of a scientific (i.e. subjectless) discourse on ideology" (Althusser 1971, 162).

Such theoretical praxis, the stepping back from ideology while within ideology, must be ongoing, a matter of permanent "self-criticism" (164) since, merely in virtue of being written, new forms of description are implicated in ideology ("The author and reader of these lines both live 'spontaneously' or 'naturally' in ideology," 160). This strategy of perpetual revolution results in the many deferrals and self-qualifications scattered throughout the ISA essay, including the wording of its subtitle, "Notes towards an Investigation," and its many unredeemed promises: "That the author . . . is completely absent as a 'subject' from 'his' scientific discourse . . . is a different question *which I shall leave on one side for a moment*" (160, 121, my emphasis).[7]

Unfortunately, Althusser's discussion of the mirror thesis in the ISA essay fails to display such hallmarks of the scientific. In particular, it fails to display a practical "awareness" of its own ideological nature. This failure is evident in Althusser's allusion to the mirror thesis as a "deciphering into theoretical language" of the experience of subjection, an allusion that patently fails to step back from, indeed denies, the ideological nature of the idealist terminology in which his thesis is expressed (168). It is true, of course, that Althusser makes some allowance for the ideological, or at least descriptive, nature of the language framing the thesis.[8] He

---

7. Althusser's redefinition of "the scientific" is as innovative as his reconceptualization of ideology, although its radical nature is more easily overlooked. He allows that scientific discourse is also ideological, thus disposing of one of the key oppositions of traditional Marxist thought, between ideology and science (a category that Marxism appropriates for itself).
8. Althusser also concedes that his argument here is, as he puts it, "rhetorical" ("I shall use a rhetorical figure and 'make it speak,'" 165).

describes this language as a "special mode of exposition" that is "'concrete' enough to be recognized but abstract enough to be thinkable and thought, giving rise to knowledge" (162). But this concession seems to be more by way of a covert attempt to forestall the accusation of ideological stain than a display of awareness of such stain.

Briefly, in virtue of Althusser's failure to acknowledge the ideological nature of the mirror thesis, it belongs to the category of protoscientific propositions (what he calls Generalities 1) rather than the category of the scientific (what he calls Generalities 3). In saying this, I am not simply reiterating the point that the mirror thesis is implicated in ideological terminology. On the contrary, failure to be scientific is a far more serious defect, involving not only an implication in ideology but also a failure to recognize such implication.[9]

If Althusser's attempt at a "scientific description" of interpellation fails, then what is its "correct," scientific description? In the next section, in the context of reworking Althusser's story of the policeman's call, I argue for an alternative account of interpellation that takes the Lacanian Real rather than the Imaginary as its focus. In particular, I argue that ideological effects arise from individuals confronting the Real limits to the symbolic order rather than mirror images. This alternative account of interpellation repudiates the idealist terminology bedeviling Althusser's discussion of the mirror thesis. This does not mean that my account avoids ideology as such. That, as Althusser argues, would be impossible. Nevertheless, I argue, by displaying an awareness of its own ideological nature, my account accomplishes what Althusser fails to achieve in his rendition of the mirror thesis: "to be the beginning of a scientific (i.e. subjectless) discourse on ideology" (162).

Powering the Call

The policeman walking the beat shouts "Hey you there!" Suppose a passerby hears his call while taking a nightly, predinner stroll around the

9. Conversely, as Althusser points out, even the most scientific discourses, including his own ISA essay, may be steeped in ideology: "the author and reader of these lines both live 'spontaneously' or 'naturally' in ideology. . . . Ideological effects [exist] in all discourses—including even scientific discourse. . . . Ideology has no outside" (160, 161 n. 16, 164). Thus Althusser redraws the traditional Marxist opposition between ideology and science. For him the important issue is not the avoidance of ideology—that is impossible—but rather the adoption of a scientific discourse, which displays its scientific nature by a practical awareness of its own (inevitably) ideological nature. Such awareness transforms the discourse into a site of perpetual struggle, situated in an ever recurring gap between an old ideological enframing and its critique, a struggle that installs a new ideological frame.

block. In an instant, even though she apparently has nothing on her conscience, she comes to a startled halt, seized by a guilt which she displays for
all to see. This is not intended as an empirically accurate description of the
way in which people actually respond to policemen shouting. On the contrary, in most circumstances a single shout by a policeman, however embarrassing, will be insufficient to produce the constitutive effects achieved by
more sustained interactions with Ideological State Apparatuses. As Althusser himself admits, his story of the policeman's call is a piece of "theater," a fictional model that provides a convenient stage on which to explore
what happens when interpellation by a full-fledged Ideological State Apparatus takes place (163). In Butler's terms, then, Althusser's figure of the policeman may be seen as merely "exemplary and allegorical," a synecdoche
for an Ideological State Apparatus (Butler 1997, 106).

But what, it may be asked, is a self-avowed piece of "theater" doing in
what aspires to being a scientific account? The important point is not the
theatricality of the story but rather Althusser's admission that it depends
for its credibility upon theatrical truth effects that are ideological in the
sense that they provoke the response: "Yes, that's it, that's the way it really
is" (Althusser 1971, 161, 166). In short, at this stage of his argument Althusser's account finally displays a practical awareness of its own ideological nature. In so doing it guarantees its own scientific status and, in
that respect at least, improves upon the earlier, purely experiential (and
thus ideological) treatment of the mirror thesis.

In the context of Althusser's piece of theater, we may ask what strikes
the passerby as she pursues her nightly stroll and hears the shout, "Hey
you there!" What moves her to reconstitute herself through what Althusser refers to as her "one-hundred-and-eighty-degree turn"? It is, I
suggest, not the policeman's personal authority or even the power he embodies as a representative of the law, but rather a tension arising between
the implicit accusation of criminality and the palpable appearance of innocence of the passerby's behavior ("I was just walking down the street,
minding my own business," she might protest). Such tension arises not
merely from a personal sense of innocence. On the contrary, as Althusser
remarks, "large numbers . . . have something on their consciences" (174).
Rather, the tension results from a conflict between, on the one hand, a
meaning of innocence which attaches to the action of strolling one's
neighborhood streets and, on the other, a meaning which turns a policeman's shout, whatever its intent, into an accusation of guilt.

The stroll's innocence is not merely a matter of the stroller's state of
mind. Instead, it is determined by a meaning framework, a widely accepted, publicly sanctioned set of associations between home, hearth,
mealtime, relaxation, and so on, in terms of which a nightly, predinner

walk in the neighborhood more or less unavoidably takes on a certain quality of innocence, although not in a strictly legal sense. Such meaning is neither indefeasible nor unequivocal. For instance, an indigent street person might see such a stroll as a self-indulgent exercise of bourgeois privilege, an arrogant assertion of the rights of property. This effective loss of innocence is reinforced by the obscurity of the law, which raises the possibility that an "innocent" stroll may pose all sorts of legal problems: unwitting trespass, violation of a traffic ordinance, and so on.

Despite such destabilizing cross-currents, the meaning of innocence enjoys a certain fixity, the result in part of work by interests who stand to benefit from the general acceptance of a bourgeois ideology that presents the "home" as a site of certain rights and privileges. The aphorism "A man's home is his castle" nicely captures the spirit of this pervasive ideology, which structures our practices as well as consciousness. In Lacanian terms, this ideological meaning acts as a point of suture at which the passerby's identity along with a corresponding account of her activities as "an honest citizen minding her own business" are sewn up for the time being. On this point, Marxist arguments for the existence of hegemonic structures converge with Lacan's claim that relatively stable meanings are necessary as temporary resting places from the otherwise continuing diffusion of meaning along chains of signifiers.

Similarly, the accusation of guilt implicit in the policeman's shout is determined not by some intention on his part (he may have merely wanted to draw attention to an approaching car) or even by the passerby's startled response, but rather by a meaning framework that assigns the role of arbiter of guilt to the institution of the law embodied in the figure of the policeman on the beat. This meaning too may be destabilized by various cross-currents. For example, in some circumstances the image of the police as defenders of the State and propertied interests tends to work against their positioning as fair and reasonable judges of guilt and innocence. Nevertheless, the meaning of guilt is relatively stable, a rhetorical as well as a practical and political achievement buttressing the hegemonic order.

These apparently opposing evaluations by intersecting meaning frameworks create a tension at the site of the policeman's call. From a strictly logical point of view of course there is no contradiction, since the stroll's innocence is established by its associations with home and hearth, while the policeman's accusation of guilt has a legal basis.[10] Nevertheless, the

---

10. In any case even if the senses of guilt and innocence were totally commensurable, the policeman's accusation does not entail my actual guilt (at most it entails that I am accused of being guilty).

meaning of innocence renders the policeman's accusation of guilt inappropriate in some strong sense, careless to the point of arrogance, a gross abuse of power, as we might say. In short, the policeman's call functions as a site at which certain aspects of the meanings or "identities" that the passerby is offered, as middle-class burgher, citizen under the law, and so on, are not only brought into conflict but also internally destabilized, each meaning in turn becoming the site of rival interpretations struggling to assert themselves. The structural similarity with Laclau and Mouffe's concept of antagonism is clear: "Antagonisms constitute the limits of every objectivity, which is revealed as partial and precarious *objectification*" (Laclau and Mouffe 1985, 125).[11] My point here does not depend upon an exact correspondence with Laclau and Mouffe's concept. Nevertheless, for convenience, I adapt their term "antagonism" to describe the structural instability that emerges at the site of the policeman's call.

An argument by Judith Butler suggests an alternative, more general account of the formation of antagonisms as sites of interpellation. An interpellation, she asserts, is an exercise of power, power in what Foucault would call "the mode of subjection" (Butler 1997, 95). In particular, it may be seen as an attempt to impose a particular identity defined in terms of the social meanings that frame it. She then argues, following Foucault, that any such exercise of power creates resistance. If, as seems not unlikely, such resistance takes shape as a counteridentity, also defined in terms of particular social meanings, and if this, in turn, creates a reactionary counterresistance, and so on, then an antagonism forms at the site of the call. Of course, not all interpellations will generate such "perpetual spirals of power and resistance" (to use Foucault's term). On the contrary, in the final section of this chapter I suggest a variation upon Butler's argument which allows that resistance may remain inchoate, a site of the Real in Lacanian terms. Nevertheless, insofar as such resistances form, they provide a mechanism for the formation of antagonisms at the site of interpellations, of which the story of the policeman's call may be seen as a special instance.

The antagonisms that gather at sites of interpellation do not inhibit their constitutive effects. On the contrary, I argue, they function as a driving force. In particular, in Althusser's story, I suggest, it is not the persuasive propositional content of the policeman's call, the "ideas" he transmits, that interpellate, but rather a tension within the "lived" representations structuring the addressee's practices, a tension between the guilt embodied in her reaction to the call and various practical associations which

11. For a general discussion of the notion of antagonism, see Laclau and Mouffe 1985, 123–127.

attach a meaning of innocence to the ritual of a nightly predinner stroll. As Butler explains it, "Interpellation works by failing, that is, it institutes its subject as an agent precisely to the extent that it fails to determine such a subject exhaustively" (197). I turn now to my key question of how this process works, of how the subject emerges in response to such tensions.

An Althusserian Attempt

As a first attempt to answer this question, I adapt Althusser's mirror thesis. The reaction of the passerby to the policeman's call, whether she turns and runs or comes to a startled halt, carries with it an interrogative inflection, expressing uncertainty about the investment others have in her situation. It covertly poses a question: What do you want, you the law-abiding citizenry who underwrite the law and observe this embarrassing little encounter? What do you want done in this situation to which you have contributed by your serious and inscrutable expectations? (The effect will be the same even if the streets are empty of spectators.)

At the level of surface semantics, the question "What do you want?" is directed at the policeman, but in the last instance the functionary to whom it is addressed is "the Subject," in this case the law, which knows what is wanted because it is the one that wants it (Althusser 1971, 181). Although the question is directed to the Subject, it is the passerby's to answer, since the Subject is in part at least a fictionalized projection of herself. To be specific, she responds to her conception of what the law might want of her rather than simply what its concrete representatives (policemen, statutes, lawyers, and so on) say. She must answer on the Subject's behalf, not only because the Subject is her creation but also because it constitutes a point of identification for her. In short, because the Subject provides her with a specular image of herself, questions directed at it must also be taken on board.

Of course, she does not have to go along with what the Subject wants of or for her. That is, even though she wants to be like it, she need not identify with what it wants for her. In brief, she may be a "bad subject" and reject the image in terms of which she construes it as addressing her (181). She may, for example, earnestly protest her innocence in the face of the policeman's public declaration of her guilt, even seeking reparation for the injury he has done her. In either case, however, insofar as she recognizes him as representative of the one to whom she is subject, she cannot be indifferent to him. In response to his desire, so the argument goes, she must form a desire of her own, which, in its form, in the specific nature of its relation for or against his desire, carries traces of its origins.

This Althusserian account is suggestive as far as it goes, but it still leaves unanswered the basic question of how antagonisms, such as the one created by the policeman's call, constitute new forms of subjectivity, including new desires. I turn to Lacan for an answer.

Lacanian Desire

In Chapter 1, I argued that desire emerges as an aspect of a three-cornered game involving a *subject*, an object of desire, and a little "other object," what Lacan calls *objet petit autre* (*objet a* for short), which stands in the way of subjects getting what they want. Engaging this little other object, circling it, affords subjects a degree of pleasure—it "go[es] some way to satisfying the pleasure principle"—and thus distracts them from their continuing state of lack (Lacan 1981, 62).

The pleasure produced in the course of the game is the result of what Freud calls the "drive" (*Trieb*). Subjects misrecognize their own agency in this process. In particular, in treating the object of desire as that which "motivated" their actions, they mistake their pleasure as the result of getting what they want. This misrecognition belongs to the Freudian category of repression (*Verdrängung*). In precipitating subjects into desire and the related category of agency, the misrecognition is also an aspect of what Althusser calls "ideology in general." This does not mean that agency is an illusion, but rather that it is accompanied by a false history, which misrecognizes it as being prior, as indeed being the cause of the process rather than an effect. I argued in Chapter 1 that such a pattern of misrecognition and the resulting production of desire are repeated whenever subjects come up against a repetition (*Wiederholung*) of their primal lack.

Antagonisms, as I presented them in the previous section, are likely sites of such repetitions. They are tensions within the social framework of meanings, which, by raising the question, "What does the Subject want of me?" reveal a gap in the subject's self-mastery, his knowledge of who he is. This gap, I suggest, is a convenient site for repeating another, namely, the primal gap created by the mother's absence or, more fundamentally, a lack of independence from others.

The possibility of such repetition depends upon the following homology. The primal scene involves the child's lack of control over, and thus alienation from, what he experiences as part of himself or herself, for example, the mother. An antagonism, such as the tension generated at the site of the policeman's hail, involves a not dissimilar lack of control. For instance, the passerby's response in running away is refracted through the gaze of the Other and reincorporated by her as a sign of a hitherto unrecognized guilt to which, through her response, she retrospectively owns up. In both situations, the primal scene of lack as well as the interrupted stroll, a similar structure is manifested: a part of the self is separated, only to be reincorporated in an unfamiliar, that is, hitherto unrecognized, and alienated (othered) form.

Such structural similarity may seem a tenuous basis upon which to ground a relation of repetition in the Freudian sense. Freud has shown, however, that repetition needs little in the way of objective similarity. Even the slightest resemblance may result in a transfer of libidinal charge associated with the primal scene onto a new situation, thereby transforming it into a repetition. In that event, Lacan argues, the new situation becomes the site of what Freud calls "unrealistic anxiety" (anxiety without an appropriate object).

The story of the policeman's call can now be brought to some sort of closure. As I indicated earlier, the point of this story has not been to understand the real effects of the policeman's shouting, but rather to provide a convenient framework within which to develop a plausible mechanism for explaining the call's constitutive impact and, in particular, its production of desire. In brief, the mechanism I suggest traces a causal trajectory along pathways that detour through the unconscious, from call, to antagonism, to primal scene, and thus on to desire. To be specific, an antagonism develops at the site of the call. By preparing a site for a repetition of the primal scene, this antagonism not only stimulates desire but also leaves telltale traces of anxiety in its wake. I do not assume that this mechanism drives all real-world interpellations. Instead, in the following chapters I show how variants of it throw light upon a selection of concrete interpellative situations drawn from different social and cultural settings.

Butler Troubles

In her book *The Psychic Life of Power* Butler introduces a reading of Althusser which overlaps mine at key points. Specifically she claims, as I do, that gaps in representations rather the contents of representations create interpellative effects ("Interpellation works by failing, that is, it institutes its subject as an agent precisely to the extent that it fails to determine such a subject exhaustively"—Butler 1997, 197). My position differs significantly from Butler's, however.

Following Freud, Butler argues that the formation of a subject involves the constitution of a conscience ("Conscience doth make subjects of us all," 107). As it does for Freud, conscience plays a double role. First, it is the site of a particular psychic structure: a split (*Spaltung*) between the ego-ideal (a point from which the individual reflexively sees him or herself as desirable) and the ideal ego (an image in terms of which the individual wants to see him/herself). Second, the conscience is the site of a narcissistic investment that subjects have in their own integrity, an integrity that the child comes to misrecognize when it sees a mirror image of itself held up by its mother:

> In Freud's view, the formation of the conscience enacts an attachment to a prohibition which founds the subject in its reflexivity. Under the pressure of the ethical law, a subject emerges . . . who takes him/herself as an object, and so mistakes him/herself, since he/she is, by virtue of that founding prohibition, at an infinite distance from his/her origin. . . . And this prohibition is all the more savory precisely because it is bound up in a narcissistic circuit that wards off the dissolution of the subject. (103)

By a complex series of transformations, some of which are only implicit, Butler links this Freudian conception of the subject not only to Althusser's concept of interpellation but also to Lacan's distinction between the symbolic and the imaginary as well as to Foucault's economy of power and resistance. First, she inflects the narcissistic desire for identity—to find a "wholesome" image for oneself—into the symbolic domain, as a desire to find or make a name for oneself: "Called by an injurious name, I come into social being, and because I have a certain inevitable attachment to my existence, because a certain narcissism takes hold of any terms that confers existence, I am led to embrace the term that injures me" (104).

Second, she identifies Althusserian interpellation with the symbolic process of being "called" or classified under an injurious name, which she connects, in turn, with the "founding prohibition"—in Freudian terms, the law of the father. Thus, when the subject is called as guilty, even if that call is legally or socially grounded, the guilt in question is invested with unconscious resonances of primal injunctions against incest, masturbation, and so on: "For Foucault, a subject is formed and then invested with a sexuality by a regime of power. If the very process of subject formation, however, requires a preemption of sexuality, a founding prohibition that prohibits a certain desire but itself becomes a focus of desire, then a subject is formed through the prohibition of a sexuality, a prohibition that at the same time forms this sexuality—and the subject who is said to bear it" (103).

According to Butler, the latter "view disputes the Foucaultian notion that psychoanalysis presumes the exteriority of the law to desire, for it maintains that there is no desire without the law that forms and sustains the very desire that it prohibits. Indeed, prohibition becomes an odd form of preservation, a way of eroticizing the law that would abolish eroticism"

(103). In short, Butler takes the prohibition associated with the Oedipal law of the father to be operating covertly in the domains of the juridical and social law whenever the latter function in an interpellative mode. The interpellation at issue here, understood as a symbolic mandate with unconscious resonances, is accusatory rather than merely normative. That is, rather than simply telling its audience what they should do, it addresses and warns them as de facto transgressors ("You sinners!" "Hey you there!" and so on).

Butler also identifies interpellation with the workings of "power" in the Foucaultian sense of discipline: "The Althusserian notion of interpellation . . . is clearly a disciplinary one" (95; and see too the opening sentence of the previous quotation from Butler). This allows her to theorize resistance somewhat differently than Lacan. In particular, she follows Screen theory in taking the imaginary as the site of resistance to interpellation: "Lacan restricts the notion of social power [interpellation] to the symbolic domain and delegates resistance to the imaginary" (98). This view, for which Screen theory has provided a vehicle, dates back to the early Lacan of the 1950s. It constructs an opposition between the imaginary domain, which Lacan identifies as the domain of narcissism, and the symbolic domain in which, according to Butler, interpellation operates. Specifically, Butler claims, the narcissistic wish to be recognized in terms of a particular linguistic category—the wish to have it said who I am—functions as a source of resistance to interpellation.

Butler gives this Lacanian position a novel Hegelian twist, however, by thinking of interpellation as a sublation of the desire for nomination. To be specific, the desire for a name may be thought of as encountering a limit or, in Hegelian terms, as being "negated" by the desire for an injurious name, since such a name cannot be desirable. Interpellation—the taking up of an injurious name—emerges, then, as a sublation of the desire for nomination. It follows that the imaginary desire for nomination opposes the symbolic process of interpellation, not in the simple sense of negating or contradicting it, but rather in the dialectical sense of sublating it, that is, incorporating its radical negation. In short, interpellation emerges, from a productive tension between a desire for nomination and resistance to an injurious name. From this dialectical structure a further paradox emerges: "Only by occupying—being occupied by—that injurious terms can I resist and oppose it" (104).

Butler claims that this paradoxical conclusion of her line of argument marks a point of agreement with Foucault and departure from Lacan.[12]

---

12. "Foucault formulates resistance as an effect of the very power that it is said to oppose. This . . . marks a departure from the Lacanian framework" (Butler 1997, 98).

That is, according to Lacan, Butler claims, the conflict between the narcissistic desire for nomination (which is on the side of the imaginary) and interpellative pressure in favor of an injurious nomination (on the side of the symbolic) must end in the defeat of the imaginary: "The imaginary thwarts the efficacy of the symbolic law but cannot turn back upon the law . . . resistance appears doomed to perpetual defeat" (98).

By contrast, for Foucault (with whom Butler sides on this issue) no conflict between power and resistance ends in such dismal fashion. Instead of the tediously repetitive defeat of the imaginary by the symbolic mandate of the law, Foucault offers us "perpetual spirals of power and resistance." Butler locates subjects at the site of this endless conflict—an open spiral of imaginary sublations of symbolic mandates—through which individuals reflexively spiral around the question of who they are. With the help of Hegel, Butler thus manages to cross Foucault with Lacan. The apparently agreeable result is that, by restoring a degree of effectiveness to the imaginary, the "fixed" Lacanian subject ("fixed" in the sense that the defeat of the imaginary is inevitable) is liberated, rendered fluid.

But Butler's conclusion here sells Lacan short. It fails to take into account Lacan's historical shift in emphasis from the imaginary to the Real. For the later Lacan (of the 1960s) the opposition to the symbolic arises not from the imaginary, as Butler claims, but rather from the Real: those anxiety-provoking points of failure of the symbolic order which always and already inhere in the symbolic and trouble it. This suggests a somewhat different version of Butler's argument. Opposition to the symbolic is located at the site of the Real, and the opposing structures are held together not as imbricated functions of the conscience but rather as a consequence of the fact that any symbolic system must eventually come up against its own limitations in the Real.

This reformulation of Butler's argument reconceives the nature of resistance to an injurious interpellation. Resistance is not fueled by a narcissistic desire for nomination. Instead its source lies in "another scene," namely, the Real, and specifically in the return of the repressed, manifested in what Jacqueline Rose describes as "something endlessly repeated and relived moment by moment throughout our individual histories . . . not only in the symptom, but also in dreams, in slips of the tongue and in forms of sexual pleasure which are pushed to the side of the norm . . . there is resistance to identity [interpellation] at the very heart of psychic life" (Rose 1986, 90–91). Butler too identifies resistance to the symbolic with such "moment by moment" repetitions, but, following the early Lacan of the 50s and his later Screen theory exponents, she classifies them as "the workings of the imaginary in language" rather than (as I do) denizens of the Real (Butler 97).

My difference from Butler is more than an academic dispute between the "early" Lacan of the 1950s and his "later" 1960s reincarnation. Instead, the future—indeed, the very possibility—of "real" resistance is at stake here. On the one hand, if Butler is correct, then a Lacanian framework entails that resistance can never win, that the conflict with power is a sham. In that case, for a real politics of resistance to be possible, a break from Lacan is necessary. (Here we see another version of the Screen theory criticism of Lacan, to which I return in the next chapter.)

On the other hand, if my characterization of resistance is correct, then a Lacanian perspective entails that neither power (symbolic interpellation) nor resistance (the Real points of failure of interpellation) have the upper hand. On the contrary, each poses and reproduces the other in what Foucault poetically describes as "perpetual spirals of power and resistance." Thus, rather than constituting a break from Lacan (as Butler claims), Foucault's account of the relation between power and resistance projects a Lacanian perspective into the microphysics of power. In sum, by identifying the Real (rather than the imaginary) points of failure internal to an interpellation as sites of "resistance," my modification of Butler's argument manages to cross Foucault with Lacan without prejudicing the privilege Lacan assigns to the symbolic or precluding the possibility of real resistance to subjectification.

There is a second, more basic difference between Butler's approach and mine, one that I have bracketed in the discussion until now. Butler models the call upon the act of addressing an individual in terms of socially or legally stigmatized names, like "Jew," "Black," "woman," and so on. She also argues for an "eroticizing of the [social/juridical] law" in accord with a Freudian erotics of prohibition (103). Thus her invocation of the "law" may be understood as a reference not only to social and/or juridical norms but also to a "founding prohibition" in the Freudian sense, that is, to the Oedipal prohibition or what Lacan calls "the law of the father." This ambiguity in reference of the law plays an essential role in Butler's argument, since it is from the psychic dimensions of the law in its social or civic senses that she understands the constitutive effects of interpellation as arising.

At this point a question arises: is Butler's bold claim of an ever present psychic and specifically erotic dimension to the law too strong? In particular, must we accept her implicit contention that whenever an address in terms of an injurious name is sanctioned juridically or socially, it will have the constitutive effects associated with a *call* in the Althusserian sense? In allowing that in "one out of ten cases" the policeman's hail may fail to make its mark, even Althusser, it seems, would find this contention a little too sweeping. For Althusser, unlike Butler, the fact that an individual is addressed in an injurious way by the civic and social law does not of itself precipitate the constitutive effects characteristic of interpellation. On the contrary, I argued in this chapter, such an address takes on a constitutive role if and only if it partakes in the dimensions of the Real, and in particular acts as a site of unrealistic anxiety. And it does this if and only if it is a repetition (*Wiederholung*) in the Freudian sense, that is, boasts unconscious chains of associations connecting it to the primal scene of lack.

In more traditional Freudian terms, the point I am making contra Butler is that on occasions the law in its juridical/social dimension may not resonate unconsciously with the law of the father. In other words, in particular cases, a juridical/social guilt at transgressing the law—failing to fill in a tax form properly, crossing the road against a red light, and so on—may not be compounded as "psychic guilt," and so avoids having any psychically constitutive effects.

Conversely not all interpellations address individuals in terms of injurious and legally sanctioned names. On the contrary, my earlier arguments suggest that interpellations may be mere "antagonisms" (in something like Laclau and Mouffe's sense) rather than antagonistic in Butler's sense of "injurious." In other words, interpellations may be points where social meanings clash among themselves rather than with their audience. In sum, it seems that, contra Butler, addressing individuals in terms of injurious names is neither a necessary nor a sufficient condition for interpellation. More specifically, if a naming is to function as an interpellation, then there must be more to its unconscious dimensions than can be guaranteed by its purely social or formal aspects.

6

The Ambassador's Body:
Unscreening the Gaze

The world of fiction film is mostly a world of intention, the well-rehearsed, and the fake: that is, Not-Reality. The comedian's trip into a swimming pool is staged, and the light streaming from that window is probably not from the sun. We all know this but we allow ourselves to forget it when the house lights go down. Sometimes, though, when a fly flies in through a window, the fiction flies out the window. Reality asserts itself over the film, the filmmakers, and the audience, whether we like it or not. In these moments when reality hijacks our treasured narrative . . . we have two options: we can merely endure it, holding our breath until the fiction returns, or we can embrace the chance encounters.

Paul Harrill, "Fly Films"

In Chapter 1, I introduced what Lacan calls "the gaze," a point from which the visible looks back at the viewer. In this chapter and the following two, with a view to furthering my investigations of interpellation, I extend my exploration of the gaze into the area of social effects. I begin by criticizing a conception of the gaze which, taken from Lacan and developed initially for cinematic images, has come to dominate much contemporary work in cultural studies.

Screen Theory

Screen theory developed in the 1970s from the work of a group of French and English film theorists including Christian Metz, Laura Mulvey, Jean-Louis Baudry, Jean-Louis Comolli, and Stephen Heath.[1] In the form in

1. Jacqueline Rose offers an interesting participant's history of the Screen theory movement in Rose 1986, chap. 9. For a more critical backward glance at Screen theory, see Silverman 1996, 83–90.

which it has come to influence cultural studies, it combines elements of an eclectic range of theoretical perspectives, including the early structuralist work of Roland Barthes, which proposes that the meanings of signifiers are determined by their position within a network of oppositions and equivalences; Louis Althusser's conceptualization of interpellation as a process of *méconnaissance* (misrecognition); and Jacques Lacan's seminal work on the mirror stage as a foundational step in the child becoming a subject.[2]

Screen theory treats filmic images as signifiers encoding meanings but also as mirrors in which, by (mis)recognizing themselves, viewers accede to subjectivity. One of its major strengths lies in its techniques for uncovering the meanings carried by images. In the context of the 1970s, this aspect of the theory contributed importantly to the development of a politics of the image, which critiqued the mass media on the assumption that the meanings that they circulate function as blueprints for the subjectivities of viewers. Such a view, divorced from the heady mixture of "high theory" and leftist politics associated with Screen theory, remains the cornerstone of much contemporary censorship practice as well as P.C. politics.

According to Screen theory, in addition to functioning as a vehicle for meanings, the filmic image operates as the site of a "gaze," meaning a place where viewers experience themselves as under scrutiny. The gaze is the mechanism through which the image imposes its meanings and thus creates constitutive effects. As in the case of Foucault's panopticon, the scrutiny characteristic of the gaze appears to come from outside the subject but in fact is a mediated form of self-scrutiny. Screen theory identifies the mechanism of the gaze with the form of self-(mis)recognition described in Lacan's account of the mirror stage. Kaja Silverman puts the position as follows:

> What Lacan designates the "gaze" also manifests itself initially within a space external to the subject, first through the mother's look as it facilitates the "join" of the infant and the mirror image, and later through all the many other actual looks with which it is confused. It is only at a second remove that the subject might be said to assume responsibility for "operating" the gaze by "seeing" itself being seen even when no pair of eyes are trained upon it. . . . This "seeing" of oneself being seen is experienced by the subject-of-consciousness . . . as a seeing of itself seeing itself. (Silverman 1992, 127)

From its inception, Screen theory suffered a major defect. Since the late 1950s, Lacan had emphasized that accession to subjectivity is not merely a matter of imag-inary self-(mis)recognition. The human subject must also

---

2. See Barthes 1973; Althusser's "Ideological State Apparatuses," in Althusser 1971, 121–173; and Lacan's 1949 essay "The Mirror Stage," in Lacan 1977, 1–7.

enter the symbolic order, that is, fall under the "law of the signifier," as well as come to terms with what Lacan called "the Real." In its visual form, the Real comprises anxiety-provoking breaks or anomalies in the visual field where the system of perceptual categories falters, a "rupture between perception and consciousness" where viewers are jolted from their comfortably established habits of viewing by failing to recognize what they perceive (Lacan 1981, 56). According to the later Lacan, images impact upon viewers through such manifestations of the Real, in particular through the effects of self-scrutiny which they bring about. Lacan's name for such effects is "the gaze." He thus directly contradicts Screen theory's concept of the "gaze" as an externally projected form of self-scrutiny arising from a system of mirror effects.[3]

From the point of view of Screen theory, this Lacanian reworking of the gaze suffers a major drawback. By emphasizing points of rupture in the visual field rather than images with specific ideological meanings, it undermines the simple politics of the image so important to media and film theorists of the 1970s as well as more recent critics of less radical persuasion. On this basis Lacan's views are accused of being systematically apolitical, that is, excluding the possibility of a politics of the image. This criticism, to which I reply in detail later, has become a central plank in contemporary critiques of Lacan as well as other "poststructuralists," such as Jacques Derrida. (I have already discussed one aspect of this critique in the reply to Butler in the previous chapter.)

Silverman's commentary on Lacan in *Male Subjectivity at the Margins* exemplifies such critiques. She accuses Lacan (as well as Freud) of taking a conception of human subjectivity characteristic of contemporary white, middle-class, European males and generalizing it to all times and places:

> Not surprisingly, given the ideological thrust of his essays on sexual difference, we can see the same kind of universalizing project at work in Freud's account of the symbolic father as we find in Lévi-Strauss's account of the exchange of women. . . . Freud consequently made it impossible to conceptualize the incest taboo outside the context of a phallocentric symbolic order. . . . Lacan also equates culture with the Name-of-the-Father. "In all strictness the Symbolic father is to be conceived as 'transcendent'" . . . he [Lacan] observes. (Silverman 1992, 36–37)

Her criticism is not merely that Freud's and Lacan's views are ideological and, specifically, patriarchal, but also that, by universalizing a particular

---

3. Lacan develops his theory of the gaze in *Seminar XI: Four Fundamental Concepts of Psychoanalysis*, first published in France in 1973 and in the United States in 1978.

conception of human subjectivity, they deny that mechanisms of subjectification incorporate ideological effects. Against this she asserts a political imperative which resonates directly with a 1970s politics of the image: "What must be demonstrated over and over again is that all subjects, male or female, rely for their identity upon the repertoire of culturally available images, and upon a gaze which, radically exceeding the libidinally vulnerable look, is not theirs to deploy" (153).

This chapter responds to such criticism by considering two cases discussed by Lacan: his own youthful encounter with a glint of light reflecting from a seafaring sardine can, and the historical reception of Holbein's painting *The Ambassadors*.[4] In both cases, I show how the gaze depends upon ideological factors. In particular, I argue that such factors provide the raw material from which chains of unconscious associations are forged, chains that connect elements of these visual objects with the primal scene of lack. Such chains of associations invest the objects as sites of unrealistic anxiety, a necessary condition if, as Lacan claims, they are to function as sites of a gaze. It follows that there is no truth to Silverman's complaint that Lacanian mechanisms of subjectification, of which the gaze is one, rule out a causal role for ideology.

What is true, however—and here the basis of Screen theory's criticism of Lacan becomes clear—is that according to Lacan the meanings of images are not in any straightforward sense "reflected" in viewer subjectivities. It follows that filmic images cannot be critiqued simply on the basis that, by encoding ideological meanings, they reproduce existing ideological structures. This does not mean that a Lacanian perspective is apolitical. It does, however, require a more complex politics of the image than Screen theory offers.

It is also true, and here I agree with the critics, that sometimes Lacan presents the gaze as if, like the glint of light reflecting from the sardine can, it were an objective structure, to which all viewers, past, present, and future, passively respond in the same way. I argue that, on the contrary, in its Lacanian form the gaze is a relational structure poised delicately between a visual object and individual viewers, its effects mediated by their differing positions within their disparate ideological horizons. Thus, there is no single transhistorical "audience" all of whom experience the effects of its gaze in a similar way. On the contrary, as in Lacan's encounter with

---

4. The point that Lacan fails to confront in his successive analyses of this particular painting is the patently ideological nature of its gaze. It could be argued that the phantasy that informs but also conceals this recurring failure is a "scientism" with which Lacan seeks to invest his theoretical discourses, a scientism that cannot easily accommodate the fact of the ideological nature of the objects it studies.

the sardine can, different viewers have different responses, only some of which fall under the category of the gaze. For instance, Lacan's sea-faring companion, Petit-Jean, laughs off the encounter, and seems to miss the gaze entirely. He gets the joke, as we might say, but not the gaze, whereas for Lacan, things are quite the other way around.[5]

I also argue that in his account of Holbein's painting, Lacan errs by focusing exclusively on the famous anamorphic projection of the skull. It is true that this formal element of the picture constitutes one potential site for the gaze, but it is by no means the only one. I present two others. One is the picture's "hyperrealism," and the other an instability in its psychological distance from the viewer. Both raise the possibility that if, as Lacan claims, the picture "looks back" at its viewers, then it is in a highly overdetermined way, from the canvas as a whole, rather than, as Lacan claims, from a single formal element, namely, the image of the skull.

Despite these concessions to Lacan's critics, my theoretical account of the gaze remains firmly Lacanian: I reject Screen theory's account of the gaze as specular in favor of Lacan's rival claim that the gaze is a site at which the Real disrupts the visual field. My differences from Lacan reside in an attempt to historicize his work by showing how ideological factors mediate the effect of visual objects upon their viewers.

The Gaze

In conversation with Gustav Janouch, Franz Kafka asserted that "sight does not master the pictures, it is the pictures which master one's sight. They flood the consciousness" (Holland 1989, 65–66). This remark captures in embryonic form Lacan's conception of the gaze. Looking at pictures, Lacan says, is not simply a matter of receiving independently impressed images and mastering them by decoding their meanings. Instead, the viewer's eye strains to pick out shapes in a flood of light which threatens to overwhelm it. Lacan's name for the unmasterable flood of light and the field of its effects is "the gaze." The gaze challenges us to form an image and make sense of what we see; by means of a mechanism I discuss later, it also places us under scrutiny.

Lacan discusses the gaze in a story about a boat trip he took with a group of Breton fishermen when he was in his twenties. It was a sunny day, and a tin can floated on the sea, reflecting sunlight into his eyes. "You

5. Elizabeth Cowie points out that for Lacan not all images "feed the gaze." Instead, as Lacan says, some have a "pacifying, Apollonian effect . . . something that involves the abandonment, the *laying down*, of the gaze" (Lacan 1981, 101, cited in Cowie 1997, 289).

see that can?" one of the fisherman, Petit-Jean, said with a laugh, "Do you see it? Well, it doesn't see you!" The young Lacan was not amused. He recounts his reaction: "The can did not see me . . . [but] it was looking at me all the same . . . and I am not speaking metaphorically. . . . I, at the moment—as I appeared to those fellows who were earning their livings with great difficulty . . . looked like nothing on earth. In short, I was rather out of place in the picture. And it was because I felt this that I was not terribly amused" (Lacan 1981, 96).

Thus the light not only unsettled his visual field but also made him feel under scrutiny; it challenged his sense of self. He came to feel, as he says, "out of place" in the picture as the indeterminacy characteristic of the glint of light spilled over onto its viewer. Lacan identifies this challenging glint of light with the gaze, which, he says, is "always a play of light and opacity. It is always that gleam of light—it lay at the heart of my little story. . . . In short, the point of the gaze always participates in the ambiguity of the jewel" (96).

In general terms, then, he restricts the gaze to points of distortion in the visual field where the appearance of objects threatens to disintegrate into a play of light and shadow, where, by unmasking light as the raw material from which appearances are fashioned, viewers glimpse their own active contribution to what they see. Thus the gaze is like the moment in a movie when the mechanics of image production come into view. By showing the grain of the film, a fly landing on the camera lens, or an actor behaving out of character, the movie affords a glimpse of its own nature as constructed image. In terms of film theory, the gaze is the point at which the illusion of realism wavers. In cognitive terms, it is a point where the visual field breaks out of the symbolic system in which its objects are conceptualized.

More specifically, Lacan insists, the gaze belongs to the order of the Real, meaning that it is not only a point where we cannot see "properly" because our visual field refuses to conform with the relevant symbolic conventions, but is also a site where the subject experiences an excessive or "unrealistic" anxiety, such as the young Lacan's evident discomfort at the glint of light. Such anxiety, according to Freud, is associated with repetitions (*Wiederholungen*), that is, events connected by chains of unconscious associations to the domain of the repressed, those traumatic primal moments when, by experiencing need, infants recognize themselves as sites of lack.

Not all anomalies in the visual field constitute moments of anxiety. For example (and here I turn to the incident described in the this chapter's epigraph), the sight of an actor in a film behaving "out of character," straining to ignore the fly that has blundered onto the film set and landed on his nose, may occasion viewer amusement rather than distress. In such cases, psychic investment in the transparency of the representational fiction is not great enough for viewers to experience anxiety when it is destroyed. This in turn raises the question of why the young Lacan makes such heavy weather of his encounter with the glint of light. Why does this particular failure to make out what he sees cause him so much distress?

His anxiety arises, I suggest, from the following chain of associations connecting the glint of light with the primal scene. The fisherman's sardonic remark, "You see that can? . . . Well, it doesn't see you," thrust upon the young Lacan an unwelcome realization of himself as without a place among the men whom he admired and counted as friends. He felt at a loss or, as he says, "rather out of place in the picture" (96). Thus, at a structural level the joke resembled the primal scene of loss. The glint of light, in turn, resembled the joke, since both were sources of discomfort. And since the joke was uttered in proximity to, and took as its topic, the glint of light, the former was also a contiguous effect of the latter. Thus a chain of metaphoric and metonymic associations connected the primal scene of lack to the joke, which, in turn, was connected to the glint of light, thereby raising the possibility that all three events converged at an unconscious level. The excessive discomfort stimulated in the young Lacan by the light, evidenced not only by its immediate disruptive effect but also more crucially by its memorialization more than twenty years later in his writings, suggests that such a convergence in fact occurred. The glint of light thus took on the dimensions of the gaze, as not only a distortion of his visual field but also a repetition and source of "unrealistic anxiety" for the young Lacan.

In this story of Lacan's day at sea, the ideological is present as a thinly disguised class hostility expressed and enacted in the fisherman's joke. Under this disguise, ideology functions as a mediating link in a chain of unconscious associations connecting the primal scene of lack to its subsequent repetition in the encounter with the glint of light. In short, the glint carries ideological traces not as encoded meanings (as Screen theory suggests) but rather through its unconscious associations.

Like children who miss their mothers, the young Lacan sought distraction from the yawning symbolic void created by the glint of light, a void that carried unconscious echoes of primary lack. Such distraction, Lacan tells us, is implemented through entrance to a new pleasurable field of practices, "the subject's answer to [the] absence . . . created on the frontier of his domain—the edge of his cradle—namely a *ditch* around which one can only play at jumping" (Lacan 1981, 62). So, like the child who plays with a cotton-reel as a pleasant distraction from the absence of the mother, the young Lacan reacted to his seagoing encounter by squinting, moving his head from side to side, shielding his eyes, and so on. These openings and closings of his visual field—looking, looking away, and looking again—produced a mixture of pleasure/unpleasure characteristic of engagement with the scopic drive (a point to which I return in the next section). Here, then, is what distracted the young Lacan from the unconsciously invested recognition of his own bourgeois status as a well-educated young man *en vacances,* playing at fishing and "out of place" in the working-class world of the fishermen whom he called friends.

In my reconstruction of Lacan's day at sea, ideology functions as a mediating link in a chain of unconscious associations between the primal scene of lack and the glint of light. The chain, in turn, provides a bridge across which anxiety flows onto the glint of light, thus setting in motion the anxious movement of the eyes by which the young Lacan seeks relief from confrontation with the Real. The resultant pleasurable dynamic of looking and looking again is constitutive of the gaze, revealed here as an anxiety-provoking but ultimately pleasurable distortion of the young Lacan's visual field.

Several key questions remain to be answered. How can this relatively minor episode in Lacan's personal history be generalized to provide a model for more far-reaching psychosocial effects? How, for example, does Lacan's account of the gaze in the context of his personal and highly idiosyncratic reaction to a glint of light carry over to the public reception of mass-mediated imagery? And how does the glint create the feeling of being under scrutiny characteristic of the gaze: "The can did not see me . . . [but] it was looking at me all the same"? In the next section, as I engage with Silverman's work, I criticize Screen theory's answer to the last question, and I suggest an alternative. Before doing so, however, it is important to notice a certain ambiguity which affects the Lacanian conception of the gaze and is endemic to his writings at large.

In the story of his youthful adventure at sea Lacan locates the gaze equivocally between the actual upwelling of light, its subjective effects as a distortion of his visual field, and its objective cause, the glinting surface of the tin can. In Lacan's writings, this ambiguity takes the more general form of an uncertainty about the *objet a,* of which the gaze is a special case. Is it a concrete "objective" entity such as the cotton-reel in the famous *Fort-Da* game described by Freud, or a field of "subjective" effects constructed around a "lost object," such as the absence in the child's life opened up by loss of access to its mother's breast? Where, in particular, are we to locate the *objet a* in the continuum stretching from the breast, a retrospectively fictionalized cornucopia around which a certain narrative of lack is constructed, to the concrete objects that are its metaphoric substitutes? In Chapter 1, I attempted to answer this question in general terms, but here, except where clarity of exposition requires, I make no attempt to resolve this creative ambiguity in Lacan's architectonic. In so doing I follow Lacan's own strategy of refusing to define the *objet a* (282).

"Being Looked At" by Screen Theory

According to Silverman, and Screen theory more generally, the gaze is a means of constituting individuals as subjects by "projecting" images onto them: "the gaze . . . has . . . power to constitute subjectivity. . . by projecting the screen [her term for the image] on to the object. . . . Just as Lacan's infant can see him or herself only through the intervention of an external image, the gaze can 'photograph' the object only through the grid of the screen" (Silverman 1992, 150). She also insists, and here she draws a contrast between herself and Lacan, that images projected by the gaze are "culturally generated" and in a quite traditional sense "ideological": "Although *Four Fundamental Concepts* does not do so, it seems to me crucial that we insist upon the ideological nature of the screen by describing it as that culturally generated image or repertoire of images through which subjects are not only constituted, but differentiated in relation to class, race, sexuality, age, and nationality" (150).[6] In short, for Silverman the gaze operates like Foucault's panopticon: it is a disciplinary apparatus by which "subject positions"—that is, socially prescribed images of how to be a subject—are transmitted to individuals who, in responding to them, are constituted as subjects.

In the perspective of Screen theory, individuals respond to such images as if recognizing themselves in a mirror: "That's me, that's who I really am!" As with specular recognitions in general, however, there is a gap between the individual and the image. That is, although the process of looking at the image masquerades as passive, work is always involved in making the image one's own, so that one sees oneself in the image. This work and the corresponding gap between image and viewer are erased in the process of looking, thus retrospectively concealing the constitutive nature of the act of recognition.

The specular recognitions that Screen theory proposes should not be understood merely as acts of identification with a character or viewing position encoded in the image. On the contrary, as John Fiske and others have argued, the viewer is engaged in a complex relation of "implication-

---

6. The distinction she draws here between her position and Lacan's is an aspect of the criticism of Lacan that I am questioning, namely, a criticism for omitting ideological factors from the process of constituting subjects.

extrication" with the image, allowing a pleasurable variation between identification and resistance in relation to its encoded positions (Fiske 1987, 169–178). Even when viewers manage to find points of identification for themselves within a media text, they do so, Fiske argues, not with encoded positions but rather with the "play of similarity and difference along the axes of nation, race, class, gender, power, work, etc." (178). In other words, insofar as a viewer's engagement with the text involves an act of identification, it is a matter of situating oneself within a space of possible positions, the boundaries of which are established by textually encoded subject positions.

In short, the recognition "That's me!" involves the more general "That's where there's a place for me!" rather than simply "That's who I am!" The experience of being scrutinized, of being "under the gaze," results from the specular nature of this process, from the fact that in looking at the image one seems, at least retrospectively, to be looking at oneself; or, more correctly, one is being looked at from where one has been and, to some extent, still seems to be.

This second-generation Fiskean Screen theory account of the gaze is plausible in the case of a range of mass media images, especially advertising. It runs into major difficulties, however, in accounting for the effects of the glint of light encountered by the young Lacan. Because the glint did not encrypt an ideologically loaded image with which he could identify, it is difficult to see how Screen theory can explain the young Lacan's experience of being under surveillance, let alone account for the presence of a gaze. It is true, of course, that the glint did have unconscious associations with ideological meanings. But such associations are not germane to Screen theory, which concerns itself only with meanings encoded according to generally accepted pictorial conventions rather than amorphous glints of light creating unconscious associations in individual viewers. I suggest an alternative to the Screen theory account, one that not only does justice to Lacan's story of his youthful adventures at sea but also explains his feeling of being under scrutiny. This alternative account is based upon the later Lacan's conception of the gaze as an *objet a* and denizen of the Real, rather than Screen theory's specular conception, which is grounded in the early Lacan's theory of the mirror stage.

Because of its unconscious resonances, the glint of light distorting the young Lacan's visual field fascinates him. He steps back and forward, squinting, refocusing, anxiously changing point of view in order to rework what he sees. By inducing him to review what he has seen, the glint of light creates a split within his point of view. More specifically, in coming to see the distorted nature of what he sees, he is made aware of himself as a viewer, and in that respect he finds himself under scrutiny, a scrutiny that, although self-induced, appears to come from somewhere else—from the region of the glint of light. In the same way, when viewers of a film see a fly bump into the camera lens, they are made aware of themselves as viewers, as subjects of/to an illusion, which, in turn, means that they experience themselves as under scrutiny, a self-scrutiny that appears to come from elsewhere, namely, the direction of the film. In sum, the experience of being under surveillance is an effect of viewers adjusting their sights in response to a failure to see clearly, rather than, as Screen theory claims, the effect of a specular (mis)recognition in response to an externally projected image.

The combined seeing and being seen constitutive of the gaze not only cause the young Lacan's feeling of being under scrutiny but also cater to his voyeuristic and exhibitionistic needs to see and be seen. This circulation of satisfactions, according to Lacan, lies at the heart of the scopic drive, which like all drives (according to Freud) produces pleasure:

> You grasp here the ambiguity of what is at issue when we speak of the scopic drive. The gaze is this object lost and suddenly refound in the conflagration of shame, by the introduction of the other. Up to that point what is the subject trying to see? . . . What the voyeur is looking for and finds is merely a shadow, a shadow behind the curtain. . . . What one looks at is what cannot be seen. If, thanks to the introduction of the other, the structure of the drive appears, it is really completed only in its reversed form. . . [i]n exhibitionism. . . . It is not only the victim who is concerned in exhibitionism, it is the victim as referred to some other who is looking at him. (Lacan 1981, 183–184)

Thus the gaze explains not only the young Lacan's feeling of being under scrutiny but also the pleasure that, distracting him from his anxieties, transforms the gaze into an object of fascination to which, even as he squints, he cannot shut his eyes.

My account of the gaze differs from Screen theory's in four key respects. First, by emphasizing the role of the Real rather than focusing on the imaginary and symbolic, it refers to Lacan's later work rather than sharing Screen theory's preoccupation with his early theory of the mirror phase. Second, it explains Lacan's seagoing encounter with the glint of light. Third, it suggests that a gaze carries ideological meanings via chains of unconscious associations rather than encoding them according to generally accepted, public conventions. Fourth, by invoking the gaze as the object around which the scopic drive turns, it explains the intimate connection between the gaze and the production of pleasure.

My account of the gaze also fleshes out and generalizes the suggestions for an interpellative mechanism which I made in the previous chapter. The gaze, like the antagonism created by the policeman's call, comprises a formal incoherence which functions as a site of encounter with the Real, and more specifically a repetition of the primal scene of lack. Whereas the incoherence associated with antagonisms is constituted directly by contradictions between social meanings, in the case of the gaze the incoherence inheres in a physical disruption of the visual field, which takes on contradictory ideological meanings via chains of unconscious associations.

First Gaze

Hans Holbein (the Younger") painted *The Ambassadors* in 1533, the year after he settled in England. The picture portrays two Frenchmen: Jean de Dinteville, seigneur de Polisy (1504–65), and Georges de Selve, bishop of Lavour (1509–42). The picture was a private commission by de Dinteville upon the occasion of a secret mission to England by de Selve in support of his friend de Dinteville, who had been unsuccessfully negotiating on behalf of the French king with Henry VIII concerning the highly sensitive question of relations with Rome. (Henry was about to break with the Catholic Church over the question of his divorce from Catherine of Aragon and marriage to the already pregnant Anne Boleyn.)

In the lower foreground of the painting is an anamorphically projected image of a skull, an object which comes into focus only when the viewer steps to the side of the picture and looks at it awry. Lacan claims that this distorted image is "the gaze as such, in its pulsatile, dazzling and spread out function" (Lacan 1981, 89). He contextualizes this assertion with a few remarks concerning the "furious polemics" to which the production of anamorphic images gave rise in the sixteenth century, when researches into geometrical perspective and the invention of Dürer's "window" (the perspectival device pictured in Dürer's famous woodcut) enabled the development of mechanical techniques for perspectival painting.

What justifies the claim that Holbein's anamorphic image of the skull constitutes a gaze in Lacan's sense of the term? And for which viewers does it constitute a gaze? More specifically, how can we make the transition Lacan suggests from the blinding effects of the glint of light upon the young Lacan during his day at sea to the visual impact of formal tensions in Holbein's portrait upon its various and varied historical viewers?

Rather than focus exclusively upon the skull image, as Lacan does, I turn first to two other less remarked formal elements in the painting which, I argue, also constitute potential sites for a gaze.

The art critic and historian John Berger points out that *The Ambassadors* dates from the inception of the tradition of oil painting on canvas in Northern Europe circa 1500. It also coincided with the beginnings of the free market for art, which gradually came to displace the medieval patronage system through which artists earned their living (Berger 1972, 84). Gold leaf and expensive pigments became *de rigeur* for the artist-craftsman as paintings themselves became costly objects, sought after by a new class of connoisseurs and entrepreneurs with an eye for expensive materials rather than a predilection for classical allusions.

The oil painting was valued not only for the intrinsic value of its materials but also for what it represented. Berger cites Claude Lévi-Strauss on this point: "Rich Italian merchants looked upon painters as agents, who allowed them to confirm their possession of all that was beautiful and desirable in the world. The picture . . . represented a kind of microcosm in which the proprietor recreated within easy reach and in as real form as possible, all . . . to which he was attached" (86).[7] In order to "recreat[e] within easy reach and in as real form as possible" those things to which the nouveaux riches were attached, the oil painting mediated the connection between representation and represented in a new way. A new realistic style of painting simulated not only the look but also the tactility of surfaces, "importuning the sense of touch," as Berger remarks in connection with *The Ambassadors*:

> Every square inch of the surface of this painting, whilst remaining purely visual, appeals to, importunes the sense of touch. The eye moves from fur to silk to metal to marble to paper to felt, and each time what the eye perceives is already translated, within the painting itself, into the language of tactile sensation. . . . Except for the faces and hands, there is not a surface in this picture which does not make one aware of how it has been elaborately worked over—by weavers, embroiderers, carpet-makers, goldsmiths, leather workers, mosaic-makers, furriers, tailors, jewellers. (90)

The art historian Jurgis Baltrušaitis indicates that in the case of *The Ambassadors* the "realism" of this new style of painting verges upon the excessive: "Everything is so realistic as to verge on the unreal. The numbers,

7. The painting itself, as a commodified object, thus became an apt subject of representation. The many paintings of paintings from this period indicate this dual role of the painting as both representation and represented (Berger 1972, 85–87).

the letters, the globes, the texture of the clothes are almost deceptively life-like. Everything is astonishingly present and mysteriously true to life. The exactness of every contour, every reflection, every shadow extends beyond the material it represents. The whole painting is conceived as a *trompe l'oeil*" (Baltrušaitis 1976, 93). The excess of realism is not like the selective magnification of individual details in naif paintings.[8] Instead, a subtle plethora of small details is twinned with overly sharp visual definition, with the result that even from a distance a dense panorama of folds and textures is revealed which could—in reality—only be seen upon much closer inspection. In Susan Stewart's useful terminology, the result of such excess is "to increase not realism but *the unreal effect of the real*. . . . It does not tell us enough and yet it tells us too much" (Stewart 1993, 26–27).[9] Such a hyperrealistic style provides a vehicle for an abstract form of representation which Jean Baudrillard calls the "simulacrum," that is, a simulation that, unlike imitation, depends for its effect upon acknowledging its own status as an appearance.[10] In particular, admitting its deceptive nature by an exaggerated, hyperrealistic form, *The Ambassadors* signals that its painted surfaces are, so to speak, "too good to be true." Like another Renaissance genre of painting, that of *trompe l'oeil*, it captivates us by acknowledging and playing with its own deceptive nature: "What is it that attracts and satisfies us in *trompe l'oeil*? When is it that it captures out attention and delights us? At the moment when, by a mere shift of our gaze, we are able to realize that the representation does not move with the gaze and that it is merely *trompe l'oeil*" (Lacan 1981, 112).

Certain elements in Holbein's painting, specifically the flat, lackluster rendering of the flesh of the ambassadors, violate the form of the simulacrum, however: "Every square inch of the surface of this painting, whilst remaining purely visual, appeals to, importunes, the sense of touch. . . . *Except for the faces and hands*, there is not a surface in this picture which does not make one aware of how it has been elaborately worked over" (Berger 1972, 90, my emphasis). Recent restoration work has established that the contrast between the image of the ambassadors' flesh and other

---

8. I have in mind here the naif paintings of trees which show a whole tree while impossibly distinguishing between individual leaves.

9. Note that the excess which I am alluding to here is not merely a matter of more detail coming to light as the viewer moves closer to the painting. On the contrary, by including detail that remains invisible until one moves in close, a painting may merely simulate reality to the point where approaching it, like getting closer to objects in real life, reveals more to the eye. Rather, the excess I have in mind involves the painting's hyperrealistic quality, which works against any "reality effect."

10. Baudrillard 1983, 150. Thus the simulacrum differs from other types of simulation, such as the fake, which conceal their status as appearances.

elements in the picture is the result of variations in the mixture of paints. Dinteville's tunic, for example, is rendered vividly in a glossy layer of lampblack in oil with additions of pine resin. Grey, formed by working a little lead white into the wet paint, is employed only sparsely in highlights to relieve the basic black of the tunic. By contrast, the mid-grey primer shows through the top layer of paint in which the faces of the ambassadors are rendered, producing what Susan Foister, Ashok Roy, and Martin Wyld (1997, 83) refer to as a "slight deadening effect." The rendering of the hands, using a warm white-vermilion mix muted with a cooler shadow paint, produces a similar "deadening effect."

Interestingly the techniques for rendering flesh in *The Ambassadors* differ from those applied in other well-known paintings executed by Holbein in the 1530s. In the famous portrait *Christina of Denmark* (1538), the face and hands take on a pale luminous quality as the paint is worked thinly without the usual grey priming layer, while in the portrait of Hermann Wedigh (1532) the face is thickly painted in a high pinkish tone, in small, smoothly blended brushstrokes (Foister, Roy, and Wyld 1997, 83). In the context of these other paintings and of the hyperrealistic style of most of the canvas, the image of flesh in *The Ambassadors* is an exception, indeed a point of resistance, to the simulacral form of representation characteristic not only of this painting but also of Holbein's contemporaneous works.[11]

Marx points out that goods involved in capitalist form of exchange appear to have a "real" or "intrinsic" value and that this value has material effects upon the lives of both buyers and sellers, even when they realize that talk of such value is a fiction. Customers thus treat the "value" of a commodity as if it were a real, intrinsic property even when they know that it is an artifice created through the processes of exchange (Žižek 1989, 31). In short, the commodity too takes on the form of a simulacrum.

11. The contrasting visual definition between the ambassadors' flesh and other objects in the picture such as clothing is reinforced by an uncertainty about how well the ambassadors fill their roles. They carry their finery as if it were made for them. They are, as Berger says, "confident" and "relaxed" with each other (Berger 1972, 94). But this impression determined by their bodily deportment is in tension with a certain "wariness" that the figures display in their look toward the viewer (97). Thus an element of uncertainty is introduced. Are their gorgeous clothes a tribute to "natural" ambassadorial qualities or merely outward show? Are the men, as represented by their flesh, equal to their clothes or is it rather the clothes which make the men? The uncertainty internal to the picture's representations captures nicely the personal difficulties and lack of success attending de Dinteville's ambassadorial mission. In a letter of 23 May 1533 he writes: "I am the most melancholy, weary and wearisome ambassador that ever was seen" (Foister, Roy, and Wyld 1997, 16).

As such, any point of resistance to the simulacral form also constitutes a site of resistance to the commodity form. This, in turn, means that the image of the naked faces and hands of the ambassadors constituted a site at which one of the forms governing the capitalist relations of exchange central to the lives of the bulk of Holbein's contemporaries *broke down*. At an abstract structural level, this breakdown in social relations resembled the failure to relate to others that, according to Lacan, haunts all human existence from its earliest moments. This resemblance, as in the story of the sardine can, opened the possibility of an unconscious, metaphoric connection between the image of the ambassadors' flesh and the primal scene of lack. For viewers who made such a connection, the image of the flesh functioned as a repetition in the Freudian sense and thus as a site to which unrealistic anxiety attached. For such viewers, the image of the ambassadors' flesh took on the status of a gaze, that is, a point invested with unrealistic anxiety where the perceptual symbolic order falters. As in the case of the glint of light that blinded the young Lacan, ideological factors contributed to the unconscious connection along which anxiety traveled in order to invest this element of the painting as a gaze.

Second Sight

A second gaze, also ideologically mediated, haunts Holbein's painting, unsettling the spectator's attempt to find a proper distance from which to view the canvas. With the exception of the ambassadorial flesh, all the items pictured are goods on display, crying out to be touched: "The surface verisimilitude of the oil painting tends to make the viewer assume that he is close to—within touching distance of—any object in the foreground of the picture" (Berger 1972, 97).[12] Yet the conventions of sixteenth-century public portraiture, exemplified by Holbein's painting, insisted on a formal distance between sitter and viewer. To this end, the ambassadors look "aloof and wary. . . . The presence of kings and emperors had once impressed in a similar way. . . . Equality must be made inconceivable" (97). Berger argues that "it is this [distance] and not technical inability on the part of the painter—which makes the average portrait of the tradition appear stiff and rigid" (97). Renaissance portraiture, he

12. This cry is more by way of a hysterical seduction than an open invitation, since a prohibition to touch ("Don't touch the merchandise") often extends up to the moment of purchase, which thus takes on the magical quality of a honeymoon. The function of the prohibition is not only to heighten the emotional investment in the act of purchase but also to defer the always disappointing moment when the purchase is complete and the goods are transformed into possessions.

claims, "never resolved" this difficulty in establishing a psychological distance from the viewer (98). In the case of *The Ambassadors* the difficulty is reinforced by a formal tension between the nearly life-size scale of the figures of the ambassadors, which implies a distant viewing position, and the details on their clothing, which entail a view from closer in.

A similar unsettling of viewer position is evident in the grotesque series of images painted by Arcimboldo in the late sixteenth century. From close up, Arcimboldo's paintings appear as chaotic juxtapositions of realistically painted images of pieces of fruit, flowers, instruments of war, and so on. By contrast, from a distance the individual images are seen to be elements of a human face. Thus, simply by changing position, viewers cause an incongruous jump from one domain of reality to another, from vegetable to man, for instance. The different domains of reality are held together by an aesthetic logic internal to each painting: the face titled "Spring" is made up of fresh fruits, and so on through all the seasons, a logic which the paintings' relations to each other confirm. The coexistence of these different levels of reality within one painting unsettles the viewer position. So, for example, it is impossible to determine whether the painting "Spring" should be viewed close up, so that individual pieces of fruit come into view, or from a distance, when the face of Spring appears. As in *trompe l'oeil*, the charm of the painting arises precisely from moving between the two perspectives.

The difficulty in determining an appropriate distance from which to view paintings such as these reflects a real contradiction within the social relational field characteristic of sixteenth-century European merchant capitalism. By dint of their occupation, merchants counted as commoners. By establishing a personalized system of exchange as well as commonality of interest with their quality customers, however, they created a superior status for themselves. This contradiction was an aspect of a more general set of tensions created at all levels of class structure by a radical expansion of the activities of the market. In principle at least, everyone was free to buy what they liked from whomever they liked, and, as money and goods changed hands, different social strata interacted, approaching each other in unaccustomed, personal ways.

The formal difficulty in settling upon a distance from which to view Holbein's painting echoed or, as Marx would say, "reflected" these ideological difficulties which viewers experienced in establishing a position for themselves in the new social space created by the expansion of the market. At a structural level, this difficulty resembled the primal difficulty individuals experienced in finding a place for themselves in the world of others. Insofar as, for some viewers, this resemblance became the basis for an unconscious connection, unrealistic anxiety attached to their difficulties in settling upon a viewing position, which thus took on the dimensions of a gaze. Like the gaze associated with the image of the ambassadors' flesh, this gaze was constituted through an ideologically mediated connection.

It may be objected that the formal difficulty in establishing a viewing position to which I have alluded is more a matter of the picture violating an aesthetic convention than an "objective distortion" of the sort displayed by the glint of light in the story of the young Lacan's fishing trip. The key issue, however, is not the origin of such visual effects but rather their function: in unsettling the observer's visual field such effects create conditions for a gaze. Such unsettling may happen as readily in response to violations of aesthetic preferences as more "objective" forms of distortion. In other words, viewers' purely "subjective" aesthetic response may precipitate a faltering of their visual field that is no less effective from the point of view of creating a gaze than the visual disruption created by an "objective" glint of light. Lacan may be seen as making exactly this point in juxtaposing his little story of a day at sea to an account of the "subjective" distortions created by "those little blues, those little browns, those little whites . . . that fall like rain from the painter's brush" (Lacan 1981, 110—the reference here is to Cézanne).[13]

The Third Eye

The bulk of objects pictured in *The Ambassadors*—navigational instruments, a book of arithmetic, a lute, and so on—are drawn in linear, single-point perspective, properly viewed from the front of the picture. The image of the skull, by contrast, is brought into focus only through surrendering a frontal view and moving to the side of the picture—putting the ambassadors to one side, so to speak. Thus the frontal viewpoint brings into focus the mundane ambitions and achievements of man—commercial, cultural, scientific, and religious—while the lateral view brings into focus death and the end to earthly vanities.

By situating the image of the skull, a traditional *memento mori*, in formal opposition to images of objects symbolizing worldly activities and aspirations, Holbein's painting evokes a traditional contrast between death and mundane ambition. The opposition is no sooner presented than it is undermined. The rich tones of the silver cross, symbolic of resurrection and

13. He also juxtaposes this account of the gaze with descriptions of "natural" or "objective" effects such as snakes dropping their scales, birds their feathers, and trees their leaves (114).

eternal life, half hidden behind the curtain against which the ambassadors stand, suggest that life ("real" life) resides on the side of overcoming worldly ambitions.[14] The dead quality of the ambassadors' flesh complements this suggestion by hinting that death ("real" death) lurks under the rich vestments of the ambassadors.

In this way, Holbein's painting recapitulates the Renaissance theme of the Vanities, which ran through the work of Holbein's humanist contemporaries such as Cornelius Agrippa, Sir Thomas More, and Erasmus of Rotterdam, the latter two of whom were patrons as well as important intellectual sources for Holbein.[15] Man's real life, they said, lies not in the flesh but in the transcendence of worldly temptation.

Holbein's painting thus anticipates the moral of Lacan's nice discussion of the forced choice "Your money or your life." Lacan points out that there is no real choice here since to die means giving up your money in any case (212). Holbein's picture hints at a similar deadlock. If, like the ambassadors in Holbein's painting, man depends upon observation and reasoning (including philosophical theology) as the path to knowledge, then he cannot understand death, since to do so requires experiencing it personally, thus leaving behind not only the world but also all possibility of understanding. In the end it seems there is no choice about knowing death: the death's-head must escape comprehension. Perhaps that is why the ambassadors look so wary, their eyes missing not only the skull before them but also the crucifix behind them. If they ever get to the point of knowing death, then, like the viewers who move sideways in order to look awry at the image of the skull, they too will have fallen off the edge of the picture.

According to humanism, the way out of this deadlock is for man to give up vain and foolish dependence upon his own limited techniques for gathering knowledge, and instead place faith in the word of God. Cornelius Agrippa eloquently puts forth this view in the conclusion to his *Declamatio*: "For the word of God is the way, the rule, and the target at which, whoever does not wish to err should aim, and thus attain the truth. All other knowledge is at the mercy of time and oblivion and will perish; for all the sciences and the arts will vanish away and others will replace them."[16]

---

14. A cross hidden behind the curtain was a traditional symbol in sixteenth-century iconography. The curtain represented the veil of appearances, hiding the truth and the light (Baltrušaitis 1976, 100).

15. On these points see Baltrušaitis 1976, chap. 7, which Lacan cites as his source on these matters.

16. H. C. Agrippa, *De incertitudine et vanitate scientarum et artium atque excellencia verbi Declamatio*, Antwerp, 1530; cited in Baltrušaitis 1976,100.

This humanist position, at which Holbein's picture hints by its inversion of the traditional opposition between life and death, contradicts an ideology in terms of which the daily lives of a key segment of Holbein's audience were structured. The field of social practices integral to the new form of merchant capitalism involved a radical expansion of man's access to and domestication of the world around him. The ambassadors represented in Holbein's picture typified the new class of men who lived by and promoted these new possibilities. As Berger puts it, they "were convinced that the world was there to furnish their residence in it" (Berger 1972, 96). The objects surrounding them—instruments for navigation and tools of the arts and sciences—symbolized these enhanced capacities for knowledge and control. All visible things were to be comprehended in human terms. Nothing, however different or alien it appeared, was permitted to escape the symbolic net constituted by scientific, theological, and cultural knowledges. The catch-phrase "man is the measure of all things" captured the spirit of this new ideology.

But this ideology, as humanism pointed out, could not accommodate death. Death fell outside human understanding, belonging to what Lacan, in his reworking of Freud's analysis of the dream of the burning child, describes as a "rupture between perception and consciousness" (Lacan 1981, 56).[17] Thus the image of the skull functioned doubly as a transgressive element. First, as an anamorphosis, it transgressed the conventions of single-point linear perspective implemented elsewhere in the picture. Second, it symbolized death, which transgressed the "man is the measure" ideology by which an important segment of Holbein's audience lived. By evoking human mortality as well as being anamorphotic, the image of the skull, metonymically linked death and anamorphosis.

But death threatened the integrity of the forms of daily life, not because life opposed death (on the contrary, humanism interrogated this simplistic opposition) but rather because the daily round of activities was structured in terms of an ideology ("man is the measure") which could not accommodate death. Thus the death's-head image bore a structural resemblance to the primal scene of lack, because it also threatened the integrity of subjects' lives. In this case too, then, a possibility exists of an ideologically mediated chain of unconscious associations between the primal scene and a formal element of the painting, namely, the anamorphosis. Insofar as this possibility was realized for particular viewers, the image of

17. Baltrušaitis argues that the existence of death as a limit to human understanding constituted a contradiction within humanist writings that paired a commitment to man's ability to acquire knowledge with a religiously inspired skepticism associated with the doctrine of the Fall.

the skull became a site of unrealistic anxiety, and thus took on the dimensions of the gaze, a physical disruption of their visual field that, via its associations, provoked an encounter with the Real.

In this chapter my brief has been purely explanatory: to advance a plausible mechanism by which, through unconscious associations, formal tensions within *The Ambassadors* produce the effects of a gaze in Lacan's sense of the term.[18] Because the associations in question are ideologically mediated, the existence of the relevant gaze is historically contingent and may, indeed, vary from viewer to viewer, depending upon his or her particular position on the ideological horizon. This argument demonstrates that although Lacan himself may fail to historicize the construction of the gaze in particular cases, his general theoretical views do not preclude such a possibility. Despite its modesty, this conclusion suffices as a means of refuting critics, such as Silverman, who accuse Lacan of proposing conceptions of the gaze and subjectivity which leave no space for ideological or historically contingent effects in their constitution.

This is not to say that my analysis is uncritical of Lacan. On the contrary, I disagree with his sweeping claims concerning the existence, extent, and source of the gaze for particular visual objects. Specifically, I disagree with his implicit claim that *all* (or nearly all—"nine out of ten," as Althusser might say) who look at *The Ambassadors* experience it looking back at them, that the gaze of this painting is, as it were, an objective structure on view for all to see. I also argue against Lacan that formal devices other than the anamorphic image of the skull may function as sources for this painting's gaze.

Although my account allows that the gaze of a particular painting affects some viewers but not others, it does not explain how and why this happens. In particular, like Althusser, I have offered no account of what distinguishes the "one out of ten" who, according to Althusser, fails to attend to the policeman's call. Nor have I discussed how interpellation operates in linguistic rather than visual contexts. In the next two chapters I begin an exploration of how these questions might be addressed by tracing the effects of the gaze upon particular members of the readership for two written texts, Robert Boyle's *New Experiments Physical Mechanical* and Gustave Flaubert's *Madame Bovary*.

---

18. My analysis fails to predict which of the painting's formal elements are responsible for its gaze and who will feel its effects. Such predictive failure—or, as Karl Popper would call it, "unfalsifiability"—is characteristic of Freudian analyses and the *Geisteswissenschaften* more generally. Despite Popper's arguments, this unfalsifiability is not an epistemic defect, since for all such disciplines explanatory power rather than predictive success or technical control is the epistemically relevant value.

7

The Vice of the Virtual Witness

SIR FORMAL TRIFLE: *Upon my sincerity, I wholly eschew all oratory and compliments with persons of your worth and generosity. And though I must confess upon due occasions I am extremely delighted with those pretty, spruce expressions wherewith wit and eloquence use to trick up human thoughts, and with the gaudy dress that smoother pens so finely clothe them in, yet I never use the least tincture of rhetoric with my friends, which I hope you'll do me the honor to let me call you. (Aside) I think I am florid.*

Thomas Shadwell, The Virtuoso

Boyle's New Experiment

Robert Boyle, born in 1626, youngest son of the earl of Cork, was a brilliant scientific experimentalist, an accomplished man of letters, and a key member of the early Royal Society. Boyle's Law, which proposes a relation of inverse proportionality between the pressure and volume of a gas, was discovered by and named after him. It continues as a topic of high-school physics texts today. Boyle was also responsible for the development of the air pump, a major tool of the new experimental sciences in the seventeenth century. The breadth and quality of his experimental work in pneumatics, chemistry, and other areas of the natural sciences were admired by contemporaries at home and abroad. For example, after having read Boyle's latest "chymical" work while boating up the Thames, Samuel Pepys writes: "I can understand but little of it, but enough to see that he is a most excellent man" (Diary, June 2, 1667). Upon reading Boyle's *Hydrostatical Paradoxes Made Out by New Experiments for the Most Part Physical and Easy,* Pepys's reaction was even more flattering, referring to the work as "of infinite delight" (Hall 1966, 166).

Such admiration was, however, neither universal nor unqualified. On the contrary, the fun poked at the scientific experimentalist Sir Nicholas Gimcrack in Thomas Shadwell's play *The Virtuoso* (1667) suggests that the work of the Royal Society, especially of its amateur correspondents, was the target of public ridicule. Pepys's diary entry for February 1, 1664, reports a visit to the duke's chamber where the king spent "an hour or two laughing . . . at Gresham College. . . . Gresham College he mightily laughed at, for spending time only in weighing of ayre, and doing nothing else since they sat" (Shadwell 1966, xxi). In the context of such royal amusement the note of qualification sounded in the first of Pepys's remarks cited above ("I can understand but little of it") takes on added significance. Boyle's practical work may well have been admired by many, such as Pepys (who consulted Boyle about a pair of spectacles), but it seems that Boyle's writing left something to be desired.

In 1659 Boyle wrote a monograph, *New Experiments Physico-Mechanical*, describing experiments performed by him over the preceding two years. The book appeared in 1660 as his first published scientific work. Part of its novelty lay in its prose style when describing experiments:

> We then took a lamb's bladder large, well dried, and very limber, and leaving in it about half as much air as it could contain, we caused the neck of it to be strongly tied. . . . This bladder being conveyed into the receiver, and the cover luted on, the pump was set on work, and after two or three exsuctions . . . the imprisoned air began to swell in the bladder . . . [and] before we had exhausted the receiver near so much as we could, the bladder appeared as full and stretched, as if it had been blown up with a quill. (quoted in Hall 1966, 326)

Boyle continued to employ and develop this style of writing in subsequent books, which he published at the rate of about one a year until his death in 1691. The style was, he confessed, "prolix" as well as "circumstantial," that is, unfashionably verbose and characterized by a proliferation of small, apparently inessential details: "I have declined that succinct way of writing . . . [and] delivered things, to make them seem more clear, in such a multitude of words, that I now seem even to myself to have been in divers places guilty of verbosity" (*Proëmial Essay*, quoted in Shapin and Schaffer 1985, 63).

Like the metaphysical poets (John Donne, George Herbert, and Boyle's contemporaries Andrew Marvell, Thomas Wilmot, and Henry Vaughan) Boyle employed a hypotactically complex prose: long, winding sentences punctuated by nested layers of appositive subordinate clauses, which Boyle himself describes unflatteringly as "making sometimes my periods or parentheses over-long" (Shapin and Schaffer 1985, 63–64).[1]

---

1. See Shapin and Schaffer 1985, 64 n. 86, for the relation between Boyle's prose and Dryden's.

Also like the metaphysical poets, Boyle employed a "simple and pure," even home-spun, vocabulary grounded in observation (Eliot 1972, 285), although Boyle's references to mundane objects, unlike those of the poets, were not to be interpreted metaphorically. Indeed, he eschewed all metaphoric inflation of meaning. As he says in the *Proëmial Essay*, he rejects a "florid" and "rhetorical strain" in favor of a "naked way of writing" (Shapin and Schaffer 1985, 66). Even the similes he employed—for example, "as if it had been blown up with a quill"—were firmly rooted in familiar, observable phenomena.

The experimental accounts often appeared in the first person, as if recounting a sequence of personally experienced events: "We carefully weighed out a small lump of our shining matter, amounting to three grains, and having purposely broken it into divers lesser fragments, perhaps six or seven at least, we laid them upon a flat bottomed glass, that was broader at the top than the bottom, and shallow too (not being near an inch deep) that the matter might be more fully exposed to free air. This glass we placed in a South window, laying it very shelving" (*Icy Noctiluca*, 1681, quoted in Hall 1966, 317). But variations on this basic style also occurred throughout Boyle's writings, for instance, imperative or impersonal styles of narration: "Take good syrup of violets, impregnated with the tincture of the flowers, drop a little of it upon a white paper (for by that means the change of colour will be more conspicuous and the experiment may be practised in smaller quantities) and on this liquor let fall two or three drops of spirit either of salt or vinegar" (*Experiments and Considerations Touching Colours*, 1664, quoted in Hall 1966, 292). On occasions such descriptions were focalized through the eyes of a first-person narrator; in other instances through the eyes of an effaced, external narrator, as in the Homeric tradition of mimesis described by Eric Auerbach: "Fully externalized description, uniform illumination, uninterrupted connection, free expression, all events in the foreground, displaying unmistakable meanings, few elements of historical development and of psychological perspective" (Auerbach 1968, 23). In all variants, however, whatever their syntactic or narrative form, the experimental accounts seemed grounded directly in the author-narrator's personal observation of experiments that he had conducted or supervised personally.

The effect of such dry and convoluted prose focused through the eye of a single observer was to conjure up images directly in the mind's eye of the reader, as if they were seeing or, better, remembering seeing the experiments for themselves. As Steven Shapin and Simon Schaffer put it, the descriptions transformed readers into "virtual witnesses," that is, "trigger[ed] in the reader's mind a naturalistic image of the experimental scene" so that "it would be as if that reader had been present at the proceedings" (Shapin and Schaffer 1985, 60, 62–63).

Boyle's prose not only produced an illusion of reality. It was also persuasive; it created belief in the appearances conjured in the mind's eye. To this end, it incorporated several traditional rhetorical devices: the familiar trope of *descriptio* (detailed description) but also, in order to enhance authorial ethos, a wordy display of modesty ("I cannot but fear that my discourses . . . want many choice things wherewith the learned writings of others might have enriched or embellished them") as well as selfless concern for the reader: "I thought I might do the generality of my readers no unacceptable piece of service, by so punctually relating what I carefully observed that they . . . need not reiterate themselves an experiment to have as distinct an idea of it" (preface to *New Experiments Physico-Mechanical,* quoted in Hall 1966, 328, 325). In short, "Boyle's texts were constructed so as to provide a source of virtual witness that was agreed to be reliable." As Shapin and Schaffer observe, the aim was to write "experimental reports in the correct way [so that] *the reader could take on trust that these things happened*" (1985, 62, 61, my emphases).

The first-person form of Boyle's narratives aided in this rhetorical function. By making the words of the text appear as their author's personal testimony, Boyle's standing as a gentleman of high moral character and a brilliant scientist could be marshaled in support of his text. In this context, as Shapin argues, Boyle's exemplary life and personage took on the dimensions of a rhetorical artifact (1994, 127, 185).

The persuasive function of Boyle's text was augmented by eschewing the traditional scholastic philosophy of essences in favor of a more "commonsense" empiricist ontology restricting reality to what was empirically accessible. This modest metaphysics (the end of metaphysics, some would say) foreshadowed Hume's skeptical repudiation of all that is neither "abstract reasoning concerning quantity and number" nor "experimental reasoning concerning matter of fact and existence."

The distinctive nature of Boyle's prose is illuminated by a useful opposition introduced by W. J. T. Mitchell, between what he calls "realism" and "illusionism":

Illusionism is the capacity of pictures to deceive . . . or otherwise take power over a beholder; in . . . *trompe l'oeil* . . . for instance, the point is to provide a simulation of the presence of objects . . . to trigger a responsive experience in the beholder. Realism, by contrast, is associated with the capacity of pictures to show the truth about things. It doesn't take power over the observer's eye so much as stands in for it, offering a transparent window onto reality, an embodiment of a socially authorized and credible "eyewitness" perspective. The spectator of the realist representation is not supposed to be under the power of the representation, but to be using representation in order to take power over the world. (Mitchell 1994, 325)

In terms of this distinction, the literary project of mimesis chronicled by Auerbach was concerned with illusionism rather than realism. Boyle's project involved *both* illusionism and realism. As Shapin and Schaffer point out, these two aspects were not independent. Illusion was supposed to take on a persuasive role, thus contributing to the text's realism in Mitchell's sense of the term.

Boyle was neither frank nor clear about the role of such realism in his project. And for good reason. Admitting the persuasive function of his prose style would have meant exposing it to the criticism that highly embellished styles of writing and rhetoric generally attracted. Such criticism is exemplified by the following remarks by Francis Bacon, spiritual father of the Royal Society: "An affectionate study of eloquence and copie of speech . . . grew speedily to an excess . . . ; men began to hunt more after words than matter; and more after the choiceness of the phrase . . . and the sweet falling of the clauses, and the varying and illustration of their works with tropes and figures, than the weight of the matter" (Bacon 1996, 139). Although he goes on to say: "But yet notwithstanding it [rhetoric] is a thing not hastily to be condemned, to clothe and adorn the obscurity even of philosophy itself with sensible and plausible elocution." In short, it is excess of rhetoric rather than rhetoric as such that is to be eschewed.

The introduction to Thomas Sprat's commissioned *History of the Royal Society* also denounced "Eloquence as a thing fatal to Peace and good Manners." And even among critics of the Royal Society, a strong distrust of excessive rhetoric was apparent. Indeed, the high-flown orator was sufficiently a figure of disrepute to make a theatrical appearance. Sir Formal Trifle, a character in Shadwell's *The Virtuoso*, provided a butt for criticizing excessive use of rhetoric: "Is there so great a rascal upon earth as an orator, that would slur and top upon our understandings and impose his false conceits for true reasoning and his florid words for good sense?" (I, i, 236–239).

Such criticism of the abuse of rhetoric extended to all verbal techniques of persuasion. Bacon, for example, criticized the a priori philosophizing of the Schoolmen—Aristotelians, Platonists, and so on—who sought to persuade purely by the presentation of grand metaphysical schemes without recourse to experience (what Bacon called "experiment").[2] The latter criticism was also taken up by the Royal Society, as evidenced by Boyle's implicit criticism of mathematicians: "I am to excuse myself to mathematical readers. For some of them, I fear, will not like, that I should offer for proofs such physical experiments, as do not always demonstrate the things, they would evince, with a mathematical certainty" (*Hydrostatical*

---

2. In the seventeenth century, the meanings of "experience" and "experiment" were not yet fully distinguished in the modern way.

Paradoxes Made Out by New Experiments for the Most Part Physical and Easy, quoted in Hall 1966, 170). In place of purely verbal mathematical demonstration, Boyle offered "experimental proof."

Concern over the abuse of ornamental devices in speech was reinforced by Puritan rejection of all kinds of decoration. Such concern constituted a key element in a Restoration sensibility that proper modesty—"prudence" or "civility," as Shapin calls it—should rule in all things: "courtesy texts repeatedly counseled gentle readers, if they wished to be credible, to perform their relations without boasting, passion, or pedantry" (Shapin 1994, 221).

Such advice left considerable scope for legitimate applications of rhetoric, as exemplified both by Bacon's highly rhetorical polemics on behalf of science as well as by pedagogical and polemical passages in Boyle's writings. Bacon went so far as to accord an important place to rhetoric both in the art of invention and in countering the seditious influence of the affections (in the "coloring of the worse") (Bacon 1996, 239).[3] Sir William Petty, an important member of the Royal Society, also accorded a key place to rhetoric in the process of education (Petty 1927, 2:3–8). Even Sprat, who polemicized against rhetoric in his *History of the Royal Society*, allowed a place for rhetoric in literature, asserting that the new experimental philosophy would offer literary language a rich new field for constructing similes and comparisons (Sprat 1667, 324, 414–417).

Within scientific writing itself, however, rhetoric was to be avoided: observation together with reason (albeit without the formal excesses of the "mathematicians") were to be the grounding principles of scientific belief.[4] Why, then, did Boyle transgress these principles by creating a new rhetorical style of writing, and how did he cope with the fact of his transgression? These questions set the agenda for the remainder of this chapter.

Explaining Virtual Witness

In Boyle's period, the gathering of testimony by reputable witnesses was a crucial step in authorizing claims of all kinds, religious, legal, and scientific: "In Chancery no less than at common law rank counted: the

---

3. See also Bacon 1996, 139, 140, 190, 210–219, 223–224, 237–241.
4. Bacon's instructions for constructing his tables of positive and negative instances included specifying honestly "whether the author was a vain-speaking and light person, or sober and severe" (*Preparative towards a Natural and Experimental History*, quoted Shapin 1994, 222). Following this Baconian principle, Boyle specified that "cited Testimonies ought to be considerately and candidly deliver'd," and he questioned reports delivered in a "dogmatical," "violent," or "confident" manner (*Use of Reason and Natural Philosophy*; unpublished Boyle Papers, quoted in Shapin 1994, 222).

word of a gentleman of good standing would be accepted against that of a maidservant even if supported by other witnesses" (Hill 1987 269). Not only the reputation but also the number of witnesses was important: "For, though the testimony of a single witness shall not suffice to prove the accused party guilty of murder; yet the testimony of two witnesses, though but of equal credit . . . shall ordinarily suffice" (Boyle, *Some Considerations about Reason and Religion,* quoted in Shapin and Schaffer 1985, 56).

Boyle multiplied witnesses for his experimental claims by performing experiments in a social space, namely, the Royal Society's assembly rooms at Gresham College, London, to which access was monitored by keeping a register "to be sign'd by a certain Number of the Persons present, who have been present, and Witnesses of all the said Proceedings, who, by Subscribing their Names, will prove undoubted testimony" (Hooke, *Philosophical Investigations and Observations,* quoted in Shapin and Schaffer 1985, 58). Boyle's reports often incorporated lists of witnesses together with their credentials: "those excellent and deservedly famous Mathematics Professors, Dr. *Wallis,* Dr. *Ward,* and Mr. *Wren* . . . whom I name, both as justly counting it an honour to be known to them, and as being glad of such judicious and illustrious witnesses of our experiment" (*New Experiments,* quoted in Shapin and Schaffer 1985, 58). Elsewhere Boyle invoked a more highly born witness: "the experiment having been tried both before our whole Society, and very critically, by its royal founder, his majesty himself" (*Hydrostatical Discourse,* quoted in Shapin and Schaffer 1985, 218). Such records indicate that in the scientific arena, no less than at law, questions of who was a witness in good standing reproduced "the social and moral accounting systems of Restoration England" (Shapin and Schaffer 1985, 59).

As Christopher Hill has pointed out, however, the tradition of legitimating beliefs by citing witnesses of good reputation was under considerable pressure in Restoration England. Protestant views insisted that personal witness, not the opinion of religious authorities, was the proper path to knowledge of God. Experience, not the word of others, however reputable, was to be the touchstone for a person's knowledge claims: "Thomas Collier, preaching to the Army at Putney in 1647, offered to confirm one of his points from Scripture, 'although I trust I shall declare nothing unto you but experimental [experienced] truth.' 'Experience goes beyond all things,' Coppin declared. The Antinomian Henry Pinnel contrasted the way 'a man knows a thing by reading it' with 'experimental certainty of it in himself'" (Hill 1987, 368).

Boyle and the Royal Society may be seen as responding to this challenge to traditional epistemological practices by adopting an "experimental philosophy" that grounded belief in personal experience and experimentation (although, as we have seen, they were also concerned to multiply witnesses of good standing). In Marie Boas Hall's words, the Society's members "tried strenuously [not] . . . to believe as true what they had not seen with their own eyes" (Hall 1966, 28). By performing experiments in their own homes, the Society's correspondents grounded their beliefs on the basis of modest generalizations (inductions) from their own experience, with due attention to the possibility of counterexamples (what Bacon called "negative instances").

Boyle adopted a similar strategy in his religious apologetics, such as *The Excellence of Theology* (1674, but written in 1665) and *The Usefulness of Experimental Natural Philosophy* (1663, written as early as 1647). Here he promulgated a naturalistic approach to theology, one that sought proofs for the existence of God not in philosophical argumentation but rather in empirical study of the natural world to discover signs of divine providence (Hall 1966, 48–52).[5] In both theology and natural philosophy, it seems, Boyle aimed to eschew purely verbal argumentation, including the testimony of others, in favor of direct and personal experience.[6]

The empiricism mandated by Boyle and the Royal Society created difficulties in implementing another aspect of their charter. The Society was committed to making science a more public activity, a commitment apparent in the following quotation from Boyle's writings: "Such a treatise for the kind, as that which follows . . . may perhaps . . . persuade a greater number of differing sorts of readers, than a far more elaborate [one]" (*Some Considerations Touching the Usefulness of Experimental Natural philosophy*, quoted in Hall 1966, 158). Boyle explicitly cites Bacon as the inspiration for this commitment: "[This book] may serve to beget a confederacy, and an union between parts of learning, whose possessors have hitherto kept their respective skills stranger . . . which how advantageous it may prove towards the increase of knowledge, our illustrious Verulam [Bacon] has somewhat taught us" (*Some Considerations Touching the Usefulness of Experimental Natural philosophy*, quoted in Hall 1966, 162–163).

This Baconian project for a public science resonated with various ideologies in Restoration England, where the matter of the production and

5. Such an approach came into prominence in the eighteenth and nineteenth centuries, under the rubric "natural theology."
6. This is not to say that theology and philosophy were one and the same for Boyle. On the contrary, he argued that natural philosophy was justified insofar as it contributed to theology, a point expounded upon at length in publications such as *The Excellence of Theology, compared with Natural Philosophy (as both are Objects of Men's Study)* (1674). Robert Hooke, one of Boyle's early assistants, and later Curator (or Demonstrator) of Experiments at the Royal Society, confirmed this distinction between theology and philosophy: "The business and design of the Royal Society is to improve the knowledge of natural things . . . by Experiment (not meddling with Divinity, Metaphysics, Morals, Politics, Grammar, Rhetoric, or Logic)" (quoted in Hall 1966, 28).

ownership of knowledge was an important public and political issue, manifesting itself in the question of the language in which to write theology. Knowledge and in particular theology, it was argued, were not to be the exclusive preserve of scholars, the upper class, and the priesthood, all of whom were educated in Latin, but should also be available to the masses who read in the vernacular.

The seriousness with which such principles were taken by Boyle and his immediate successors, such as Hooke and Newton, is evident in an increasing shift from Latin to English as the written language of science. (English had been used as a language for science since the mid-sixteenth century, despite frequent complaints that it lacked the necessary terminology.) Newton's *Principia,* for example, published in 1687, first appeared in Latin, whereas the first edition of the *Opticks,* in 1704, appeared in the vernacular. Although fluent in the language, Newton did not write a Latin version of the *Opticks,* instead paying an impoverished disciple, Samuel Clark, five hundred pounds to do the job (Westfall 1990, 648).[7]

The empiricism and emphasis upon personal witness characteristic of the new experimental philosophy created difficulties for the public dissemination of scientific works such as Boyle's *New Experiments.* Not only did these works fail to communicate with the general audience whom they targeted (in this context Pepys's comments cited in the opening section of this chapter are germane), but they also struck a serious difficulty of principle. The texts relied for effect upon readers trusting their experimental accounts. For the most part, however, such accounts, like many reports of exotic events received by the Royal Society, were not and could not be supported by the intended readers' personal experiences, few of whom enjoyed the social or scientific status to be invited to the Royal Society's public experimental performances, let alone had access to the major financial resources and technical skills needed to repeat experiments for themselves. As Boyle tells us: "Such trouble as I met with in making those trials, and the great expence of time that they necessarily require (not to mention the charges of making the engine, and employing a man to manage it) will probably keep most men from trying again these experiments" (preface to *New Experiments Physico-Mechanical,* quoted in Hall 1966, 325).

It seems, then, that if its projected readers were to follow mandated empiricist principles, Boyle's text could not make its experimental claims rationally credible to the majority. In short, Boyle was caught on the horns of

7. Note that although learning Latin was part of acquiring an "education," many of the "educated" middle- and upper-class readers whom the Royal Society hoped to enroll in the cause of science would have lacked any great fluency in the language.

a dilemma: either he sacrificed the Baconian project to create a public science or he forced his readers to transgress empiricist principles in coming to believe what they read.

Boyle's new prose style was, I suggest, a response to this dilemma. By a series of cleverly judged rhetorical devices, including the trope of *descriptio,* his prose created such "clear and distinct ideas" of the experiments in readers' minds that they believed in them *as if* they had witnessed them personally. Readers were transformed into "virtual witnesses," and thus were enabled to conceal from themselves their failure to satisfy the empiricist requirement of personally witnessing what they believed.

Shapin and Schaffer offer a somewhat different rationale for Boyle's prose. For Boyle and his contemporaries, Shapin and Schaffer point out, the number of witnesses was an epistemologically relevant factor. Thus, because it appeared to multiply witnesses, virtual witnessing took on the dimensions of a rhetorical strategy. Since every new reader comprised a new virtual witness, "through virtual witnessing the multiplication of witnesses could be, in principle, unlimited" (Shapin and Schaffer 1985, 61). Shapin and Schaffer see a special role for this rhetorical strategy in virtue of the expanded audience for science, an audience who for the most part lacked the opportunity or ability to directly witness or replicate Boyle's experimental performances: "Yet, because of natural and legitimate suspicion among those who were neither direct witnesses nor replicators, a greater degree of assurance was required to produce assent. . . . Boyle's literary technology [of virtual witnessing] was crafted to secure this assent" (61).[8]

By contrast with Schaffer and Shapin, I take virtual witnessing as a rhetorical strategy which, by simulating the effects of personal witness, conceals the violation of empiricist principles needed to render Boyle's texts credible to its readers. Whereas Shapin and Schaffer explain Boyle's rhetorical strategy in terms of a traditional epistemology favoring multiplication of witnesses, my explanation invokes the new empiricist epistemology.

In which ever way it is explained, however, the strategy of virtual witnessing created a major difficulty. Because of its persuasive dimension, Boyle's new prose style violated the prescription against rhetoric in experimental descriptions. Boyle would have been well aware of this violation. He and many of its readers were well schooled in classical rhetoric, one of the elements of the medieval Trivium which continued to provide the framework for University education. Boyle attempted to conceal the violation by a va-

8. On this point see *New Experiments Physico-Mechanical,* 1–2, quoted in Hall 1966, 325; Shapin and Schaffer 1985, 60, 62. Here too the emphasis appears to be not so much upon simulating personal witness as on the multiplication of witnesses.

riety of strategies. He avoided mentioning the term "rhetoric" in reference to his own writing, and by emphasizing its lack of ornamentation—in particular, apologizing for failing to heed the "precepts of rhetoricians" who required a more embellished style—he implicitly denied his writing's rhetorical nature: "I cannot but fear that my discourses . . . want many choice things, wherewith the learned writings of others might have enriched or embellished them" (*New Experiments Physico-Mechanical*, quoted in Hall 1966, 328).

From a formal point of view, however, such strategies only compounded the problem, since the indirect denial of its own rhetorical nature involved Boyle's writing in yet another piece of rhetoric, namely, the familiar Aristotelian trope of enhancing authorial ethos by refusing to engage in sophistry or rhetorical niceties. Nevertheless, from a rhetorical point of view, the strategies seem to have been effective. They emerge as formally self-defeating but nonetheless persuasive rhetorical ploys, sliding ambiguously between the obvious truth that Boyle's rhetoric was unconventional (for texts of philosophy) and the false claim, the merit of which he sought to persuade his reader, that his writing was rhetoric free.

In addition to both concealing and denying its rhetorical nature, Boyle's text offered a formal justification for its prose style: "I thought I might do the generality of my readers no unacceptable piece of service, by so punctually relating what I carefully observed, that they may look upon these narratives as standing records in our new pneumatics, and need not reiterate themselves an experiment to have as distinct an idea of it, as may suffice them to ground their reflexions and speculations upon" (preface to *New Experiments Physico-Mechanical*, quoted in Hall 1966, 325). In other words, Boyle claimed that his prolix prose was intended not to persuade but rather to provide readers with a clear enough impression of the experiments to "ground their reflexions upon" without going to the trouble and expense of repeating the experiments for themselves.

Of course, this claim came perilously close to admitting the rhetorical nature of his prose. Boyle skirted this further admission by claiming that the point of giving readers "distinct ideas" was to enable them to repeat the experiments for themselves: "I thought it necessary to deliver things circumstantially that the person I addressed [the experimental accounts] to might without mistake, and with as little trouble as possible, be able to repeat such usual experiments" (quoted in Hall 1966, 325). Even the most straight-laced empiricist could approve the latter justification.[9]

9. Replicability does not play the same methodological role here as in the modern context. Its importance for Boyle lay in enabling readers to observe his experiments for themselves and thus come to believe his accounts on the basis of personal witness.

A related justification appeared in Boyle's later essay *On the Practical Uses of Natural Philosophy*, published in 1671 (although written some six years earlier):

> the generality of those readers, to whom we would give good impressions of the study of nature, being such as will probably be more wrought upon by the variety of examples, and easy experiments, than by the deepest notions, and the neatest hypotheses, such a treatise for the kind, as that which follows, containing many practices of artifices and such particulars, that are either of easy trial, or immediate use, may perhaps by that variety gratify, and persuade a greater number of differing sorts of readers, than a far more elaborate piece. (quoted in Hall 1966, 158)

Here Boyle's concern was not so much that readers be persuaded of the truth of the experiments as that they receive "good impressions of the study of nature." Even the following quotation, which strongly suggests that Boyle's intention was to persuade his readers, is open to this weaker reading: "Of my being somewhat prolix in many of my experiments, I have these reasons to render: that some of them being altogether new, seemed to need the being circumstantially related, to keep the reader from distrusting them" (from *New Experiments Physico-Mechanical*, quoted in Hall 1966, 324–325). Here Boyle's stated intention is that of preventing distrust rather than creating trust; in other words, he seeks to engage his readers' interest and encourage them to suspend disbelief rather than persuade them.

Unfortunately, as Boyle himself conceded with disarming honesty, such justification for his prose was worthless, since, despite his plain and detailed instructions, few were able to repeat the experiments: "Such trouble as I met with in making those trials . . . will probably keep most men from trying again these experiments." Indeed, it was some time before any scientists, especially his continental critics, were able to perform his experiments, let alone confirm their results (Shapin and Schaffer 1985, chap. 6). Nevertheless, justifying his style of writing as a clear and accurate means of communicating instructions served the useful purpose of deflecting attention from its real function as a rhetorical device.

In sum, Boyle's strategy of virtual witnessing was a response to an empiricist epistemology that stressed the importance of personal witness rather than multiple witnesses or the word of authorities. This epistemology created a serious problem for texts, such as *New Experiments*, that described what were for the bulk of its intended readers effectively unwitnessable experiments. In this respect Boyle's texts were uncomfortably close to the esoteric and secret works of the alchemists, a fact hinted at in

Pepys's remark that he found Boyle's work "so chymical, that I can understand but little of it."

The task of virtual witnessing was to conceal this difficulty by creating in readers' minds an impression that they had personally witnessed the experiments. By concealing, denying, and justifying their own rhetorical nature, Boyle's writings addressed the further difficulty that virtual witnessing took on the dimensions of a rhetorical technique. Here, then, we see the Boylean rhetoric of science at work, complete with its own invisible meta-rhetoric, which conceals its rhetorical nature by creating an appearance of being rhetoric free.

A similar rhetoric is in use today as the plain, detailed, prose style of the modern experimental account. Its discourse of self-justification (insofar as it includes one) appeals not to considerations of audience convenience (as Boyle did) but rather to the self-evident value of the historically specific forms of "precision" and "objectivity" that it embodies. This modern scientific rhetoric is able to conceal its own rhetorical nature not only because modern readers, uneducated in rhetoric, are unable to see "plain writing" as a trope but also because Boyle's "prolix and circumstantial" rhetoric has taken on the dimensions of an official style, gaining its persuasive effect as much from the institutional authority of science as from its formal rhetorical effects.

From a contemporary perspective it thus becomes difficult to comprehend the scrupulousness displayed by *New Experiments* with respect to the question of its style. In the context of the seventeenth century, however, when the Royal Society was struggling to establish itself as the legitimate inheritor of the tradition of "natural philosophy," and when readers showed an informed wariness of rhetoric, Boyle's scrupulousness emerges as a practical necessity. In the next chapter, where I show how the rhetorical technology of virtual witnessing creates a gaze, I turn to further details of the visual aspects of Boyle's text.

8

Seeing Texts

You have two goblets before you. One is of solid gold, wrought in the most exquisite patterns. The other is of crystal-clear cut glass, thin as a bubble and as transparent. Pour and drink; and according to your choice of goblet, I shall know whether or not you are a connoisseur of wine. . . . If you are a member of that vanishing tribe, the amateur of fine vintages, you will choose the crystal, because everything about it is calculated to reveal *rather than hide the beautiful thing which it was meant to* contain. *. . . Bear with me in this long-winded and fragrant metaphor; for you will find that all the virtues of the perfect wine-glass have a parallel in typography.*

Beatrice Ward, The Crystal Goblet

When we talk about "looking at" a book we usually mean one of two things. First, we may mean literally viewing it: inspecting its cover, typeface, layout, and so on. In this context a gaze may arise in a perfectly straightforward way. For example, the glittering gold leaf of an illuminated medieval manuscript may physically impact the eye in the same way that a glint of light assaulted the young Lacan during his day at sea. But such a gaze has nothing to do with the propositional content of the text, and in any case has little relevance for the modern printed book, the visual appearance of which has been standardized to the point where it has little impact.

Indeed, such invisibility has been elevated to the level of a norm. In her book *The Crystal Goblet: Sixteen Essays on Typography,* Beatrice Ward adopts an avowedly "modernist" stance (which she defines in terms of attention to function rather than form) when she writes: "A page set in 14-pt. Bold Sans is, according to the laboratory tests, more legible than one set in 11-pt. Baskerville. A public speaker is more 'audible' in that sense when he bellows. But a good speaking voice is one which is inaudible *as* a voice. It is the transparent goblet. . . . Type well used is invisible *as* type, just as the perfect talking voice is the unnoticed vehicle for the transmission of words, ideas" (Ward 1955, 13).[1] Her argument is that since the function of printing is "to convey specific and coherent ideas," printing should be "readable" rather than "legible." By this she means that the typeface should be invisible *as* type, that is, should enable readers to take in ideas without distracting them through ornamentation or being visually intrusive in any way. Here the thread connecting Boyle's Restoration sensibility to modernism is clear.

We may also talk about "looking at" or "viewing" a text in a quite different way, as a metaphor, a colorful way of restructuring the semantic space of reading in terms of concepts associated with sight and seeing. Within the terms of this metaphor, written texts may be assigned a "gaze" in a sense that has nothing to do with physical vision. This metaphor has taken on special importance in the context of the modern novel or realist fiction more generally, which, as Peter Brooks points out, favors visual modes of description: "The dominant nineteenth-century tradition, that of realism, insistently makes the visual the master relation to the world, for the very premise of realism is that one cannot understand human beings outside the context of the things that surround them, and knowing those things is a matter of viewing them, detailing them, and describing the concrete milieux in which men and women enact their destinies" (Brooks 1993, 88).

Thus, when we talk of "viewing" a text, it seems that we do so in one of two ways, either by ignoring the text's content and referring to visual engagement with its material signifiers, or talking metaphorically about aspects of the process of reading which have nothing to do with literally seeing or having visual impressions. In both cases, the possibility of literally (as opposed to metaphorically) seeing what the text says is erased. Indeed, as Ward suggests, the "modernist" sensibility wants to erase all possibility of seeing the text, to the extent of rendering its material signifiers "transparent."

Despite normative pressures against visualizing written texts, there is one tradition of writing, what Auerbach calls mimesis, for which reading does involves literally viewing what it says. Mimetic writing incorporates vivid or, as we say, "realistic" descriptions that stimulate visual impressions in readers. The impressions result not from perceiving or even remem-

---

1. For Ward's self-definition as "modernist" see Ward 1955, 12. This chapter's epigraph, taken from the preceding page, gives a fuller illustration of the metaphor of the crystal goblet. I am grateful to Adrian Marshall for pointing me toward this delightful mixture of high Tory party nostalgia and British modernism. For a more academically satisfying account of the historical roots and complexities of the matter of typography see Drucker 1994.

bering but instead operate through the faculty of imagination—the mind's eye.[2] The visual field created by such writing may, on occasion, take on the structure of the gaze. I shall discuss this possibility by returning to Boyle's *New Experiments* and introducing a discussion of Flaubert's *Madame Bovary*.

Emma's Body

Gustave Flaubert's *Madame Bovary* (1857) is taken by many as the first "realist novel." Like Holbein's *The Ambassadors* and Boyle's *New Experiments*, its descriptions are characterized by an excess of detail. The descriptions of Emma through the eyes of the men who know her focus in great detail upon apparently unconnected and trivial aspects of her appearance, as if reporting the half-hidden details upon which a fetishistic observer's eye might stumble and linger—a lock of hair curling onto the nape of the neck, a shoe, the corners of her mouth:

> Her eyelids seemed perfectly fashioned for those long ardent looks that drown the eye; while deep breathing dilated her fine nostrils and lifted the plump corners of her mouth, shadowed in the light with a faint black down. . . . About her neck the dropping coils of her hair; they twined in a great mass, neglectfully. . . . Something subtle that ran straight through you breathed out even from the folds of her gown and from the curve of her foot. Charles, just as in the first days of his marriage, found her delicious and irresistible. (Flaubert 1992, 157)

These little things—these partly obscured corners and edges of her body—like the trinkets with which she litters her life, catch the eyes of the men whom she charms and fascinates in a way that they find hard to understand:

> The less Charles understood of these things, the more they beguiled him. They added to the pleasures and comforts of his fireside. It was like a sprinkling of gold-dust along the narrow track of his life. . . . In Rouen she saw ladies wearing bunches of trinkets on their watch chains; she bought some trinkets. For her mantelpiece she wanted a pair of large blue glass vases, and a little later, an ivory work-box, with a silver-gilt thimble. (47)

Only her clothing, it seems, occupies the eye in a more systematic way: "She would be wearing her dressing-gown unbuttoned, revealing, between

2. A written description may also trigger visual memories, but that is not my focus here.

the copious folds of her corsage, a pleated chemisette with gold buttons. Round her waist she had a cord with big tassels, and her little wine-red slippers had large knots of ribbons, spreading down over the instep" (47). Even with respect to her clothes, however, the view seems to flit from detail to detail. When Léon, her lover to be, joins her in conversation for the first time, "she was wearing a little cravat made of blue silk, that made her tube-pleated batiste collar stick up like a ruff; and, whenever she moved her head, half her face was screened by the fabric or else was pleasingly revealed" (67). This punctuated regime of description is repeated in connection with the "dear room" in which the lovers' rendezvous takes place:

> There was a great big mahogany bed in the shape of a boat. The curtains made of red oriental stuff, hung from the ceiling, curving out rather too low over the wide bed-head. . . . The warm room with its plain carpet, its frivolous decorations, its tranquil light, seemed quite perfect for the intimacies of passion. The arrow-headed curtain rods, the brass fittings, and the big balls on the fender would gleam suddenly, whenever the sun shone in. (215)

The scopic economy thus mirrors the empty peregrinations of the lovers' conversations, which move randomly from phrase to phrase, centering upon nothing more substantial than vague shared sentimental attachments: "one of those vague conversations in which every random phrase always brings you back to the fixed center of mutual sympathy. Paris, theatres, titles of novels, new quadrilles, and the society they knew nothing of" (67). In short, as Brooks argues, the look implicit in the narratorial descriptions in *Madame Bovary* is fetishistic, fastening upon details not because they are salient but rather because, at an unconscious level, they distract from what cannot be seen (Brooks 1993, 103).

When Emma's body is described in more comprehensive terms, it is in vacuous, conventional, even stereotypical language, which on occasion makes explicit reference to the romantic art and literature from which it is culled: "She was the lover in every novel, the heroine in every play, the vague *she* in every volume of poetry. On her shoulders he found the amber colours of *Odalisque au bain;* she had the long body of some feudal chatelaine; and she looked like the *Pale woman of Barcelona,* but supremely she was the Angel" (Flaubert 1992, 215). In short, except for a few details which prick their sensibilities—the "faint black down" and the "folds of her gown"—Emma is perceived by her lovers in terms of a collage of banalities: a virtuous, even virginal woman whose conquest seems to serve primarily as a mark of the manliness and worldly status of her seducer: "Never had he met with such grace of language, such modesty of dress, such tableaux of drowsy maiden-innocence. He admired the exaltation of her soul and the lace on her skirts. Besides was she not a *lady*, and a married woman! A real mistress" (215). Thus the ostensible site of desire, Emma's body, is represented as a disturbing void, a site of failure of representation, veiled only by a thin tissue of *clichés* and an erratic trail of glittering points to which the eyes of her bourgeois lovers are irresistibly drawn. The critical thrust of Flaubert's text, as Fredric Jameson remarks, is constituted by this evacuation of the site of desire.[3]

In Barthes's terms, then, Flaubert's descriptions take the *studium-punctum* form characteristic of the "true" photograph (Barthes 1993, 26–27): the bulk of the novel's descriptions verge on the stereotypical (the *studium*), but these are interrupted by *punctums*—lyrical phrases that, by lavishing detail upon small, apparently insignificant detail of appearance, transgress the dominant descriptive regime. In this way, Flaubert sought to capture the fetishistic quality of the bourgeois gaze, constituted by its fascination with trivia, forever seeking distractions from what it never dares to consider, namely, the fundamental emptiness of its own existence.

Transcending the vulgarities of bourgeois thought, the *punctums* in Flaubert's text redeem his writerly project by providing distance from bourgeois sensibility. But they were also points of danger, for Flaubert sought to capture in words ephemeral objects that fascinated the bourgeois sensibility but were impossible to mention. Flaubert explicitly dwells upon this danger. He was, he writes in a letter to a friend, "afraid of becoming another Paul de Kock or producing a kind of chateaubriandized Balzac. . . . How to render trivial dialogue that is well written? . . . I pass alternately from the most extreme emphasis to the most academic platitude" (quoted in Bourdieu 1996, 93).

Flaubert's anxiety spills over into the content of his text. For the bulk of the book, the more intimate contours of Emma's body are a site of invisibility, which is doubled since it masquerades as visibility. As Brooks argues, because of the words lavished upon her appearance, readers think they know Emma's body well. It is only when they attempt to construct a picture of how she appears that, as Brooks points out, the book's failure to provide a representation of her body becomes evident: "The reader's sense of the presence of Emma's body is so intense and so memorable that it comes a something of a surprise, upon rereading the novel, to find that there is very little in the way of full length portraiture of Emma" (Brooks 1993, 90).[4]

3. See Jameson's discussion of Flaubert in Jameson 1981.
4. This structure of invisibility, which conceals itself behind a mask of visibility, resembles the Victorian taboo against sexuality which Foucault describes in the first volume of his *History of Sexuality*, a taboo so profound that any mention of the taboo was itself proscribed. Arguably this taboo arose from the same bourgeois prudishness that Flaubert sought to capture in *Madame Bovary*.

In a passage near the end of the novel, however, when the ill-fated affair with Léon is almost over, Emma's sensuality suddenly thrusts itself into the light, figured as the site of an unnamable horror, an excessive emptiness, which foreshadows the death of passion as well as Emma herself ("pale and silent . . . that brow covered in cold drops"):

> Emma came back to him more inflamed, more voracious. Her undressing was brutal, tearing at the delicate laces on her corset, which rustled down over her hips like a slithering snake. . . . Pale and silent and serious, she fell upon him, shivering . . . on that brow covered in cold drops, on those murmuring lips, in those wild eyes, and in the clasping of those arms, there was something excessive, something empty and lugubrious, which Léon felt sliding, imperceptibly, between them, as if to push them asunder. (Flaubert 1992, 230)

In this passage, Flaubert graphically anticipates the Lacanian "Thing" (Freud's *"das Ding"*): a horrifying, inchoate void, the disgusting underbelly of pleasure, associated here with an ambiguously phallic female sensuality, erupting and sliding through the phantasmatic trappings of a fragmenting (male) symbolic order.

Until that juncture in the text, the polite and prudish bourgeois conventions of description (the *studium*) coexisted with the violent little breaks (the *punctums*) upon which Emma's lovers focused. But at that point the little spots, the *punctums*, suddenly swell up, consume, and take over the whole of Emma's body, which, by failing to take a determinate visualizable form, stands nakedly revealed as a point of failure in the symbolic order.

The horrifying terms in which this encounter is described suggest that at this point in the novel the author's anxieties concerning the production of his text coalesce with something less controlled, more visceral, which haunts his imaginings. The phrase "something excessive, something empty and lugubrious" may be seen as a hidden metaphor for the loathsome bourgeois banalities, "a kind of chateaubriandized Balzac," which Flaubert consciously struggled to avoid in writing *Madame Bovary*. But it also resonates with a more basic, sexual, and specifically phallic anxiety that seems to find form and surface at this point in the text, from which it then disseminates, retrospectively and prospectively shrouding all other encounters with Emma's body in unrealistic anxiety (unrealistic because of the hidden nature of its object).

Thus, for its author, it seems, the *punctums* of *Madame Bovary* take on the dimensions of a gaze: a site of unrealistic anxiety where the symbolic order falters. To be specific, it seems that for Flaubert the points of overdescription of Emma's person mark the boundaries of a gaze emanating from a horrifying emptiness at the center of her body, toward which his writing gestures but which finally it cannot describe.

The Virtual Gaze

Shapin and Schaffer claim that reading Boyle's descriptions of scientific experiments creates visual impressions which simulate the effects of "witnessing": "The technology of virtual witnessing involves the production in the *reader's* mind of such an image of an experimental scene as obviates the necessity for either direct witness or replication" (Shapin and Schaffer 1985, 60). These visual effects, I argued in Chapter 7, arise from Boyle's style of writing, a hypotactic excess of detail unrelieved by verbal flourishes, which he refers to apologetically as "prolix and circumstantial."

The writing's unremitting excess, the tedium of reading the plain, detailed descriptions, forces readers to "step back" from what they read, to dip in and out of a text that otherwise would overwhelm them. This effect is reinforced, indeed guided, by changes of descriptive depth within the narrative itself. Some items are described in detail, as if at the center of the narrator's focus, while others are reduced to the status of props, merely named, as if glanced at in passing. A good example is Boyle's experiment with the lamb's bladder (quoted on p. 120). Here the process of "exsuction" and the bladder itself, "large, well dried, and very limber," are described in some detail, while two other items, the pump and the receiver, as well as the process of conveying the bladder, are mentioned in passing. This variation in descriptive depth imposes a duality of perspective on the narrative, the close-up alternating with the distant. In short, readers may be thought of as looking and then looking again from a more distant perspective at what they have seen already from closer in.

The looking in question is an act of visual imagination, of course, rather than seeing in any literal sense. Nevertheless, according to Shapin and Schaffer, readers do form visual impressions of what they read, which, although lacking the "realistic" quality of bona fide perceptions, are no less visual than dreams or memories. In particular, by imaginatively looking again at what they have seen, Boyle's readers "review" their own "seeing." Thus, they not only "see" but also, in a reflexive turn, put themselves and in particular their own "seeing" under review.

New Experiments, like *Madame Bovary*, incorporates elements to which its author's anxieties attach. Boyle's anxieties seem to target the text's style rather than particular narrative moments, however, and thus diffuse over the work as a whole. This does not imply that Boyle dwells any less fulsomely ("prolixly") upon selected details than Flaubert: "a flat bottomed glass, that was broader at the top than the bottom, and shallow too (not being near an inch deep) that the [contained] matter might be more fully exposed to free air" (*Icy Noctiluca*, quoted in Hall 1966, 317). Unlike Flaubert, however, Boyle's descriptive focus on particular items is not an occasion for anxiety but rather reflects the items' salience to his more general project of providing recipes for repeating experiments. So, for example, in the last quotation he gives details about the shape, dimensions, and material of a dish because these are judged relevant to the experiment's successful conduct.

Instead, in Boyle's text unrealistic anxiety attaches to the question of his written style. Boyle expresses this anxiety in elaborate, multiply layered, and internally incoherent statements which struggle with the issue of the rhetorical nature of his writing. On the one hand, he avoids mentioning, indeed implicitly denies, his style's rhetorical nature; on the other, he justifies its rhetorical effects. (I return to these paradoxical manifestations of his anxiety later in this chapter.) In short, Boyle's writing combines the two elements constitutive of the gaze: it leads readers to step back and look again at what it describes, and it functions as a site of unrealistic anxiety. Because the resultant gaze attaches to features of the text as a whole, to its style rather than to localized points, it takes on what Barthes (referring to the *punctum* rather than the gaze) calls its "less Proustian expansion," which "while remaining a 'detail' . . . fills the whole picture" (Barthes 1993, 45).

The gaze associated with *New Experiments* is characteristic of memory rather than perception. At each point in Boyle's narrative a stage of an experiment is described. These descriptions include subtly oscillating time references, which imply that the narrator knows about events both later and earlier than the stage of the experiment he is describing. For example, the description of tying up a lamb's bladder includes a reference to its being "well dried" and "limber," thus implying prior experience of drying and manipulating the bladder. At another point in the same quotation, the receptacle for the gas ("the receiver") is said to have been in a state "before we had exhausted [it] near so much as we could." Here the description includes foreknowledge of events yet to come: by continuing the process of exsuction more air would be exhausted from the receiver. Such foreknowledge together with the past tense of the narrative strongly suggest that rather than reporting impressions resulting from observing the experiment, the narrator is recalling events from his past. Thus Boyle's descriptions simulate the effects of memory both by the selective nature of their focus and by their temporalization.[5] In the following sections, I confirm

5. The past tense of the narrative is strictly speaking irrelevant to this point, since the issue is not the narrator's relation to the impressions he is relaying but rather the relation of the impressions themselves to the moment of their conception.

the existence of this gaze in *New Experiments* by tracing its effects in Boyle's phantasies about his own writing. I also undertake a similar confirmation for Flaubert's *Madame Bovary*.

Unrealistic Anxiety, Desire, and Phantasy in Bovary

Flaubert's prose was motivated, it seems, by two interlocking desires. Wanting to discredit literary rivals, specifically the first-wave "realist" school associated with Gustave Courbet and Jean Champfleury, he remarks in the preface to *Madame Bovary* that the "irritation produced in me by the bad writing of Champfleury and the so-called realists has not been without influence in the production of this book," adding elsewhere that he "wrote *Madame Bovary* to annoy Champfleury" (Bourdieu 1996, 88, 93). He also tells us that he wanted to write beautifully. These desires, we may speculate, found expression in a parodic project designed to highlight the bourgeois dreariness and mediocre sentiments characteristic of Champfleury's work by rewriting them in a beautiful way, "to blend lyricism and the vulgar. . . . I wanted to show that bourgeois dreariness and mediocre sentiments could sustain beautiful language" (96, 93).

I argued that this project was not without its anxieties. Although determined to complete *Madame Bovary*, Flaubert questioned whether it would bear any resemblance to his original intentions: "What this book will be, I don't know; but I can say that it will be written" (quoted in Bourdieu 1996, 96). Such an attitude bespeaks what Freud calls unrealistic anxiety.

Freud explains such anxieties by suggesting that from earliest childhood subjects are dogged by threats that inhibit the satisfaction of "instinctual wishes." He distinguishes five different stages in which such threats appear: birth, loss of the mother, object loss in the genital stage associated with the paternal injunction and castration threat, loss of love or punishment by the stern superego (associated with the danger of "separation or expulsion from the hoard"), and death or fate (Freud 1993, 294–297).

Freud makes clear that the inhibited wishes—what he also calls "certain feelings and intentions within us"—may not be at the forefront of the child's mind but instead may be posited retrospectively as causes of the threats. More generally, "the loved person would not cease to love us nor should we be threatened with castration if we did not entertain certain feelings and intentions within us" (303–304).

The same threats which inhibit wishes also generate anxieties that would overwhelm the child were it not for ways of controlling them. Similarly, Freud tells us, toothache, like anxiety a danger signal, threatens to overwhelm the sufferer and become a danger in its own right unless controlled by, for example, the sufferer indulging in various "symptomatic" distractions such as hitting his head.[6]

Such control of anxiety, Freud tells us, is achieved in two quite distinct stages: first, the "instinctual wishes" are repressed, decathected at a conscious level by masking them behind phantasy structures of opposing conscious desires. Second, through a process of symptom formation, although repressed, the instinctual wish returns and is realized in disguised form. According to Freud, the function of this combination of repression and return is to attain the instinctual wish while shifting attention away from the otherwise paralyzing threat that its realization creates.

At an unconscious level, the wish and corresponding threat remain active, producing anxieties which are free floating because the dangers to which they respond have been hidden from view. Such "free" anxieties make their way along unconscious pathways and manifest in what Freud calls an "unrealistic form," attached to new objects which retain unconscious connections with the original dangers. Because the new objects no longer match the objects to which they were a response, these second-level anxieties appear, in Freud's terms, "unrealistic." In short, unrealistic anxiety is a reaction to a hidden threat that is covertly connected to an overt source of anxiety by a chain of unconscious associations.

This account of unrealistic anxiety, based upon his work on animal phobias in children—for example, the Little Hans case—appears in Freud's later writings beginning with the "Inhibitions, Symptoms and Anxiety" essay of 1926: "The anxiety felt in animal phobias is, therefore, an affective reaction on the part of the ego to danger, and the danger which is being signalled in this way is the danger of castration. This anxiety differs in no respect from the realistic anxiety which the ego normally feels in situations of danger, except that its content remains unconscious and only becomes conscious in the form of a distortion" (Freud 1993, 282).[7]

Such anxieties are managed by and precipitate a process of "symptom formation." This involves developing ritual-like behaviors, what Freud calls "symptoms," that are positioned by unconscious trains of associations as disguised realizations of repressed wishes. According to this conception (which generalizes the earlier definition of "symptom" developed by Freud in the context of his work on hysteria) the symptom is a dis-

---

6. Toothache is itself regarded as a symptom in the more usual medical sense of this term, that is, as a diagnostic sign. The behavior by which the sufferer distracts himself from pain thus becomes a symptom of a symptom.

7. Freud's earlier view, which appears as late as the 1923 edition of *The Ego and the Id*, is that the cause of anxiety is the freeing of energy resulting from decathexis accompanying repression (Freud 1993, 283–287).

guised return of an instinctual wish.[8] Because its connection with the wish is hidden, the symptom does not trigger a threat of danger and therefore avoids setting off the alarm bells of anxiety. Symptoms thus provide subjects with a means of realizing their unconscious wishes while keeping anxiety in check: "It is plain, then, that . . . the obsessional act of washing of the hands [was] to obviate outbreaks of anxiety. In this sense every inhibition which the ego imposes on itself can be called a symptom" (302).

Because it constitutes a return of the repressed, the symptom takes on a transgressive quality, covertly breaking through the masking phantasy of conscious desires which function as a defense against the unconscious wish and its associated danger. Freud also argues that since, unlike the unconscious wish it represents, the symptom is uninhibited, it is subject to what he calls "a compulsion to repeat." It is as if the cathecting energy originally associated with the wish is turned into a source of kinetic energy driving the resulting symptom (312). The paradoxical combination of transgression and compulsion to repeat is a key distinguishing mark of the symptom.

If the disguise concealing the symptom's identity as a return of the repressed is too thin, the symptom may becomes a site of renewed anxiety (or, as Freud calls it, "unpleasure"). Such supplemental anxiety is especially likely in cases of obsession, although it may also occur in cases of phobia: "The mechanism of phobia does good service as a means of defence and tends to be very stable. A continuation of the defensive struggle, in the shape of a struggle against the symptom, occurs frequently" (283). Usually, however, in the case of phobia the symptom, an avoidance of the phobic object, seems totally free of anxiety, which focuses instead upon the phobic object. In such cases, anxiety arises in connection with the symptom only when the subject is somehow prevented from enacting it. Thus, Little Hans may be said to be anxious *to* avoid horses, but not anxious *about* avoiding them. Or, to make the same point in a slightly different way, he is anxious about horses rather than about avoiding them.

In the case of obsession, by contrast, matters are not so clear-cut. The symptom is not simply the avoidance of a phobic object upon which the bulk of anxiety is focused through a train of unconscious associations connecting it to the primal situation of danger. Instead the symptom develops in relation to the superego, as a substitute formation for a wish that has been repressed because it transgresses the superego's commands.

Flaubert's writing of *Madame Bovary* illustrates the latter possibility. Flaubert did not doubt his ability to write ("I can say that it will be

8. In the *Three Essays* of 1905, Freud conceives of the symptom as a "sign of, and substitute for, an instinctual satisfaction which has remained in abeyance . . . a consequence of the process of repression" (Freud 1993, 242).

written"). Instead his anxieties and doubts attached in an indeterminate way to the project as a whole, to the question of its possibility ("what this book will be, I don't know"). His simplest course of action would have been to give up or modify his goals. Instead he persisted in the face of doubt and uncertainty. In short, the project's execution took on the appearance of a "compulsion to repeat."

In virtue of its parodic nature, the book realized in disguised form exactly what Flaubert consciously desired to avoid, namely, an alignment with Champfleury. The transparency of this disguise (to others) is evident from his contemporaries' reactions—despite vociferous protests by its author, *Madame Bovary* attained the status of an exemplary "realist" text. Flaubert's writing thus functioned as a disguised means of transgressing his conscious desire to evade the mark of "realism." In short, Flaubert's persistent struggle to write *Madame Bovary* evinced the characteristics of a symptom, that is, a paradoxical combination of transgression with compulsive repetition. Correlatively, the accompanying anxieties, which, I argued, found a point of focus in the punctal encounters with the margins of Emma's body, assumed an unrealistic dimension.

The symptomatic nature of Flaubert's writing of Bovary implies that it was motivated at an unconscious level. The most plausible candidate for such motivation is a covert wish to be like Champfleury. What the deeper unconscious roots of this wish might have been I can only speculate: perhaps an Oedipal relation with the impotent figure of Champfleury, who, as a founding figure of the "realist" movement with which Flaubert was associated publicly, bore the "name of the father."[9] Whether or not one accepts this paternal identification, the Oedipal resonances of the unconscious desire motivating Flaubert in the context of crafting *Madame Bovary* seem clear enough, finding expression in the description of the ambiguously phallic Thing that Léon encounters beneath the sheets: "something lugubrious."

The unconscious wish to be like Champfleury, masked by an opposing conscious desire to write beautifully and a vitriolic criticism (denial) of "realism," found suitable expression in the parodic form of Flaubert's project. In Freudian terms, the project functioned as a phantasy structure defending against, but also sustaining, an unconscious wish. This structure, in turn, provided a setting for a new conscious desire to rewrite Champfleury's vulgar themes in "lyrical fashion," a desire encapsulated in the apparently oxymoronic formula "Write the mediocre well," to which Flaubert constantly returned "in an . . . obsessional fashion" while writing *Madame Bovary* (letter to Louis Colet, quoted in Bourdieu 1996, 94 n. 96).

9. As Lacan emphasizes, the bearer of the name of the father is always impotent (Lacan 1977, 315).

Boyle's Desire

Boyle explicitly desired to spread the good word of science to a more general lay audience and encouraged his readers to witness and repeat experiments for themselves: "The generality of those readers, to whom we would give good impression of the study of nature . . . will probably be more wrought upon by the variety of examples and easy experiments. . . . Such a treatise for the kind, as that which follows, contain[s] many practices of artifices and such particulars, that are either of easy trial, or immediate use" (*Some Considerations Touching the Usefulness of Experimental Natural Philosophy*, quoted in Hall 1966, 158). He also expressed a desire to write well, in the accepted philosophical mode: a "close and concise way of writing" which "manifest[s] those truths more distinctly . . . and yet without exceeding that brevity, my avocations and the bounds of an essay exact of me" (*Of the Usefulness of Experimental Natural Philosophy*, quoted in Hall 1966, 141).

These two desires conflicted, since the general reader, whom Boyle desired to reach, could not be persuaded by a "close and concise" style. Boyle resolved this rhetorical difficulty by sacrificing the desire to write philosophically, developing instead a new "circumstantial and prolix" prose: "I confess, that it was out of choice, that I declined that close and concise way of writing, that in other cases I am wont to esteem. For writing now not to credit myself, but to instruct others . . . " (*Hydrostatical Paradoxes Made Out by New Experiments for the Most Part Physical and Easy*, quoted in Hall 1966, 170).

Schooled in traditional rhetoric, Boyle must have been well aware of the rhetorical function served by the new style of writing. Nevertheless, as I indicated above, he both avoids mentioning this fact and (paradoxically) denies it. "I cannot but fear," he writes in the preface to *New Experiments*, "that my discourse . . . wants many choice things wherewith the learned writings of others might have enriched or embellished them" (quoted in Hall 1966, 324, 325). As I also pointed out, these strategies of avoidance and denial are combined with a contrary strategy of justifying the new style, thus undermining the attempt to deny its rhetorical nature. By this contradictory combination of strategies, Boyle betrays an anxiety that is unrealistic in precisely the Freudian sense of persisting against good reason.

According to Freud, such unrealistic anxiety indicates that Boyle's actions conceal an unconscious wish masked by and opposed to his conscious desire. The obvious candidate for this wish is a predilection for the self-same rhetorical forms against which Boyle protests. (Such protests, a form of denial—*Verneinung*—are, as Freud notes, among the simplest mechanisms of defense.)

The presence of this unconscious wish is doubly confirmed insofar as it explains two otherwise puzzling features of Boyle's rhetoric. The first is Boyle's choice of the Aristotelian trope of "plain speaking," uncommon in philosophical disquisitions of the time, which persuades by appearing to avoid engagement with rhetoric. By deploying this trope, Boyle is able to realize covertly an engagement with rhetoric—a goal that he unconsciously desires but which he must also deny, lest he offend his own sensibilities as well as those of his colleagues in the Royal Society.

Boyle's strange apology for not heeding "the precepts of rhetoricians" can be explained similarly. In the light of the Royal Society's well-known hostility to rhetoric, Boyle's apology must be read nonliterally, as to some extent insincere or at least disingenuous, an indirect way of denying his text's complicity in rhetoric. But the apology also served an unconscious function of permitting Boyle, under the cover of insincerity, to express safely what he dared not say openly and may have been reluctant to admit even to himself: regret at not being able to use his rhetorical skills.

In short, the tensions within the phantasy structure of Boyle's conscious strategies and desires suggest the presence of an unconscious wish that he explicitly denies, namely, an interest in rhetoric. No less than *Madame Bovary*, *New Experiments* is, it seems, the site of its author's unconscious investment.

Afterword: A Historical Trajectory

I have shown how a Lacanian framework explains the strange contrast between the violence of Flaubert's protests against "realism" and the widespread perception that he belonged to, indeed was doyen of, the "realist" school. Flaubert's protests can be understood as aspects of a phantasy structure that manifested an unconscious wish to resemble Champfleury, a resemblance that the public perception of his work acknowledged but which Flaubert himself denied.

From a Lacanian perspective, commitment to such a phantasy structure is no casual matter, since it is essential to maintaining the drive through which pleasure is produced. Which drive is detectable in Flaubert's engagement with *Madame Bovary*? Earlier in this chapter I argued that *Madame Bovary* was the site of a scopic drive structure, which turned around a gaze stimulated by lyrical descriptions of the margins of Emma's body. Thus an explanatory connection can be drawn between two apparently unrelated aspects of the novel: on the one hand, the unconscious desire of its author; on the other, the formal *studium-punctum* structure underwriting its gaze. A similar connection can be made in the case of

Boyle's *New Experiments*. That is, Boyle's unconscious desire to be a rhetorician may be seen as part of a support system and thus evidence for the scopic drive structure and corresponding gaze associated with the work's "prolix and circumstantial" prose.

The choice of works in the last three chapters may seem eclectic: Holbein's masterpiece *The Ambassadors*, produced at a moment (1533) near the beginning of the tradition of oil painting on canvas, a painting that, by borrowing from the subgenre of anamorphic projections, played with and undermined the Albertian system of perspective which came into prominence in the fifteenth century; Boyle's *New Experiments Physico-Mechanical*, first published in 1660, which, by repudiating the florid style of contemporary learned treatises as well as the formal argumentation of "mathematicians" and arcane concepts of "chymists," lays claim to being the origin of modern scientific rhetoric; and a nineteenth-century novel, Flaubert's *Madame Bovary* (1857), often taken to mark the beginning of modern "realist" fiction.

These texts are linked by a formal concern for "realism" in the broad sense of creating lifelike appearances—what Mitchell calls illusionism (see Chapter 7). Within this broad similarity, however, key differences emerge. Flaubert's novel strives for lifelikeness by imparting a certain degree of "truth" about bourgeois life. Its concern is with "reality effects," however, rather than truth as such—with fictionalized caricature rather than verisimilitude in the narrow sense. In short, although it is in certain respects "true to life," *Madame Bovary* is a work of patent falsehood, "fictional" in a sense that characterizes the modern "realist" novel generally.

Holbein's and Boyle's works, by contrast, strive not only for aesthetic reality effects but also for credibility, that is "realism" in the narrow epistemological sense suggested by Mitchell rather than the traditional literary sense of the term. In Boyle's case, I argued, this persuasive dimension comprised a point of difficulty since it opened him to accusations of being rhetorical. Holbein's painting, by contrast, readily embraced its persuasive function. Indeed, it was integral to the work's *raison d'être*, commissioned by one of its subjects, de Dinteville, as a public record of his ambassadorial mission to England. As Derek Wilson puts it in a recent biography of Holbein: "De Dinteville, who took the painting back to France with him, wanted an impressive record of his mission . . . an elaborate and costly painting covering ten oak panels and measuring 207 by 209.5 centimetres" (Wilson 1996, 196–197). In this context, the painting's circumstantial details, such as the unusual tile floor painstakingly copied from Westminster Abbey, may be understood as integral to its function as a convincing record of de Dinteville's presence in England. Holbein's reputation as a portraitist depended upon such persuasive techniques. Henry VIII was pleased with Holbein's portraits precisely because they provided reliable pictures of their models, an invaluable asset in an age when such pictures played a key role in closing a deal in the marriage market.[10]

Despite sharing a formal concern with "realism," each of the works is characterized by a different visual style. Although Boyle's descriptive regime is selective, it gives an impression of comprehensiveness and plenitude by providing a tedious excess of detail. The temporalization and focus of its descriptions mean that the corresponding visual field takes on a mnemonic form. Flaubert, by contrast, provides excessive detail concerning localized, eccentric aspects of Emma's body (*punctums*), skimming over more usual points of interest. In Barthes's terms, then, Flaubert's description takes the *studium-punctum* form characteristic not of memory but rather of the "true" photograph: "Not only is the Photograph never, in essence, a memory (whose grammatical expression would be the perfect tense, whereas the tense of the Photograph is the aorist), but it actually blocks memory, quickly becomes a counter-memory. . . . The Photograph is violent: not because it shows violent things, but because on each occasion *it fills the sight by force*" (Barthes 1993, 91). Holbein's portrait of the ambassadors also employs a descriptive regime based upon excess detail. But it is a reversal or negative of the photographic form, insofar as its lavish excess of detail spreads over the canvas as a whole, relieved only at highly localized spots, such as the lifeless, lackluster images of the ambassadors' flesh. Thus, whereas the descriptive regime of *Madame Bovary* is photographic, that of *The Ambassadors*, like *trompe l'oeil*, is simulacral, playing with the revelation of its own masquerade.

The trajectory of visual styles from simulacrum to memory to photograph follows in the footsteps of broader cultural, social, and technological changes: the advent of merchant capitalism (Chapter 6), the displacement of the medieval arts of memory in favor of writing (Chapter 7), and the invention of the daguerreotype/photograph. My aim has not been to trace this history in any detail, let alone speculate about the causal relations connecting it with other histories, but rather to identify a common psychic mechanism which, in each of its successive incarnations, has sustained the gaze by connecting it to the pleasures and desires of individual viewers.

10. There is a second reason for classifying each of these works as "realist." All were iconoclastic, that is, each in its respective context of production transgressed dominant conventions of representation, and thus fell under Jameson's category of "realism" (to which I return in Chapter 10): "As any number of 'definitions' of realism assert . . . realistic representation has as its historic function the systematic undermining and demystification, the secular 'decoding' of those preexisting inherited traditional or sacred narrative paradigms which are its initial givens" (Jameson 1981, 152).

This historical analysis stands at the endpoint of a line of theoretical development that began with the discussion in Chapter 5 of an Althusserian approach to the problematic of interpellation in terms of a specular model for the constitution of subjects. In Chapter 6, I presented a refinement to this approach, which, by infusing Althusser with the later Lacan, showed how the problematic of the gaze provides a way of explaining the constitutive effects of images upon their viewers in a historically specific way. While allowing for the imbrication of ideological with unconscious factors, Chapter 6 followed a traditional Marxist trajectory of studying the ideologically mediated relation of the cultural to the social without engaging in an analysis that penetrates to the level of individual subjects. Althusser's bald assertion that "nine out of ten" of the "right" listeners will heed the call is typical of such approaches. He makes a small concession to the possibility of individual variation—one out of ten may fail to conform—but then leaves that possibility unexplained. In the present chapter I rectified this approach by showing how in the case of individual reader/viewers, the effects of the gaze disseminate into other areas of psychic life. Thus the problematic of interpellation has been successively reworked from Althusser's coarse-grained purely social approach to the point where an individual's distinctive psychic response to interpellation can be explained.

IV

INTERPASSIVITY AND
THE POSTMODERN

9

Interpassivity and the Knowing Wink: Mystery Science Theater 3000

Reification and the Postmodern

In the *Sublime Object of Ideology*, Slavoj Žižek draws attention to "a phenomenon quite usual in popular television shows or serials: 'canned laughter.' After some supposedly funny or witty remark, you can hear the laughter and applause included in the soundtrack of the show itself" (Žižek 1989, 35). Žižek then adds: "So even if, tired from a hard day's stupid work, all evening we did nothing but gaze drowsily into the television screen, we can say afterwards that objectively, through the medium of the other, we had a really good time." In Robert Pfaller's terminology, the audience who listen passively to a laugh track instead of laughing for themselves is said to be "interpassive" (Pfaller 1999).

In its original sense, the term "interpassive" was intended to describe agents who, instead of acting on their own behalf, delegate their activities to others—for instance, viewers who, having recorded a show on a VCR, do not bother to watch it for themselves since, as we might put it, something else "objectively" watches on their behalf; or an audience who, having attended a concert, read the newspaper critique instead of making up their own minds about what they have heard. Opportunities for interpassive engagements have increased through the technological mediation of everyday practices by automatic dishwashers, ATMS, vibrators, and so on. This mechanization of life means that we are able to interpassively delegate ever more aspects of our daily activities to mechanical agencies.

For instance, my contribution to washing dishes reduces to stacking, un-loading, and pushing the button of a machine which washes them on my behalf.

I generalize the concept of interpassivity by rethinking it as a property not of agents but of artifacts. In particular, a cultural artifact is said to be "interpassive" if, like a sitcom with a laugh track, it responds to itself on its audience's behalf, thus enabling the audience to delegate their response. Of course, not all members of a particular audience may (inter)-passively accept the artifact's response rather than responding for themselves. On the contrary, even those who start by passively listening to a laugh track may end up actively laughing, either because the mechanical laughter strikes them as comic or because, as Freud notes, laughter is infectious.

Interpassivity may be seen as an aspect of the process of reification theorized by Lukacs (1983, 100). The construction of a laugh track, for instance, involves removing laughter from its subjective human source and then "objectifying" or standardizing it in various ways—smoothing it out and editing it into the soundtrack. In this alienated (othered) form it is relayed back to an audience who, in the first instance at least, decathect their own laughing in favor of listening "passively" to the recorded substitute. This process follows the familiar pattern of reification, since it involves abstracting laughter from its human origins and restoring it in alienated form.

Alternatively, interpassivity, and canned laughter in particular, may be explained as aspects of a "postmodern" shift in emphasis from signified to signifier. Television shows no longer concern themselves with producing pleasure but rather with producing its free-floating signifiers such as laughter. The usual connections between the signifier (laughter) and the corresponding signified (pleasure) are disrupted. The agency producing the laughter, namely, the soundtrack, is no longer the same as the human audience who enjoy themselves.[1]

The analysis of canned laughter as either an effect of reification or a postmodern privileging of the signifier fails to answer a further crucial question: Why, and more specifically how, does interpassivity affect the production of pleasure. To put the question concretely, if I no longer laugh "spontaneously" because the soundtrack laughs on my behalf, then how does watching the show produce the pleasure traditionally associated

1. Fredric Jameson argues that reification and the postmodern privileging of the signifier are one and the same process: "'reification' and the emergence of an increasingly material-ized signifier are one and the same phenomenon—both historically and culturally" (Jameson 1992, 16).

with the personal production of laughter? At issue here is not only the peculiar mechanics of watching television but also a more general question that Marxist approaches to theories of cultural production have failed to answer satisfactorily, namely, the relation between cultural forms and the pleasures and desires of individual consumers.

One might, of course, answer these question from a Baudrillardian perspective by taking the production of pleasure in the postmodern context as nothing but the circulation of signifiers of pleasure. But I will answer them here from a Freudian and specifically a Lacanian perspective, focusing initially on the phenomenon of canned laughter and then analyzing the contemporary American television show *Mystery Science Theater 3000* (MST3K for short). In general terms I argue that the pleasure produced by interpassive cultural artifacts depends upon the workings of what Freud calls the drive (*Trieb*), which he sees as the primary mechanism for producing pleasure.

What a Laugh!

In *Jokes and Their Relation to the Unconscious,* Freud claims that the construction of jokes requires "joke-work" analogous to what in the *Interpretation of Dreams* he calls "dream-work." In dream-work, according to Freud, one reworks residues of the day's waking thoughts, which, through memory, retain their cathexis during sleep. This reworking involves constructing a series of associations, condensations, and displacements connecting the dream-thought with an unconscious wish. In this way, the dream becomes a vehicle for covertly expressing a wish, thus evading the prohibition associated with its direct articulation (Freud 1991, 217).

By analogy, joke-work involves three imbricated processes. The first is wordplay, to "put words together without regard to the condition that they should make sense, in order to obtain from them the pleasurable effects of rhythm and rhyme" (174). The resultant concatenations of fragmentary strings of linguistic signifiers are analogous to what in dreams are called the "day's residues." Second, in order to evade the prohibition against nonsense, the joker ensures that the results of his or her play conform with minimal requirements of sense: "The joke-work . . . shows itself in a choice of verbal material and conceptual situations which will allow the old play with words and thoughts to withstand the scrutiny of criticism" (180).

If that were all the joker did then the result would be what Freud calls "a jest" (178). But the true joker as opposed to the mere jester takes a third step. What she or he says must in some respect be appropriate to the occasion, even when expressed in a new and quirky way (179): "Jests," he tells us, merely "say [what] does not appear senseless. . . . [But] if what a jest says possesses substance and value it turns into a joke" (181).

More specifically, Freud distinguishes jokes from jests by suggesting that the former tap into the unconscious of the joker as well as the audience. He suggests that even the apparently most innocent, "non-tendentious" jokes are transgressive and set "themselves up against an inhibiting and restricting power" that is connected at an unconscious level to a "repressed" prohibition (183).[2] At this point in his exposition, Freud carefully stops short of claiming that all jokes have such unconscious connections, but later, in the "Theoretic Part," he tentatively advances this further claim: "Let us decide, then, to adopt the hypothesis that this is the way in which jokes are formed in the first person: *a preconscious thought is given over for a moment to unconscious revision and the outcome of this is at once grasped by conscious perception*" (223).

Freud also distinguishes between the "first-person" joker, who at least initially does not laugh at her or his own creation, and the "third-person" audience for whose benefit the joke is told, and who immediately express their pleasure in laughter (209, 238). (The "second-person" involved in the joke is the "butt" of the joke, the person at whose expense the joke is told. This second-person role is not central to jokes but essential to comic effects, which I discuss later.) According to Freud, pleasure for both the "first" and "third" persons is a spin-off from the energy freed by the joke through its evasion of inhibitions, that is, through managing to say indirectly what should not be said.

For the first-person joker the energy freed by such evasion merely compensates for the quota consumed in the joke-work, without leaving much for the act of laughing. Thus the first-person joker laughs only as a secondary effect, *par ricochet,* as it were. As Freud puts the matter: "When I make the other person laugh by telling him my joke, I am actually making use of him to arouse my own laughter" (209). This indirect mechanism for stimulating one's laughter by making another person laugh depends upon the fact that, as Freud says, "Laughter is among the highly infectious expressions of psychical states." The third-person audience for the joke, by contrast, are the lucky beneficiaries of the teller's work: they get their pleasure for free, as it were. Merely by listening, they evade the inhibition that the joke teller labors to overcome. In their case, then, all the energy freed by the joke is directly channeled into and fuels the laughter accompanying and signaling the production of pleasure.

---

2. "Among the various kinds of internal inhibition or suppression there is one which deserves our special interest, because it is the most far-reaching. It is given the name of 'repression'" (Freud 1991, 184).

Can Laugh

Canned laughter in a television sitcom presents problems for the Freudian account. Since they do not laugh *at* the jokes, the interpassive viewing/listening audience cannot be identified with what Freud calls the "third party," namely, those whose laughter serves to distinguish a joke from a mere jest. Instead, if the interpassive audience laugh, it is only as a secondary effect, either because the mechanical canned laughter is contagious or because they find it comic. Members of an interpassive audience are more like Freud's "first party." Their laughter, like the joker's, is triggered by the laughter of others. But unlike the "first party," the interpassive audience do not make the jokes. In short, canned laughter is anomalous with respect to the Freudian scheme: its audience fit none of the Freudian categories of first, second, or third party. Nevertheless Freud's distinctions between the comic, the humorous, and the joke turn out to be helpful in understanding this phenomenon.

The comic involves laughing at the expense of a "second party," for example, at the major physical disruption created by a person slipping on a banana skin. More specifically, Freud says, the comic involves a comparison "between two cathectic expenditures that occur in rapid succession and are concerned with the same function" (256). A person appears comic when an excessive expenditure of bodily energy over mental energy is apparent.[3] The pleasure generated by such recognition, which in turn fuels the laughter, arises from what Freud calls "a pleasurable sense of superiority" (256), which enables viewers to relax and drop their guard, thus freeing up a certain quota of energy they previously dedicated to paying attention to their own interests.

Of course, as Freud points out, not all such recognitions will lead to laughter (280). Among the conditions that favor its emergence he lists a certain degree of inattention: "A movement or a function cannot be comic for a person whose interest is directed to comparing it with a standard which he has clearly before his mind. Thus the examiner does not find the nonsense comic which the candidate produces in his ignorance" (283). In short, if it is to produce comic pleasure, then "the process of comparing expenditures must remain automatic," that is, must "lack the cathexis of attention with which consciousness is linked," although without neces-

---

3. By contrast, if the situation is reversed, if we recognize a certain saving of physical energy by applying mental effort, then "we no longer laugh, we are filled with astonishment and admiration" (Freud 1991, 256). Here we see the origin of at least some of the pleasure in viewing the work of art which economically conjures up a vision that we, the viewers, must otherwise work so hard to see.

sarily sinking to the level of the unconscious (284). In the Freudian topology, such lack of attention is associated with the preconscious.

The humorous, by contrast, is characterized as a species of defense. Instead of being attached to some distressing thought or feeling, cathexis is displaced somewhere else, thus avoiding the generation of unpleasure (290). The strategy of "grinning and bearing" or "laughing off" some catastrophe by withdrawing attention from it and focusing wryly or ironically upon some distant and relatively insignificant benefit of the situation exemplifies the humorous. So, a man who has just lost a leg remarks: "At least I won't have to cut all my toe-nails." In this situation too, Freud argues, inattention must be preconscious rather than deliberate (298).

In the light of these distinctions, canned laughter on the soundtrack of a television sitcom can be understood as involving a comic effect. Just as a shaggy-dog story derives its humor from the teller's exaggerated attempts to signal that his story is a winner, so too the comic effect of canned laughter derives in part from the lack of proportion between the sustained laughter on the soundtrack and the stupid, unfunny jokes.

The comic effect of canned laughter also depends upon a coincidence between the mechanical and the human—in particular on a mechanization of the human faculty of laughter. Canned laughter leads listeners to relax their efforts by suggesting that there is no need to laugh, or even pay much attention to the jokes, since those activities are being carried out effortlessly, automatically on their behalf.[4] In Freud's terms, the freeing up of energy that results from a reduction in cathexis of the listeners' attention produces a pleasurable effect combined with a secondary burst of laughter.

But none of these Freudian effects seem adequate to explain the pleasure that sustains viewers who, week after week, return to their favorite sitcom. A Frankfurt-school model of television viewers—which casts them as "cultural dopes" or "addicts" who watch what they are given to watch, and come to enjoy it from sheer force of habit, their sole pleasure lying in a mechanical repetition of the familiar—seems equally inadequate as an explanation. Such a model, geared to an outdated conception of a "mass audience," does not fit the peculiar and pleasurable rituals of the box. In particular, it is unable to account for the pleasures of channel surfing, which depend upon fickleness and an obsession with novelty rather than mechanical repetition of the familiar.

In explaining the pleasures of sitcom viewing, I draw attention to an aspect of canned laughter that has no place in the Freudian scheme adduced

---

4. According to Freud, this is an instance of a more general proposition: "Everything in a living person that makes one think of an inanimate mechanism has a comic effect" (Freud 1991, 271).

so far, namely, an element of contradiction between viewers' intellectual and practical engagements. On the one hand, viewers know with certainty that the laughter on the soundtrack is simulated, that it comes neither from them nor from anyone else actually listening to the program. (I leave aside cases where a studio audience is present at the filming of the show.) On the other hand, they find the program amusing and enjoy it as if the laughter were genuine. In this respect, then, canned laughter functions in a similar way to money. As Žižek puts it:

> When individuals use money, they know very well that there is nothing magical about it—that money, in its materiality, is simply an expression of social relations. . . . The problem is that in their social activity itself, in what they are *doing*, they are *acting* as if money, in its material reality, is the immediate embodiment of wealth as such. They are fetishists in practice, not in theory. What they "do not know," what they misrecognize, is the fact that in their social reality itself, in their social activity—in the act of commodity exchange—they are guided by the fetishistic illusion. (Žižek 1989, 31)

Žižek goes on to say that "what they overlook, what they misrecognize, is not the reality but the illusion which is structuring their reality, their real social activity. They know very well how things are, but still they are doing it as if they did not know. The illusion is therefore double: it consists in overlooking the illusion which is structuring our real, effective relationship to reality. And this overlooked, unconscious illusion is what may be called the *ideological phantasy*" (32–33). Similarly, the audience for the soundtrack "know very well how things are," that the laughter is "purely a pretense," that it does not originate from them or anyone else watching the show. They are perfectly clear on this score, by contrast with the confusion sometimes displayed in distinguishing actors from the characters they play. Nevertheless, as Žižek says, "still they are doing it"; by returning night after night, year after year, to see the show, they act as if the canned laughter were a genuine response, a true index that the show is funny. In short, the audience's response is balanced between knowing that the laughter they hear is faked and enjoying the show as if the laughter were genuine, an enjoyment signaled at a practical level not by the audience's laughter but rather by a strong commitment to watching the show.

Such a contradiction between knowledge and practice, between knowing and doing, is characteristic of a phenomenon that Freud calls the drive (*Trieb*), the primary mechanism for the production of pleasure. Lacan illustrates the drive by the phenomenon of *trompe l'oeil*: "What is it that attracts and satisfies us in *trompe l'oeil*? When is it that it captures our attention and delights us? At the moment when, by a mere shift of our gaze, we are able to realize that the representation does not move with the gaze and that it is merely *trompe l'oeil*. For it appears at that moment as something other than it seemed. . . . That other thing is the *petit a*, around which there revolves a combat of which *trompe l'oeil* is the soul" (Lacan 1981, 112).

In the course of this description, Lacan introduces a new category of objects, the *objet [petit] a*. In the special case of *trompe l'oeil*, he tells us, the *objet a* is that which "appears . . . as something other than it seemed"; specifically it is that which gives rise to an instability in the viewer's visual field, causing an oscillation in what he or she sees. In short, the *objet a* is the painting, the "representation" around which the flux of appearances constitutive of the phenomenon turns. (More correctly, the *objet a* is the visual instability caused by the painting, but we do not need to be so precise here.) This flux (or more correctly the associated libidinal flow) constitutes what Lacan, following Freud, calls "the drive." It is responsible for the production of pleasure, which fuels the phenomenon of *trompe l'oeil*. As Lacan puts it, the *objet a* is "that other thing . . . around which there revolves a combat of which *trompe l'oeil* is the soul" (112). Or, as he says elsewhere in more general terms: "To this . . . object, *objet a* . . . we must give a function that will explain its place in the satisfaction of the drive. The best formula seems to me to be the following—that *la pulsion en fait le tour*" (168—*pulsion* is Lacan's translation of *Trieb*). The term *tour*, Lacan tells us, "is to be understood here with the [full] ambiguity it possesses in French, both [as] *turn*, the limit around which one turns, and *trick*" (168). In the case of a *trompe l'oeil*, for instance, the pertinent drive structure is constituted by a "turning" and "returning" of looks, a looking and looking again, in response to an unstable illusion or "trick."

In short, Lacan's position is that the pleasure produced by *trompe l'oeil*, that which "attracts and satisfies us," is produced by a drive that revolves around the painting as *petit a*. Lacan's name for this visual form of the drive is "the scopic drive," and he calls the *objet a* around which it turns "the gaze." Conceived in this way, *trompe l'oeil* illustrates perfectly the claim that the drive is accompanied by a contradiction between what we know and what we do. That is, as viewers of *trompe l'oeil* we know very well that what we see is *un tour*, a trick or illusion, but all the same, in virtue of the pleasure it affords, the trick deceives and fascinates us.

Canned laughter, I suggest, fills a similar role to *trompe l'oeil* but in a vocal rather than visual context. In Lacan's terms, it too is a *petit a*. It is an instance of what Lacan calls "the Voice," an audible deception or trick (*tour*) within the soundtrack that "appears . . . as something other than it seems" and is encircled by a structure of vocalizations and revocalizations. To be specific, the canned laughter masquerades as laughter by the audience, and, in turn, stimulates real laughter, albeit as an attenuated secondary effect. (The rudimentary nature of the secondary laughter is an aspect of the interpassive nature of the phenomenon: we do not laugh heartily since the track does so on our behalf.)

The structure of canned laughter and its secondary spin-off constitute what Lacan calls the invocatory drive. Conceived as a vocal analogue of the looking and looking again that constitute the scopic drive, it functions as a drive in its own right (Lacan 1981, 174–180, 194–195, 274). And since according to Freud's pleasure principle, the drive in any of its forms is productive of pleasure, it follows that canned laughter and its secondary spin-off laughter are also a source of pleasure.

These suggestions concerning the psychic structure of canned laughter, specifically the hypothesis that canned laughter belongs to the category of the Voice, explain the paradoxical feature noted above: judged by their loyalty to the show, a sitcom audience's enjoyment is well in excess of what we might expect on the basis of their desultory secondary laughter. Their excess pleasure, I claim, comes from the operation of the invocatory drive circulating the canned laughter. It follows that despite its desultory quality, the secondary laughter stimulated by the soundtrack and overlaying the audience's purely passive response is essential to the sitcom's production of pleasure. Without it, an invocatory drive structure would not take shape, and the show could not produce the pleasure that sustains viewer involvement over years of reruns.

This account of canned laughter leads to a reevaluation of what Pfaller calls "interpassivity." Listening to a soundtrack, we have seen, stimulates laughter as a secondary effect (*par ricochet*) and thus creates pleasure through the operation of an invocatory drive structure with canned laughter at the center functioning as the Voice-object (*objet a*). Thus, far from constituting a passive delegation of one's response to others, listening to the soundtrack is part of a complex although not necessarily intentional strategy in pursuit of pleasure. This complex phenomenon, an imbrication of the passive delegation and the active pursuit of pleasure through a set of secondary effects, provides a template for interpassivity as a self-sustaining phenomenon.

MST3K and the Scopic Drive

The phenomenon of interpassivity is not restricted to canned laughter. It also crops up in other contemporary media productions, such as the television show *Mystery Science Theater 3000*. Originally (in the late eighties) a local cable access program produced in Minnesota, it quickly created a large cult following on both coasts, especially among college students. Subsequently it made it into "big-time" national television, where it was featured on Comedy Central. Currently it is produced (with minor changes in format) for the Sci-Fi channel.

The program features reruns of old B-grade movies and employs an innovative double framing device, a device later adapted by programs such as Beavis and Butt-Head and MTV interactive music videos. The innermost of the frames is a blacked out strip at the bottom of the television screen, in which three figures are silhouetted against the movie: Mike Nelson and his two robot friends, Tom Servo and Crow, who, we are informed in a separate song and dance introductory sequence at the beginning of the program, are being chased across the galaxy by an evil and powerful woman, Pearl. She forces them to watch a steady diet of bad old movies ("cheesy," Pearl calls them). The three figures duly watch the films and exchange a series of smart-ass, media-wise jokes.

The figures are provided with a rudimentary *mise en scène:* a row of movie theater seats on which they sit during the screening, their backs to the television audience as if they were sitting in a row of seats in front of us in a cinema. The gestures of the robots are minimal, without any real attempt to achieve realistic body or lip movements synchronized with their speech. The three figures look at the screen displayed before them, chat about what they see, and occasionally get up and move offscreen to make comfort visits to an indeterminate surrounding location. While they are in the inner frame, they never acknowledge our presence "behind" them.

The movie screening is interrupted by breaks, which function formally as a second, outer frame for the inner one. Mike and his robot friends appear on the bridge of the spaceship in which they are traveling, and we are treated to a full-screen, full-color elaboration of the show's premise that they are being pursued across the galaxy by the evil Pearl. At the same time the robots chat with Mike, revealing and occasionally commenting upon their own "true" identity as puppets, as well as critiquing their performances in the inner frame as if they were actors playing the parts of the robots. During these breaks, by contrast with the movie screening, the presence of the audience is frequently acknowledged. The evil Pearl, for instance, makes extensive use of conspiratorial looks at the audience, and Mike reassures viewers when a commercial break is about to begin: "Back in a minute."

The dialogue of the characters is consistent throughout this dazzling series of transformations: a hybrid between Beavis and Butt-Head type wisecracks and the juvenilia of a bunch of computer nerds heavily at risk from OD-ing on late night reruns. The following extract from a sequence during which the figures watch the clean-cut, good-looking scientist hero being teased and seduced by the blonde heroine is typical:

ROBOT 1: [*Commenting about the hero*] He's a moist, pillowy Dwayne Hickman type.
[*The on-screen couple kiss*]
ROBOT 2: I believe I'm experiencing stagflation.
[*The on-screen picture shifts to a scowling, sinister figure half hidden behind the curtains, watching the embrace*]
MIKE: Freeze-hold on his eyebrows.
ROBOT 1: [*Commenting about the hero's romantic technique*] He just holds his kisser up there and she does all the work.

From a structural point of view MST3K is interpassive insofar as the show itself, via the framing figures, responds to the screened movie on the audience's behalf. As in the case of the laugh-track on the sitcom, this raises the possibility that the viewers passively watch the program instead of responding themselves. This brings us to our problem: in such cases how can we explain the pleasure that sustains audience involvement, and, specifically, how does the complex framing of the show contribute to the evident audience enjoyment?

Part of the answer to this question (as in the case of canned laughter) appeals to the frame's comic effect. As Freud argues, bad jokes, such as the framing figure's wisecracks about the movie, enjoy a comic potential in their own right: "We can . . . decide whether . . . to call such productions . . . 'bad' jokes or not jokes at all. . . . Jokes of this kind undoubtedly produce a comic effect. . . . Either the comic arises from the uncovering of the modes of thought of the unconscious . . . or the pleasure comes from comes from the comparison with a complete joke. . . . It is not impossible that . . . the inadequacy of . . . a joke is precisely what makes the nonsense into comic nonsense" (Freud 1991, 278). But more is involved than bad jokes. The frame in MST3K calls to our attention, and laughs on our behalf, at a comic disparity between the (presumed) serious intentions of the targeted movie's producers and the pathetic results of their efforts. In other words, the framing narrative provided by MST3K functions as an elaborate comic cue, a *mise en abîme*, which suggests that the targeted movie is to be mined for comic potential. Such devices, Freud indicates, are commonplace in the comic genre: "In the last resort it is the recollection of having laughed and in the expectation of laughing that he [the reader of a comic book or the viewer of a farce] laughs when he sees the comic actor come onto the stage before the latter can have made any attempt at making him laugh" (283).

Freud also contends that "the generating of comic pleasure can be encouraged by any other pleasurable accompanying circumstances as though by some sort of contagious effect (working in the same sort of way as the fore-pleasure principle)" (285). In this light, the comic pleasure produced by the framing characters' pathetic jokes in MST3K may be seen as seeds or catalysts for other comic effects at the expense of the movie's producers.

What Freud calls "humor," as distinct from comedy or jokes, also plays a part in MST3K. Under normal circumstances, the poor quality of the movie and its dated feel would bring about a negative affective response on the part of contemporary, hip viewers to whom MST3K is directed. The framing narrative expects this response, and more or less effectively turns it to advantage by channeling the audience's cathexis from their own negative affect into new directions. Specifically the frame turns the tedious aspects of the movie, such as the clumsiness and pretentiousness of its producers, into points of interest for the audience. Thus the show enables the *"economy of expenditure upon feeling"* that Freud (1991, 300) takes to be characteristic of the humorous. But, important as they are, these effects do not exhaust the sources of pleasure in the show.

The location of the framing figures encourages an impression that we are watching over their shoulders. This results from an obvious homology between the figures' position (blocking our view of the screen) and the position occupied by a real audience sitting in front of us in a theater.[5] Together with the fact that the figures ignore our presence, this impression creates an illusion of "realism" in the inner frame. I do not mean that the illusion is credible—on the contrary, we know it is just a fiction. Rather, I mean that we relate to the events portrayed in the inner frame voyeuristically. In other words, while knowing they are a fiction, we experience the robots *as if* we were watching them watch a movie. Thus a wedge is driven between our knowledge (the robots are fictional) and the quality of our perception (even so, they look real). (This formal sense of the term "realism" differs from Jameson's, to which I shall refer in the next chapter.) In short, as in its classical Hollywood form, the illusion of "realism" is concerned with "reality effects," specifically a voyeuristic point of view, rather than credibility.[6]

5. This impression is helped by the inclusion of a real man among the figures.
6. I am not claiming that the inner frame's realism is totally unqualified. On the contrary, its poor production values—the robot figures are crude caricatures rather than conforming to "realistic" representations of robots—draws attention to the inner frame's artifices, and thus undermines its illusion of realism. In this context it is clear that, as I indicated above, lack of realism is not simply a matter of lack of credibility. On the contrary, in one respect at least, the frame's credibility is enhanced by the transparency of its masquerade—at least it's honest about its own status as a simulation, we might say.

While creating an illusion of realism with respect to the fiction of the robots, the inner frame in MST3K undermines the realism of the movie that the robots are watching with us. By bringing to our attention its clumsy effects and bad script, the robots' comments destroy the possibility of a voyeuristic relation to the movie. In short, MST3K sacrifices the movie's realism as part of a strategy for reinscribing realism at the level of the inner frame within which the screening takes place. Later I argue that such sacrificial displacement of realism from the movie to its frame is borrowed from a similar strategy in the contemporary world of advertising, where, to use Robert Goldman's terminology, "ads which are not ads" embed their promotional claims in a frame that reflexively questions the integrity of those claims.[7]

The outer frame of MST3K, by contrast with the inner one, is the site of systematic failures of realism, induced by addressing the audience directly and thus expelling them from the comfortable voyeuristic stance of seeing without being seen. For instance, Pearl winks conspiratorially at the audience, Mike blandly reassures us he will be "back in a minute," and the puppets reflexively joke about their own status as fictions: "Look at my butt; I've got no butt." Paradoxically these failures of realism in the outer frame support the realism of the inner frame. Viewers are directly addressed—"interpellated" in the formal sense—as ones who are in the know. The knowledge they are supposed to have is that they are watching what is, in the words of the song in the opening sequence, "Just a show." "Relax . . . forget the science facts," the song instructs us. Thus, despite its own manifest lack of realism, the outer frame functions as an elaborate *mise en abîme* supporting the inner frame's realist illusion. In the next section, I show how this feature of the show also functions as a vehicle for ideology. But now I return to my original question: what are the sources of pleasure in viewing MST3K?

The show's multiple frames, which include the commercial breaks and television screen itself, are the site of multiple *trompe l'oeil* effects, as viewers move in and out of a succession of illusions: the robots expose the movie's crude visual artifices, the robots in turn are exposed as puppet

---

7. Goldman 1992, chap. 7. This is not to say that the movie screened in MST3K is totally divorced from all effects of realism. On the contrary, even though we "see through" the movie's pathetic attempts at realism, MST3K's interpassivity (the fact that it criticizes the movie on our behalf) causes us to moderate certain aspects of our critical response. In particular, the boredom that would be created by watching the movie "cold," without the benefit of the MST3K frame, is dispelled to some extent, and we find ourselves watching it against our better judgment. In brief, in the context of its MST3K screening, the movie takes on a sort of perverse fascination for the viewer who watches it not with the blind enthusiasm of the fan but rather with a degree of suspension of awareness of the film's artifices that entails a partial return of realism.

simulations, and we see that it's all "just a show." What draws us to MST3K, I claim, is the pleasure resulting from the oscillations of our eyes, which, despite our sure and certain knowledge of the truth of the matter (the figures are only puppets that we are watching on television—who could doubt it?) flit restlessly in and out of the layers of masquerade which the show so agreeably lays before us.

In the same way, even after we discover what appears to be a window on the wall is merely *trompe l'oeil*, we continue to be drawn into the illusion. This is not because we have any doubt about what is reality and appearance, but rather because falling in and out of the illusion creates a pleasure we are loath to forgo. As Lacan elegantly makes the point, and here I repeat a quotation given above: "What is it that attracts and satisfies us in *trompe l'oeil*? When is it that it captures our attention and delights us? At the moment when, by a mere shift of our gaze, we are able to realize that the representation does not move with the gaze and that it is merely *trompe l'oeil*" (Lacan 1981, 112). The pleasure in such effects, Lacan argues, is produced through the scopic drive. Thus the mechanism by which MST3K diverts us is among the most basic by which the human eye takes its pleasure in the world of appearances.

Ideology in the Text

In the previous section I discussed a mechanism by which the interpassive MST3K produces pleasure, a mechanism which has less to do with its humor and bad jokes than with the multiple *trompe l'oeil effects* associated with its frames. As well as functioning as a site for the production of pleasure, MST3K plays an ideological role. In this section I explore the connection between the show's erotic and ideological effects.

The illusion of realism is ideological, implicated in the forms of engagement essential to contemporary consumer capitalism. It is manifested in relations between shoppers browsing in the modern shopping mall and the glamorous commodities displayed before them, replete with glittering promise to make the purchaser envied/desired by others (Berger 1972, 132–149). At an intellectual level the shoppers are cynical, knowing that the commodities cannot deliver what they promise, but even so they put down their money and take their chances. "By the early 1980s," Goldman writes, "a new crisis of believability unfolded. . . . Who could take seriously the claim that an authentic self is available via consumption of commodity aesthetics? But who could distance themselves from this socialized desire to be special, to stand out?" (Goldman 1992, 222). In a similar way, Jameson argues, virtually from its inception the "domestic realism"

of the classic Hollywood film of the 1930s, including the formal characteristics which I grouped together under the heading "realism," was seen as
idealized fiction and, following the Great Depression, escapism (Jameson
1992, 174–175). All the same, at a practical level audiences suspended their
disbelief, paid for tickets, and entered its dreams.

In short, Hollywood realism and the cinematic consumerism of the
shopping mall depend upon a common structure, namely, the ideological
misrecognition (*méconnaissance*) that Žižek associates with the workings
of money and the commodity form more generally: "I know very well
how things are, but still (up to a point) I am doing it." In particular, the
Hollywood illusion of realism, which takes as its content the impression
that from an objective, third-person point of view I am watching real
events unfold before me, is the site of a fundamental split. On the one
hand, it involves an intellectual recognition that the illusion is a fiction; on
the other, at the level of practice it incorporates a misrecognition leading
one to act as if the illusion were truth.

Žižek ascribes a further dimension of misrecognition to ideology:
"What they 'do not know,' what they misrecognize, is the fact that in their
social reality itself, in their social activity . . . they are guided by the
fetishistic illusion" Žižek 1989, 31). In short, they fail to recognize the conflict between what they do and know. Realism may be seen, then, as ideological *not* in virtue of its illusory nature or even the form of its illusion—
what I referred to earlier as its voyeurism—but rather in virtue of the
ideological form of misrecognition through which it is set in place: "I
know very well how things are, but still (up to a point) I am doing it."

For all its radical chic, MST3K depends upon exactly such an ideological structure, albeit with a novel postmodern twist. Through the critical
comments made by the figures in the inner frame, it encourages viewers
to act upon their knowledge that the movie's special effects are crass, its
plot unbelievable, and so on, thus undermining any attempt to engage
with it realistically. It does this, however, only as a means of reintroducing
realism at the level of the inner frame: "I know the figures are just puppets, but still (up to a point) I am watching the movie with them." I argue
next that MST3K's strategy of sacrificing the movie's realism in favor of
the frame's is echoed in a genre of postmodern advertisements that developed during the 1980s in response to a shift in consumer sensibilities.

The Not-Film

Direct-sell ads of the 1950s and 1960s overtly sang the praises of their
products, thus requiring a certain suspension of disbelief with respect to

their own first-order content. In the United States of the 1980s, Goldman points out, growing consumer cynicism with respect to advertising claims meant that such direct-sell ads became less effective as instruments of persuasion (although a surprisingly large number of them survive at the budget end of the advertising market, apparently targeting "working-class" audiences).[8] This failure of the old-style ad posed a rhetorical challenge: how could ads work as instruments of persuasion in a milieu in which they were no longer trusted? More specifically, how could consumer cynicism about ads be turned to advertisers' advantage? A new genre of ad—what Goldman refers to as "the not-ad" or "the ad which is not an ad"—developed in response to this challenge (Goldman 1992, chap. 7).

The new ads highlight their own status as advertisements. By offering viewers what Goldman refers to as "a knowing wink," they implicitly (and on occasions explicitly) allude to their generic lack of credibility (181). Goldman illustrates such ads by the 1985 "Out on the Street" spot made for Levi 501 Jeans, in which an urban, ethnic, working-class character "good-naturedly places his palm between his face and the camera to shield his face . . . and then he unexpectedly steps outside the camera's frame, off the side-walk, and then back with a grin. Playfully transgressing the camera's boundary rules initiates a self-reflexive awareness about the nature of this text *as* advertising, and a momentary refusal to participate in the society of the spectacle" (184). Such ads are characterized by a second-order meaning of cynicism which provides contemporary audiences with a ready point of identification based upon their common mistrust of ads. The point of the strategy is not so much to create belief in ads—that would be ridiculous—but rather to neutralize consumer cynicism by turning it back on itself, specifically by showing consumers that their knee-jerk mistrust of ads leads them into the self-referential complexities of the liar paradox.

The ads do this by partaking in self-criticism, thus implicitly raising the following unanswerable question: "If we tell you we are liars, then are we to be trusted?" If they are to be trusted, then their claim to be liars should be believed, in which case they are not to be trusted. On the other hand, if they are not to be trusted, then their statement that they are liars is not trustworthy, and so, it seems, they are not liars after all. Therefore they can

---

8. Lengthy "infomercials" for exercise equipment and shop-at-home programs may be placed in this category. The problem of determining a target audience for such productions is complicated by a distinction between an appearance of appealing to working-class sensibilities (a highly mediated ideological construction) and having "genuine" working-class appeal (a construction that will be ideologically mediated in a different way).

be trusted. In short, if they are to be trusted then they are not; on the other hand, if they are not to be trusted then they are.

This strategy of bamboozling cynics by thrusting them into the logical thickets of paradox has a modest aim: not to create trust in ads (that is a lost cause) but rather to render obscure and thus shift focus from the difficult question (difficult for advertisers) of whether ads are to be believed. By throwing into confusion the cynic's response, the new ads pave the way for a range of auxiliary devices by which they construct meanings for products.

The auxiliary devices do not employ direct argumentation, of course, since to do so would simply reintroduce the difficult question of whether ads are to be trusted. Instead, the new ads continue a range of techniques developed in the 1960s and 1970s, which depend upon forging multiple connections of a visual kind between an image of the product and an already desired referent image (a beautiful woman, a tropical island, and so on). Thanks to such direct image-to-image connections, desirable meanings transfer from referent to product. The transfer in question depends not upon the logical forms of persuasion employed by direct-sell ads but rather upon establishing the sorts of associations that Freud shows at work in dreams. That is, the ads forge associations between things by physically connecting their signifiers rather than drawing logical connections between the signifiers' contents (Williamson 1978, 15–19).

A similar strategy is at work in MST3K. To adapt Goldman's useful terminology, this program is "a film which is not a film" or, briefly, a "not-film." To be specific, MST3K reworks a familiar realist genre, the Hollywood B-grade movie, which in its original context of production, like ads of the 1950s and 1960s, required a certain suspension of disbelief on the part of its viewers. Because of enhanced media-literacy, as well as radically increased sophistication in the area of special effects and the alienating effects of nostalgia in the film industry at large, these movies can no longer be watched in the same way as they were originally. On the contrary, a certain critical distance has opened up between contemporary audiences and these older movies, thus effectively foreclosing the possibility of taking up a realist attitude to them. And as in the case of the "Out in the Street" ad for Levi 501s, this foreclosure seems to clear a space for a heady possibility: a subversive, indeed liberatory moment of, to use Goldman's terms, a "refusal to participate in the society of the spectacle" (Goldman 1992, 184).

As Goldman also remarks in the case of the 501s ad, however, "instead of unmasking the ideological construction of commodity signs," the new-style media text "fashions the self-reflexive hipster into the newest—'most authentic'—sign yet" (184). And similarly in MST3K, the dismantling of the ideological structure of realism by a gesture of unmasking—"seeing through" the movie producer's silly pretensions of realism—is merely a step on the way to reinstalling realism at a more abstract level, that of the inner frame.

In sum, in MST3K the framing characters' cynical stand in which we are led to participate vicariously does not protect viewers from the ideological illusion of realism. On the contrary, in exactly the way Žižek indicates, postmodern cynicism serves as a support for ideology: "Cynical distance is just one way—one of many ways—to blind ourselves to the structuring power of ideological fantasy" (Žižek 1989, 33). This, in turn, raises the question to which I turn in the next chapter: whether it is possible for a cultural artifact, especially one like MST3K with its radically reflexive postmodern form, to break with or even subvert ideology.

10

Crash and Subversion

Cronenberg's film *Crash,* based on a book by J. G. Ballard, is set in an American city of the present. The meandering plot concerns a motley assortment of people obsessed to a potentially fatal extent with cars as instruments for sex and violence.

The lack of a well-defined story line, the high-quality glossy color print and arty shot production, a certain melancholy of the characters, and profuse imagery of streamlined mechanical devices place it squarely in the category of what Jameson calls the postmodern "nostalgia-deco" film (Jameson 1992, 222–225). Nostalgia is manifest not by setting the story in a particular historical period—on the contrary, it takes place in an indeterminate present—but rather by infusing the *mise en scène* with an art deco style which conveys a certain sense of historicity: "a certain synthesis between *modernization* (and the streamlined machine) and *modernism* (and stylized forms)" (224).

This style is introduced in the opening sequence where the immaculately beautiful and strangely remote Catherine (Deborah Unger) ecstatically pushes her bared breast against the smooth and highly polished curves of an airplane. A "suitor" (as her husband calls her lovers) interrupts her reverie (or are her actions a narcissistic display for his benefit?) and penetrates her from behind with his tongue as she caresses the metal curves. Attending this moment of mechanical *tendresse* is a certain ambiguity that the film never fully resolves. Does the scene gesture, as many critics have argued, toward a new postmodern cyborg sexuality, a partial dehumanization of the body, which the character Vaughan (Elias Koteas) explicitly refers to as the impact (literally, as it turns out, a "crashing") of modern technology upon the body? Or is the issue here what Vaughan refers to as his "real" project, a new "benevolent psychopathology" centered upon the car, and hinted at in the characters' repeated conversational references to a mysterious and sinister increase in traffic: "Have you noticed that the traffic has been getting heavier?" Or is what we see merely a fetishizing of the machine, or an elaborate narcissistic display in which the machine functions merely as a decorative prop?

The postmodern format continues in the unmotivated, apparently random coincidence in names between the author, James Ballard, and one of his characters, partially echoed in turn in the name of the actor who plays him, James Spader. It is as if the authorial signifier—the signifier of signifiers—has become unmoored and has accidentally floated into an adaptation of Ballard's own creation, even penetrating the "real" world of the actors. This little joke repeats and extends the form of the Hitchcockian gag but with a postmodern spin. Instead of the director cropping up under an assumed name, the author's name crops up under an assumed character.

Crash through a Rear Window

The postmodern is also evident in *Crash's* emphasis upon "specular obsession," a motif which, Jameson argues, the postmodern movie adapts from its modernist predecessors, where it is "motivated by the theme of voyeurism" (216). In this respect, Hitchcock's *Rear Window* is a paradigm of the modernist genre. The crippled Jimmy Stewart character sits in his darkened room, watching Grace Kelly through the window of a lighted room across the courtyard, where he has sent her to spy on a (hopefully absent) homicidal neighbor. As cinematic viewers of the scene, we identify with Stewart's point of view, specifically with his voyeurism: we too sit in a darkened room watching Grace Kelly, an identification which is strengthened by positioning the camera (with which we also identify) so that it looks over Stewart's shoulder.

The Stewart character's position is not that of the pure voyeur—the unseen watcher. He too is under scrutiny, not only by us but also indirectly by his target (the Grace Kelley figure) who, although she does not look back at him, knows she is being watched. And because we identify with the Stewart character, our scrutiny of him doubles as a scrutiny of us. The fact that it is only by ourselves that we are being scrutinized does not alter this conclusion.[1] On the contrary, the shot's skill lies precisely in the way that the frame covertly splits the viewer of the film between one who looks and one who is seen.

The result of this covert self-scrutiny is that, at the level of its form, *Rear Window* takes on a specular dimension, that is, displays to its viewers their own act of looking. Viewing the film thus takes on an exhibitionistic dimension which, in turn, unsettles the familiar voyeuristic position of invisible watcher. This specular structure is not without benefit. The combination of exhibitionism and voyeurism enables the film to function as a site for the scopic drive, conceived by Lacan as a pleasurable but also anxiety-provoking coupling of looking and being seen.

Like *Rear Window, Crash* incorporates specular obsession at the level of both form and content. By stripping the acts of seeing and being seen of any dimension of human feeling, *Crash* adds a postmodern twist, however. In the postmodern movie, Jameson claims, "the psychic subject disappears altogether . . . and along with it, the process by which looking is specifically foregrounded as a privileged element and a psychological motive" (217). In terms of this distinction, *Crash* falls squarely in the postmodern category. That is, unlike *Rear Window, Crash* presents voyeurism as a specular structure divorced from human pleasure and desire. And, unlike the Jimmy Stewart figure in *Rear Window,* the characters in *Crash* appear for the most part as strangely affectless, their emotions and motives hidden from one another as well as from us. Humans are pictured as impassive objects, hunks of aesthetically arranged hair and meat, exemplified by the cold, elaborately coiffed, picture-perfect and inhumanly beautiful Catherine. When they are pictured in action, even in the throes of sexual "passion," it is frequently as dull-eyed, stone-faced zombies caught in the grips of a drive that renders questions of motive irrelevant. Indeed, signs of passion emerge only when humans are joined to machines, as in the opening scene of Catherine's penetration while embracing the airplane. Sexuality, it seems, pertains to the cyborg rather than the human being, a theme echoed in the jerky movements and lifeless features of James's lover, Dr. Helen Remington (Holly Hunter). Her deportment and looks are eerily reminiscent of Lal, the android daughter of Mr. Data from the television series *Star Trek the Next Generation,* who although she has feelings cannot give them "natural" expression.

The alienation of humans from their motives and feelings finds focus in an episode early in the film. Two of the male protagonists, Vaughan and

1. This in turn provides a basis for a secondary identification with the Grace Kelly figure, who is also under scrutiny.

James, stand in the corridors of the hospital where the latter is being treated. They watch each other looking at medical photographs of torn flesh and shattered limbs, each only tangentially aware of the other's scrutiny. In a strange *reprise* and doubling of the window scene from *Rear Window,* and despite their proximity, each manages to take up a voyeuristic position of unseen watcher in relation to the other. Vaughan, by posing as a medical technician, conceals both his sexual interest in James and his prurient fixation upon the photographs, a masquerade of which we and James become aware only retrospectively. James, on the other hand, relies upon his "real" identity as a patient in order to conceal his voyeuristic impulses and uneasy sexual response to Vaughan.

Like *Rear Window, Crash* unsettles its voyeuristic scopic regime by looking back at viewers. However, the formal techniques by which it does this contrast with the characteristically modernist strategy employed by Hitchcock, who, when the film looks back at the viewer, favors the shot-reverse-shot technique. Through suturing viewers to a character who is internal to the narrative, this technique erases their awareness of themselves as viewers, thus reinforcing their voyeuristic reverie even while undermining it.

Crash, by contrast, avoids shot-reverse-shot sequences. Instead, the camera's look takes on an inhuman quality: the formal, geometrically precise, and oddly angled shots follow a pattern no human viewer could replicate. Highly formalized, long, linear tracking shots glide along rows of cars in a parking lot or scan the damaged limbs of crash victims, and characters are arranged in stylized, totally artificial poses, silhouetted behind one another, all facing in the same direction. For example, in several sequences the camera moves up through the roof of a car and yet continues to see what goes on underneath, as if the roof has become transparent.

By opening a gap between what is visible to the human eye and the camera's visual field, and especially by leading viewers to see in an "unnatural" way what they could not see for themselves, this use of the camera draws attention to the film's nature as film. The inhuman quality of its look refuses viewers the familiar viewing position of identifying with the camera, that is, of watching what it sees as if they themselves were watching. Viewers are thus made aware of the interpassive nature of the filmic experience, the fact that they are seeing vicariously what has been seen on their behalf.

The film thus plunges the viewer into the formal structure of the gaze. Viewers are made aware that what they see incorporates a paradoxical, alien element, which, by offering them a sight of what they cannot see, constitutes a transgression of the perceptual symbolic order. To put the paradox in concrete terms: "I (who sees) see that I can't be seeing this." This paradox, in turn, makes viewers look again at what they see, thus introducing a split between themselves as seeing and seeing what they have seen.

These formal effects are reinforced by long tracking shots of gruesome, obscene sights, for instance, a lengthy vagina-like scar under net stockings on a calipered leg. The shot is presented in an extended close-up, which glides slowly and deliberately along the length of the scar. The impression is the very reverse of identifying with the camera. On the contrary, one's difference from the camera is marked by both the shot structure and content.

This effect is created not merely by the horror of what is shown but also by the way it is shown: the camera lingers so precisely, so dispassionately, so inhumanly upon what it sees. By contrast with a Hitchcock film, there is no drama in the camera's act of seeing, no sudden cuts away from the site of horror, which, by simulating a "natural" human response, facilitates viewer identification with the camera. Instead, *Crash* creates a teeth-grinding tension between the act of looking and what is seen/shown. As in Hitchcock, viewers cannot bear to see the content of what they are shown, but *Crash* adds an extra twist: viewers cannot look in the same inhuman, dispassionate, fully focused way at the horrors which the camera sees on their behalf.

The impression of being placed under scrutiny is further reinforced by a series of *mise en abîmes*. In the course of the narrative, James and Vaughan reveal to each other their voyeurism, joining openly in looking at television clips and snapshots of violence and damaged flesh. These communal viewings of the act of viewing are haunted by a gradually strengthening, eventually consummated homoerotic bond between the two men, albeit one in which all signs of human emotion are strangely muted. Other protagonists dispassionately masturbate while seated on a couch viewing video clips of car crashes. Viewers of the film are led to identify with the point of view of these characters, not directly, as in *Rear Window,* by seeing through a character's eyes, but rather by sharing their activity of viewing violent and sexually explicit material.

In sum, for *Crash* as for *Rear Window,* viewing involves an imbricated looking and looking again, a voyeurism combined with exhibitionism that is characteristic of the scopic drive. Its stylized shots of damaged gaping flesh, like the glint of light in Lacan's story of his day at sea, make viewers uneasily aware of their role as viewers, thus constituting a gaze around which the drive turns (Lacan 1981, 95). Such shots constitute sites of a knot or singularity in the visual field around which looks anxiously circulate with a mixture of horror, fascination, and pleasure.

In viewing *Crash,* however, the scopic drive takes an extra, fetishistic twist. Instead of being incorporated within the narrative (as in *Rear Window*), the characteristic ambivalence of the scopic drive between looking and looking again, between seeing and being seen, is inflected at a cognitive level, destabilizing and splitting viewers' knowledge of what they see and who they are. *Crash* refuses viewers any firm ground to which they can step back and accept what they see as "realistic," as something that *they* see for themselves. Unlike *Rear Window*, it refuses any easy identification with the camera or a character. *Crash*, to use Jameson's phrase, "plunge[s] [us] into the image itself as such" (Jameson 1981, 216) in the sense of making us aware of the split between the imagining and imagined subjects.

In particular, although viewers of *Crash* know that what they see is only a film, *even so* and contradictorily they "know" that they are implicated as objects under its scrutiny. The "knowledge" at issue here is not merely, as in *Rear Window*, a matter of *feeling* under scrutiny, feeling that the film looks back, as it were. Neither is the "knowledge" in question purely an intellectual matter. On the contrary, at an intellectual level there is no equivocation. Viewers know that in reality the film does not look back at them.

Instead, it is a matter of what Freud calls "disavowal," a contradiction between two forms of "knowledge," between what is known intellectually, on the basis of seeing, and phantasies which, in structuring people's behavior, specifically their symptoms, provide an (often unacknowledged) setting for their desires.

In his 1927 essay "Fetishism," Freud illustrates such a contradiction in the case history of a young man who

> has exalted a certain sort of "shine on the nose" into a fetishistic precondition. The surprising explanation of this was that the patient had been brought up in an English nursery but had later come to Germany, where he forgot his mother tongue almost completely. The fetish, which originated from his early childhood, had to be understood in English, not German. The shine on the nose [in German *Glanz auf der Nase*]—was in reality a "*glance* at the nose." (Freud 1953–73, 21:155)

At an intellectual level Freud's patient knows very well that his mother does not have a penis, but even so, he "knows" that she does, a "knowledge" which he manifests in terms of a long-standing symptomatic attraction to a shine on the nose which, through a chain of signifiers crossing from German (*Glanz*, meaning "shine") to English ("glance" but also "glans," as in penis), functions as a substitute for the mother's penis.[2] In

2. Freud does not mention the homophonic relation with "glans," perhaps because this is a word that is unlikely to have been in the childhood vocabulary of his patient who, we are told, came to forget his childhood acquaintance with English. But it must not be forgotten that the effects here are retrospective, so that such anachronisms are to be expected rather than eschewed.

this case, then, the nose functions as a phallic symbol, a relation suggested by its shape and, more basically, by the fetishistic condition which literally gives body to the "knowledge" of the mother's penis.[3]

In the same way, the unrealistic anxiety (anxiety without an appropriate object) created by watching *Crash* suggests that the "knowledge" created by viewing it, namely, that one is under scrutiny, is in the technical Freudian sense part of a phantasy structure. Like a symptom, it not only encodes a message but also functions as a vehicle for anxiety. On the basis of the film's systematic erosion of any position from which it can be watched, one can speculate that the unconscious roots of this phantasy structure lie in the subject's repressed knowledge that he or she is the site of lack constituted by falling short of the inscrutable expectations of the Other. In that case, the phantasy of being watched, of being under the scrutiny of a mysterious other, as in the experience of a film looking back at its viewer, may be seen as constituting a direct, perhaps almost too literal, return of repressed knowledge, a return that is responsible for unrealistic anxiety. As Lacan writes in his unpublished *Seminar X,* "Anxiety manifests itself clearly from the very beginning as relating—in a complex manner—to the desire of the *Other.* From the very first I have indicated that the anxiety-producing function of the desire of the *Other* was tied to the fact that I do not know what object *o* [*objet a*] I am for this desire" (quoted in Weber 1991, 161).

In MST3K, by contrast with *Crash,* the camera never sees in an inhuman way, even when what it sees is totally fantastic in content. Thus identification with the camera is never seriously threatened, even at those moments in the outer frame when, by a character locking eyes with and addressing the viewer, the voyeuristic illusion is shattered. This means that despite all the "seeing through" and playful slippage between frames, MST3K, like *Rear Window,* never forces viewers to confront the split implicit in seeing themselves seeing. However unstable the content of what they see, in the last instance MST3K viewers can identify with the apparently firm position defined by the camera's eye. In other words, as in *trompe l'oeil,* the splitting of the seeing subject into one who sees and one who is seen remains covert; and, as in *trompe l'oeil,* viewers are distracted from such splitting by the scopic drive's ongoing pleasures, which take shape in the gap between illusion and its seeing through, the gap across which, in the words of Lacan, "one can only play at jumping" (Lacan 1981, 62).[4] Para-

---

3. The explanandum in this case is part of the evidence for the explanans. Such circularity is harmless, indeed, characteristic of many perfectly satisfactory historical explanations.
4. For all its radical chic, from a structural point of view, MST3K is no more than a sort of automated double *trompe l'oeil,* working by an interpassive mechanism. That is, the inner frame sees through the fiction of the movie on its viewers' behalf; and the outer frame, in turn, sees through the inner frame's fictions.

doxically, then, the playfully reflexive visual games into which MST3K introduces viewers serve to stabilize rather than disrupt their position.

In sum, MST3K and *Crash* exhibit two different forms of fetishism. MST3K involves the "practical fetishism" defined by Žižek, which governs both the ideological mechanism of *méconnaissance* and the operation of the drive, and which manages to conceal the splitting of the subject. *Crash*, by contrast, involves fetishism in the full Freudian sense, which, through a "perverse" structure of disavowal, openly displays the splitting of the subject.[5] With a view to clarifying the political and specifically subversive dimensions of the distinction between these two forms of fetishism, I turn to Jameson's essay "The Existence of Italy" (Jameson 1992, 155–229).

Subversive Realism

Jameson claims that a tension exists within the concept of realism. In its epistemological sense, realism is taken to be a mode of truth telling, a transparent form of representation that tells things as they really are. In its aesthetic sense, by contrast, it is a rhetorical form, a mere reality-effect that simulates the truth through the application of culturally and historically bound aesthetic conventions (158–159). Jameson argues for a third conception of realism, one that restores to it the critical, radical political edge it enjoyed in the works of Bahktin and Lukacs. He suggests that a code be taken as "realist" when, in Basil Bernstein's sense of the term, it manages to become "elaborated or universal" (169). In short, realism is an effect created by treating a particular set of representational conventions as universal so that they appear to cover everything that exists.

Jameson then argues that by introducing a new universal categorical scheme, realism may function as a subversive aesthetic. By "appropriating part-structures" of speech and transforming them into a kind of interior dialect, what Jameson calls "a private language, hysterical or camp," a realist aesthetic may undermine a hegemonic form of representation. To be specific, from the bric-a-brac of the old symbolic order the subversive realist aesthetic constructs a voice for a "beleaguered collective." It thus exists at "the limits of language (or representation)," where it is characterized by a certain "excess of intensity . . . rais[ing] its voice, mobiliz[ing] pitch and intonation. . . . The individual subject seems to disap-

---

5. In Copjec's words, "Fetishism is, as Freud claims, 'particularly favorable' for studying the splitting of the ego in the process of defense; as a perversion, it *ex-planes* it, unfolds the split onto a flat surface and thus conveniently displays it for the analyzing eye. 'I know very well, but just the same [I] . . .' —here we see laid out before us the splitting of the two I's in the *statement*" (Copjec 1994, 111).

pear behind the beleaguered collective which thus speaks all the more res-
onantly through it" (173).

This construal of realism elaborates a conception to be found in Jameson's
earlier work *The Political Unconscious*. There, basing himself on Bahktin and
Lukacs, he proposes that realism (specifically narrative realism) "has as its
historic function the systematic undermining and demystification, the secular 'decoding,' of those preexisting inherited traditional or sacred narrative
paradigms which are its initial givens" (Jameson 1981, 152).

In "The Existence of Italy" Jameson argues that at a particular historical
juncture—America in the 1930s—the conventions of the Hollywood
movie (to which the B-grade science fiction movie belongs) constituted a
realist aesthetic. In particular, film provided a new language, a new lens,
through which Hollywood "offer[ed] viewers glimpses of their own domestic and single-family existence" (Jameson 1992, 174). The "viewers"
Jameson refers to are, of course, the new class of factory workers who in
exchange for a promise of bourgeois status bought commodities manufac-
tured for the new "mass markets" created by twentieth century "Fordist"
industrial capitalism. This new Hollywood "domestic realism," as
Jameson calls it, took on a "negative or ideological moment" in the Great
Depression, when "Hollywood's images of domesticity . . . suddenly
come to be seen, not as 'realism' but as compensatory wish-fulfillment
and consolation" (174). Nevertheless, thanks to a certain conservatism
built into the nexus between capitalism and the Hollywood production
system, the conventions of domestic realism continued to enjoy a certain
hegemony as elements of a cinematic genre system, retaining their historical association with the signifier "realism" in what came to be a purely
formal sense of the term.[6] In the context of these remarks, I now return to
a consideration of *Crash* and its fellow traveler in postmodernity, MST3K.

6. According to Jameson, Hollywood "realism" and its polar opposite in the field of "high
art," namely, "modernism," characterize second-stage, monopoly capitalism, exemplified
by America in the 1930s when the newly bourgeoisified married couple, struggling free
from their working-class roots, were attempting to give voice and sight to their aspirations
in the face of advertising and a new mass market full of relatively affordable commodities
(Jameson 1992, 174, 225–226). The postmodern, by contrast, is the "cultural dominant" of
the third, late or multinational stage of capitalism associated with the 1960s (203). The
move from second- to third-stage capitalism may also be seen in terms of the switch from
Fordism to post-Fordism. For a criticism of this view see Callinicos 1989.

The epistemic sense of realism as a mode of truth telling seems to be absent from this
little genealogy of realism, but it can be incorporated easily enough by recognizing that all
dominant systems of representation attempt to persuade their audiences that they tell the
truth. In particular, the shot-reverse-shot and the "objective," third-person shot characteristic of Hollywood "realism" in the 1930s are two instances in a much longer history of
formal devices by which aesthetic modes have attempted to create "reality effects," that is,
persuade audiences that they are telling the truth.

Crash is subversive at the level of its form, in the sense that its shot production undermines the voyeurism characteristic of Hollywood domestic realism. Its form overlaps the "classic" realism of modernism, as delineated in the work of André Bazin, who, as Jameson says, "projects an ideal of film whose secret truth is no longer film, but rather photography itself, and black and white photography at that" (186). This classic Bazinian realism utilizes the tableau form and foregrounds the photographic signifier by privileging the "deep [black and white] shot, grainy with the plaster of the retaining walls and stones of the courtyard, streaked (as so often in such filmic moments) by rain . . . river water . . . empty roadways flanked by elms" (186).

Crash is distinguished not only by modernist devices such as the tableau but also by a range of postmodern techniques, such as a too precise resolution of its images and a hyperrealistic gloss and coloration that both betrays its "irreality" and, through exaggeration, foregrounds the "technicolor" filmic signifier (192). By carrying these techniques to extremes, *Crash* and the postmodern more generally register their aesthetic break from the style, irony, and plotlessness that Jameson takes to be characteristic of the unstable category of modernism (201, 213). For instance, as I indicated above, the sight gags or "in-jokes" characteristic of modernist *auteur* directors, such as Hitchcock's appearance as a minor character in his own productions, are taken to an attenuated extreme in *Crash* through a running gag of a character whose name coincides with the author's.[7]

Crash is also subversive at the level of content. It speaks in what Jameson, following Gilles Deleuze and Félix Guattari, calls "the minor"— speaks, that is, on behalf of a disaffected, fringe group separated from the "dominant" by its participation in sexual practices that, to the extent that they are recognized as belonging to a "type" rather than constituting a disparate assortment of curiosities, are deemed pathological.[8]

The visual language in which *Crash* gives voice to this minor is adapted from traditional images of copulation, masturbation, foreplay, sadism, ho-

7. This joke indicates another feature of the postmodern: the "death of the author" *qua* the modernist *auteur*-director-joker, along with his gullible audience who are content merely to be let in on the joke. Similarly, Jameson argues, we can rewrite modernist texts as postmodern "by heightening the silences around their sentences (as in Flaubert); and can even attempt, more violently, to misremember modernist films by jumping from 'image' or frame to the next in a properly discontinuous or heterogeneous fashion" (207).

8. In Jameson's words, *Crash* "acknowledges one of the prime features of the postmodern situation," namely, an "intensified collectivization, and the subsumption of all solitary rebels or isolated monads into new forms of group cohesion and affirmation" (173). He also claims that "we long mistook [this feature] to be the death or disappearance of the subject" (173).

mosexuality, fetishism, and so on. These images are combined in new and intensified ways: Catherine's ecstatic cyborg experience in the opening shots; Helen's curious lack of emotion in scenes of intense sexual arousal; Vaughan, perched in full public view on the back seat of a convertible driven by James, his lover-to-be, undressing and masturbating a woman he has picked up a few moments before in a parking lot. The film provides a space in which, by being metonymically linked within a collage of images, bizarre sexual practices and their practitioners take on a contrived collective identity. In Jameson's sense, then, the film exemplifies the subversive realist project of "intensified collectivization . . . the subsumption of . . . solitary rebels or isolated monads into new forms of group cohesion and affirmation" (173).

MST3K, like *Crash*, transgresses the conventions of Hollywood realism, but in a different way. In seeing through the B-grade sci-fi movie that it screens, it relieves viewers of the task of seeing through it for themselves. This allows them to decathect their own negative responses and slip back into an attitude of more or less passive acceptance of the movie's image production. Nevertheless, at a practical level, the movie screened within MST3K loses its generic "realism." By conspiratorially appealing to viewers to recognize the naive response that the movie not only expects but also to some extent evinces, MST3K creates a distance between viewers and their viewing experiences that is inconsistent with sustaining realism. As I argued above, however, the realism lost from the movie is reinscribed in the inner frame. In short, despite its destabilizing layers of illusions, MST3K reproduces the ideology of realism.

Crash, like MST3K, produces pleasurable effects through the workings of the scopic drive, but unlike MST3K it makes visible the mechanics of the drive. That is, in *Crash*, pleasure is produced not by the ideological mechanism that Žižek calls "practical fetishism," which hides from viewers the gap between themselves as seeing and seen. Rather, the mechanism is fetishistic in the full Freudian sense. The usually repressed knowledge of being under scrutiny surfaces at a symptomatic level. To be specific, by creating a gap between human vision and what the camera sees, the viewer is refused a comfortable point of identification. Thus whereas MST3K, assuming a conservative cast, pacifies its viewers and reproduces the ideological forms that it shares with the world of advertising, *Crash* undermines these forms. Rather than being tranquilized with the comfortable voyeuristic fare of Hollywood realism, the viewer is discommoded by induction into a fetishistic scopic regime—a subversive realism in Jameson's sense.

In sum, and here I return to themes alluded to in the Introduction, *Crash* inducts viewers into a fetishistic scopic regime that drives a wedge between the human eye, with which viewers engage the filmic image, and the inhuman mechanical eye of the camera, which watches interpassively on their behalf. Thus, in a direct physical way the film's fetishistic visual economy undermines the material processes of modernization (as well as theories of "vision") that collapse both human seeing and mechanical signal transmission/scanning into a single abstract category of "vision." The neologism by which, at a material as well as intellectual level, TV becomes "tele-vision" perfectly illustrates this collapse. *Crash* opposes this collapse through openly depending for its effects upon a separation between the human eye and the camera.

In short, fetishism in *Crash* takes on a subversive role, undermining not only the ideological forms of Hollywood realism but also the modernizing processes of abstraction by which differences, specifically differences between human and nonhuman, are erased (Sharp 1985). In this context, it is, of course, no accident that the contents of *Crash* circulate the theme of the cyborg, that is, the partial mechanization of the human body—or what one of its characters, Vaughan, refers to as "the impact [literally a crashing] of modern technology upon the body." Thus, the theme of the cyborg in *Crash* emerges as an ideological gloss which, at the level of the film's form, conceals a radical separation of the human (eye) and the machine (camera).

I have argued that through its fetishistic form and despite its foregrounding of the theme of the cyborg, *Crash* subverts a modernizing tendency to erase differences between human and machine. Thus *Crash* illustrates a subversive potential common to all forms of fetishism, namely, a propensity to restore that obvious yet paradoxical dissimilarity between a man and woman, namely, the father's possession of the phallus and the mother's lack, which modernizing processes of abstraction as well as the imbricated patriarchal order strive to suppress.

I am not claiming that the fetishistic scopic economy of *Crash* is resistant to all ideological formations. On the contrary, as Laura Mulvey argues in her influential essay "Visual Pleasure and Narrative Cinema," the fetishistic look is one of the principal strategies by which patriarchy (understood as the symbolic-Oedipal order) preserves itself in the face of the castration threat posed by cinematic images of woman's body (Mulvey 1975). Mulvey illustrates the fetishistic look by the highly aestheticized images of women, such as Sternberg's portrayals of Dietrich, that distract attention from the referent onto the image itself. Through such distractions, the cinematic image functions as a sort of metonymic substitute for that which woman is seen as lacking, and thus functions as a defense against castration anxiety. Such a strategy can be seen at work in *Crash* in the highly aestheticized "beaver shots" of Helen making love with her husband James after having been brutally assaulted by his friend Vaughan.

The other cinematic form of defense against castration anxiety that Mulvey mentions is the sadistic voyeuristic look. In the case of *Crash* this is cued by the shots of Vaughan's brutalizing encounters with women, as well as by the marks of violence visible on their bodies. Here, then, we see the full range of looks which, according to Mulvey, characterize traditional patriarchal defenses in the cinematic arena (including pornography). Which is not to say that *Crash* is unambiguously antifeminist. On the contrary, by displaying an awareness of itself as an image, *Crash* adopts one of the strategies that Mulvey identifies with the subversive feminist film. Thus here as elsewhere the question of whether fetishism is subversive or conservative cannot be answered unequivocally.

My analyses of *Crash* and MST3K indicate the bankruptcy of any one-sided approach to the question of the "the postmodern" and its political impact. At the least a distinction must be made between a fetishistic form of the postmodern, which subverts hegemonic ideological forms, and a form in which the visual reflexivity characteristic of the scopic drive is less prominent and thus takes a less perverse, ideologically conservative turn. My analyses of the gaze and the fetish provide the analytic tools with which such distinctions can be drawn.

Appendix: The Oedipus Connection

For Geoff Sharp

L évi-Strauss claims that the Oedipus myth is about the inability to con- nect two rival cosmological accounts for the origin of humanity. One of these claims that man is autochthonous, that is, born of earth. In the Hel- lenic context this view was embedded in a system of metaphors connecting man with plants, and the soil with birth, blood, and woman.[1] The other cosmological account is empirical. Drawing on common experience, it rec- ognizes that man is the product of the sexual union of man and woman: "The [Oedipus] myth has to do with the inability, for a culture which has the belief that mankind is autochthonous . . . to find a satisfactory transi- tion between this theory and the knowledge that humans are actually born from the union of man and woman" (Lévi-Strauss 1979, 216).

According to Lévi-Strauss, the function of the Oedipus myth is to recon- cile its audience to the contradiction between these cosmologies. It does so in terms of a two-step logical argument. First it proves that the contradiction between the schemes of autochthony and sexual union is identical with an- other, that between being born of same and born of different. This, in turn, is shown to be identical with a social opposition between overrating and un- derrating blood relations as marriage partners: "The Oedipus myth provides a kind of logical tool which relates the original problem—born from one or born from two?—to the derivative problem: born from different or born

---

1. Traces of such metaphors survive in English today, exemplified by the evocative "Dust to dust, ashes to ashes" at the center of various Christian funeral services.

from same?" (216). In this way the myth resolves the initial cosmological contradiction between autochthony and sexual reproduction, not by mediation but rather by a proof that the contradiction is repeated and lived out in the practices of negotiating whom to marry. As Lévi-Strauss puts it succinctly: "Although experience contradicts theory, social life echoes cosmology by its similarity of structure. Hence cosmology is true" (216).

A somewhat different but more elaborate version of this account of myth function emerges from remarks Lévi-Strauss makes elsewhere in his discussion of the Northwest Coast native American myth of Asdiwal:

> All the paradoxes conceived by the native mind, on the most diverse planes: geographic, economic, sociological, and even cosmological, are, when all is said and done, assimilated to that less obvious yet so real paradox which marriage with the matrilateral cousin attempts but fails to resolve. But the failure is *admitted* in our myths, and there precisely lies their function. . . . .
>
> . . . Such speculations . . . do not attempt to depict what is real, but to justify the shortcomings of reality. . . . Mythical thought implies an admission (but in the veiled language of myth) that the social facts . . . are marred by an insurmountable contradiction. (Lévi-Strauss 1978, 27–30)

Such remarks suggest that myths address social difficulties. In the case of the Asdiwal myth, the difficulty in question concerns inheritance and domiciliary arrangements in marriage. In the case of the Oedipus myth, by contrast, the difficulty lies in deciding between the opposing strategies of endogamy (overrating blood relations) and exogamy (underrating them), between, on the one hand, marriage within the close family circle with its attendant advantages of preserving family wealth and, on the other, marriage with distant kin, a risky but potentially highly rewarding strategy creating new obligations but also new alliances.

Myth responds to such difficulties, it seems, by naturalizing them. In particular, the Oedipus myth inflects the opposing marital strategies onto the cosmological plane by showing that they are equivalent to the rival procreative procedures of autochthony and sexual reproduction. In this way the social difficulty of deciding upon an appropriate marriage partner is shown to be equivalent to a cosmological difficulty, that is, a contradiction in the natural order, and therefore unavoidable: what can't be helped, must be borne. Myth thus assumes a solidaristic function similar to that of ideology, that of naturalizing contradictions in the social order.[2]

2. Lévi-Strauss also suggests a third account of the function of myth when he writes elsewhere: "Mythical thought always progresses from the awareness of oppositions towards

By what logic does the myth prove that the opposition between autochthony and sexual reproduction is identical with that between overrating and underrating blood relations? Lévi-Strauss offers what he calls a
"provisional formulation" in answer to this question: "The inability to
connect two kinds of relationships is overcome (or rather replaced) . . . by
the assertion that [the two] contradictory relationships are identical in as
much as they are both self-contradictory in a similar way" (Lévi-Strauss
1979, 216). Unfortunately he never improves upon this "provisional formulation," which even well-disposed critics such as the English anthro-
pologist Edmund Leach seem to find unsatisfactory. In his volume de-
voted to Lévi-Strauss in the Fontana Modern Masters series, Leach
comments: "Those who think that this is vaguely reminiscent of an argument from *Alice through the Looking Glass* will not be far wrong" (Leach
1982, 65).

But in connecting the Oedipus myth with the dreamlike narratives of
Lewis Carroll's *Alice*, Leach's critical remark is more helpful than he
seems to have intended.[3] It suggests that the logic of the Oedipus myth
depends upon the system of associations that, according to Freud, structures dream thoughts and the unconscious. The relevant associative connections are obvious. Overrating blood relations as marriage partners results in offspring born of one blood. Thus, since dream logic associates
effects with their causes, overrating blood relations is equivalent to being
born of one. Since autochthony is to be born of the earth, it too is equivalent to being born of one. Thus overrating blood relations is equivalent to
autochthony, since both are equivalent to being born of one. And conversely underrating blood relations is equivalent to being born of more
than one, that is, born of two. In Lévi-Strauss's terms, then:

overrating blood relations : underrating blood relations =
autochthony : born of the union of two.

(I provide a fuller version of this proof in the final section of this appendix.) For the following reasons, however, Lévi-Strauss cannot accept
this Freudian gloss of his myth logic.

The roots of Lévi-Strauss's thought lie not only in the structural linguistics of Ferdinand de Saussure and Roman Jakobson but also in three im-

---

their resolution" (Lévi-Strauss 1979, 224). Such references suggest that the function of
myth resides in mediating contradictions: "It is the nature of myth to mediate contradictions" (Douglas 1978, 52).

3. Leach's attitude to Freudian explanations seems to have been ambivalent at best, as indicated by the references to Freud in Leach 1982.

portant traditions in French scientific thought. The first, Durkheimian sociology, seeks a realm of objective social facts which function as proper objects for social science; the second, Comtean *science positif*, attempts to apply rigorous ("positive") scientific method to investigating social phenomena; the third, Descartes's method of analysis and synthesis, sets out to explain the variety of phenomena in the natural world as permutations of a small number of mathematically described structures. Lévi-Strauss attempts to bring these three strands together with structural linguistics. He applies canons of rigorous scientific method to determine a limited range of objective, mathematical structures that underlie the evanescent phenomena of the social world construed as a vast semiotic system, including myths and their retellings.

His work may be seen as an extension of the nineteenth-century project for a mathematical phenomenology exemplified by James Maxwell, Ernst Mach, Gustav Kirchoff, and Heinrich Hertz as well as the French physicists Jean Fourier, Augustin Fresnel, and Henri Poincaré. These scientists treated the abstract equations of the new mathematical physics of electromagnetism, thermodynamics, and optics as descriptions of a deeper reality in terms of which the messy surface of phenomenal appearances could be explained. By analogy with such an approach, Lévi-Strauss seeks to strip away the myriad idiosyncratic details of everyday collective stories and ritual activities in order to expose objective, highly abstract mathematical structures upon which such phenomena may be seen as variations. Lévi-Strauss explicitly draws an analogy between such structures and musical themes, so that the term "variation" here takes on the connotations it has in a musical context (Lévi-Strauss 1981, 647).

Such an approach sits ill with any suggestion, such as Leach's somewhat frivolous remark, that identifies the logical structure of myth with chains of connections grounded in purely *subjective* unconscious associations. In particular, if Leach's suggestion is correct, then the persuasive force of the Oedipus myth is not, as Lévi-Strauss suggests, a matter of apodictic certainty but instead depends upon "poetic" or tropological associations that work upon individual readers in a highly context-dependent fashion. As Suzette Heald and Arlane Deluz write in their introduction to a history of psychological approaches in anthropology: "While Lévi-Strauss claims Freud as a major intellectual influence, his theories of the human mind as the creator of culture have dealt with the psyche solely as an intellectual product, independent of psychoanalysis. . . . For Lévi-Strauss, it is logic not poetry which holds sway in ordering the unruly bric-a-brac of culture and its representations in mythology" (Heald and Deluz 1994, 7).

The suggestion that Freud's dream logic underwrites the inferences implicit in myth also contradicts another principle endorsed by Lévi-Strauss,

namely, that mythic thought is as rigorous as its Western scientific coun-
terpart: "The kind of logic in mythical thought is as rigorous as that of
modern science. . . . The difference lies, not in the quality of the intellectual process, but in the nature of the things to which it is applied" (Lévi-
Strauss 1979, 230).

This is a central principle for Lévi-Strauss, which serves to distinguish
his views from those of predecessors, such as Lucien Lévy-Bruhl, who introduced the concept of a "prelogical" mentality to explain why totemic
systems of classification categorize men in terms of animals.

> The idea of totemism made possible a differentiation of societies . . . by rel-
> egating certain of them *into* nature (a procedure well illustrated by the term
> *Naturvolker*), at least by classing them according to their attitude *toward* na-
> ture, as expressed by the place [they] assigned to man in the animal
> kingdom. . . . Totemism is firstly the projection outside our own universe,
> as though by a kind of exorcism, of mental attitudes incompatible with the
> exigency of a discontinuity between man and nature which Christian
> thought held to be essential. (Lévi-Strauss 1963, 2–3)

Lévi-Strauss argues compellingly that this concept of primitive thought
played a key ideological role in legitimating the regressively paternalistic
attitude to colonial subjects which grounded much French foreign policy
in the nineteenth and early twentieth centuries.[4]

4. On the relation to Lévy-Bruhl see the quotation from Marcel Mauss that Lévi-Strauss
cites approvingly in Lévi-Strauss 1963, 96. On the relation to colonial paternalism see Lévi-
Strauss 1963, 1–3. Lévi-Strauss's criticism of his predecessors implicitly denies involvement of his own views in the politically loaded metaphysical and ideological prejudices he
locates in others. Yet his own position, specifically his erasure of any substantive difference between the thought of "primitives" and that of "civilized" people, also plays an ideological role, albeit within a colonial context different from that of his nineteenth- and
early-twentieth-century predecessors. In particular, his principle of equality between native and Western thought can be appropriated to legitimate economic practices that treat
colonial subjects as full participants in the "free market" for Western (and in particular
French) aids to civilization: "What makes a steel ax superior to a stone ax is not that the
first one is better than the second. They are equally well made, but steel is quite different
from stone. In the same way we may be able to show that the same logical processes operate in myth as in science, and that man has always been thinking equally well; the im-
provement lies, not in alleged progress in man's mind, but in the discovery of new areas to
which it may apply its unchanged and unchanging powers" (Lévi-Strauss 1979, 230). My
remarks here are not intended as a nostalgic gesture toward the paternalism of an earlier
period of colonization. Instead, I am making the point that the egalitarian spirit of Lévi-
Strauss's critique of the notion of "prelogical mentality" can also be turned to ideological
ends, namely, defending a regime of colonization no less exploitative than its paternalistic
predecessor.

In sum, the suggestion that the logical structure of the Oedipus myth is identical with the logic of the unconscious presents two problems for Lévi-Strauss. It contradicts his (politically important) principle of equivalence between mythological and scientific thought, and, by introducing subjective structures into myth analysis at a fundamental level, it violates the norm of objectivity in the social sciences.

Nevertheless, the suggestion has two major advantages. First, identifying mythic logic as the logic of the unconscious fills a central gap in Lévi-Strauss's account concerning the nature of mythological proof. Second, it explains the otherwise puzzling fact that the Oedipus myth continues to speak to us today, some two thousand years after Homer.[5] It explains this amazing continuity in terms of two features. First, according to Freud, the logic of the unconscious in terms of which the myth is structured has characterized human thought from the beginning. Second, what we may take as the "conclusion" of the myth, namely, the association between incest and monstrosity, continues to have force today in the form of stories about the unfortunate results of incestuous unions, rumors about isolated hill communities of "yellow eyes," and so on. At a rhetorical level, these "facts" continue to provide support for the equivalences upon which the myth's conclusion is based, despite the failure of the cosmological views that grounded them (including the fact that autochthony produces monsters).

Some of this support, it may be argued, arises from the scientifically proven claim that breeding from small gene pools results in a failure to dilute recessive strains. The air of authority and moral indignation surrounding objections to incest is characteristic of the realm of superstition rather than science, however, which in turn suggests that the objections' continuing power resides in their social function as vehicles for drawing boundaries around marginal practices or groups rather than in their scientific validity.[6] Freud, by contrast, would suggest that, along with the myth of Oedipus, these objections and the "facts" adduced to support them derive their authority by resonating with repressed knowledge that has been at the basis of all human existence from its beginning.

---

5. Of course, the Oedipus myth does not impact upon everyone equally. The Freudian account I am offering here also explains this waywardness. Whether an individual makes an associative connection between a particular cause and effect is highly dependent upon context. This is not only because causal beliefs (such as autochthony causing monsters) may vary from person to person within and between cultures, but also because a cause is not always associated with its effects. As Freud himself observes, on some occasions a cigar is "just a cigar."

6. Indeed, it may be argued that these facts legitimate science rather than the other way around.

The Proof

Lévi-Strauss detects four key relations in the Oedipus myth:

1. Overintimacy with blood relations
2. Failure to respect blood relations
3. The slaying of monsters
4. The persistence of monsters or monstrous attributes

Each relation is present in the myth as a bundle of instances. The first is manifested in the episodes of Cadmos risking Zeus's displeasure by seeking his ravished sister, Europa; Oedipus marrying his mother, Jocasta; and Antigone burying her twin brother, Polynices, despite the King's prohibition. The second relation is manifested in the episodes of the Spartoi killing one another; Oedipus killing his father, Laius; and Eteocles slaying his brother, Polynices. The third relation is manifested in the episodes of Cadmos killing the dragon and Oedipus killing the sphinx, while the fourth is manifested not by particular episodes in the myth but rather by the names of the actors: "Labdacos" (the name of Oedipus's grandfather) means "lame"; "Laius" (the name of Oedipus's father) means "left-sided"; and "Oedipus" means "swollen foot," and hence "lame" (a reference also embodied in the episode of Oedipus losing his sandal in accordance with the oracular prophecy). These relations in turn are divided into two oppositions: between the first relation and the second (Lévi-Strauss writes this opposition in abbreviated form as "1:2") and between the third and fourth relations (3:4).

According to Greek cosmology, monsters such as dragons, the Sphinx, the Spartoi, and so on are autochthones, that is, born of earth. Therefore, the persistence of monsters, the fourth relation, is an effect of autochthony. But, according to dream logic, effects stand in for, that is, are equivalent to, their causes. Thus the fourth relation is equivalent to autochthony. But autochthony, in turn, is definitionally equivalent to being born of one, which, in turn, is logically equivalent to being born of the same, since things which are the same are also one. In sum, the fourth relation is connected to being born of same by the following chain of equivalences:

persistence of monsters (4)↔born of one (autochthony)↔born of same

By using the same logic, it is easy to show that the first relation is similarly connected to being born of same. The first relation, excessive intimacy between close relatives, causes the birth of offspring from people with the same blood. Hence, since causes stand in for their effects, the first relation is equivalent to being born of two people with the same blood.

But since according to dream logic parts stand in for wholes, a person's blood stands for the person himself. It follows that two people of the same blood are themselves the same. Thus being born of the same blood is equivalent to being born of same. In sum:

overintimacy with blood relations (1)↔born of same blood↔born of same

From these two associative chains, whose links are forged by dream logic, we see that the first and fourth relations are both connected by strings of equivalences to being born of the same. Therefore the first and fourth relations must also be equivalent to each other. That is, 4↔1.[7]

And since opposites of equivalents must themselves be equivalent, the third key relation (which is opposed to the fourth) must be equivalent to the second (which is opposed to the first). That is, 3↔2

Since 4↔1 and 3↔2, it follows that 4:3↔1:2, that is, the opposition 4:3, between the persistence of monsters and their slaying, is equivalent to the opposition 1:2, between overvaluing and underrating blood kin.
Quod erat demonstrandum.

In sum, Freud's associative dream logic provides the inferential connections missing from but required by Lévi-Strauss's account of the Oedipus myth. In particular, dream logic underwrites various links in the chains of equivalences by which the oppositions 1:2 and 3:4 are proven equivalent. Note, however, that by bringing the four key relations into a common space where the associative chains are able to do their work of establishing the relevant equivalences, the narrative of the myth also plays an important role in the proof.

7. The assumption that such equivalences grounded in metonymic and synecdochic connections satisfy the law of transitivity is, of course, invalid from the point of view of formal Aristotelian logic. The logic at issue here is not Aristotelian, however, but rather Freud's dream logic, for which chains of metaphoric connections, however lengthy, entail equivalences between their beginning and end points. Thus Leach's reference to *Alice through the Looking Glass* is appropriate, although, in the light of his hostility to Freudian approaches, unintentionally so.

Bibliography

Althusser, Louis. 1971. *Lenin and Philosophy and Other Essays.* Translated by Ben Brewster. London: New Left Books.

——. 1982. *For Marx.* Translated by Ben Brewster. London: Verso.

Apter, Emily. 1993. "Introduction." In *Fetishism as Cultural Discourse,* edited by Emily Apter and William Pietz, 1–9. Ithaca: Cornell University Press.

Auerbach, Eric. 1968. *Mimesis: The Representation of Reality in Western Literature.* Translated by Willard Trask. Princeton: Princeton University Press.

Bacon, Francis. 1996. *Francis Bacon.* Edited by Brian Vickers. Oxford: Oxford University Press.

Baltrušaitis, Jurgis. 1976. *Anamorphic Art.* Translated by W. J. Strachan. Cambridge: Chadwyck-Healey.

Barthes, Roland. 1973. *Mythologies.* Translated by Annette Lavers. London: Paladin.

——. 1993. *Camera Lucida.* Translated by Richard Howard. London: Vintage.

Baudrillard, Jean. 1983. *Simulations.* Translated by Paul Foss, Paul Patton, and Philip Beitchman. New York: Semiotext(e).

Benjamin, Walter. 1973. *Charles Baudelaire: A Lyric Poet in the Era of High Capitalism.* Translated by Harold Zohn. London: New Left Books.

Berger, John. 1972. *Ways of Seeing.* London: Penguin Books.

Bhabha, Homi. 1994. *The Location of Culture.* London: Routledge.

Bourdieu, Pierre. 1996. *The Rules of Art: Genesis and Structure of the Literary Field.* Translated by Susan Emanuel. Cambridge: Polity Press.

Boyle, Robert. 1772. *The Works of the Honorable Robert Boyle.* 6 vol. Edited by Thomas Birch. London.

Brooks, Peter. 1993. *Body Work: Objects of Desire in Modern Narrative.* Cambridge: Harvard University Press.

Butler, Judith. 1997. *The Psychic Life of Power: Theories in Subjection*. Stanford: Stanford University Press.

Callinicos, Alex. 1989. *Against Postmodernism: A Marxist Critique*. Oxford: Polity Press.

Chaitin, Gilbert. 1996. *Rhetoric and Culture in Lacan*. Cambridge: Cambridge University Press.

Copjec, Joan. 1994. *Read My Desire*. Cambridge: MIT Press.

Cowie, Elizabeth. 1997. *Representing the Woman: Cinema and Psychoanalysis*. London: Macmillan.

Douglas, Mary. 1978. "The Meaning of Myth, with Special Reference to 'La Geste d'Asdiwal.'" In *The Structural Study of Myth and Totemism*, edited by Edmund Leach, 49–69. London: Tavistock.

Drucker, Johanna. 1994. *The Visible World: Experimental Typography and Modern Art, 1909–1923*. Chicago: University of Chicago Press.

Durkheim, Émile. 1915. *The Elementary Forms of Religious Life*. Translated by Joseph Ward Swain. London: George Allen and Unwin.

Eagleton, Terry. 1981. *Walter Benjamin or Towards a Revolutionary* Criticism. London: New Left Books.

Eliot, T. S. 1972. *Selected Essays*. London: Faber and Faber.

Evans, Dylan. 1996. *Dictionary of Lacanian Psychoanalysis*. London: Routledge.

Fiske, John. 1987. *Television Culture*. London: Routledge.

Flaubert, Gustave. 1992. *Madame Bovary: Provincial Lives*. Translated by Geoffrey Wall. London: Penguin Books.

Foister, Susan, Ashok Roy, and Martin Wyld. 1997. *Making and Meaning: Holbein's Ambassadors*. London: National Gallery Publications.

Foucault, Michel. 1987. *The History of Sexuality*, vol. 2, *The Use of Pleasure*. Translated by Robert Hurley. New York: Random House.

Freud, Sigmund. 1953–73. *The Standard Edition of the Complete Psychological Works of Sigmund Freud*. 24 vols. London: Hogarth.

——. 1965. *The Interpretation of Dreams*. Translated and edited by James Strachey. New York: Avon Books.

——. 1969. *An Outline of Psychoanalysis*. Translated and edited by James Strachey. London: Hogarth Press.

——. 1975. *Three Essays on the Theory of Sexuality*. Translated and edited by James Strachey. New York: Basic Books.

——. 1989. *Totem and Taboo: Some Points of Agreement between the Mental Lives of Savages and Neurotics*. Translated and edited by James Strachey. New York: Norton.

——. 1991. *Jokes and Their Relation to the Unconscious*. Translated by James Strachey. Edited by James Strachey and Angela Richards. London: Penguin.

——. 1993. *On Psychopathology: Inhibitions, Symptoms and Anxiety and Other Works*. Translated by James Strachey. Edited by James Strachey and Angela Richards. London: Penguin.

Gamman, Lorraine, and Merja Makinen. 1994. *Female Fetishism*. New York: New York University Press.

Goldman, Robert. 1992. *Reading Ads Socially* London: Routledge.

Hall, Marie Boas. 1966. *Robert Boyle on Natural Philosophy*. Bloomington: Indiana University Press.

Harrill, Paul. 1998. "Fly Films." *Blimp* 38:20–22.

Heald, Suzette, and Arlane Deluz. 1994. Introduction to *Anthropology and Psychoanalysis: An Encounter through Culture*, edited by Suzette Heald and Arlane Deluz, 1–26. London: Routledge.

Hill, Christopher. 1987. *The World Turned Upside Down*. London: Penguin.

Holland, Norman. 1989. *The Dynamics of Literary Response*. New York: Columbia University Press.

Jacobs, Harriet. 1987. *Incidents in the Life of a Slave Girl*. Edited by L. Maria Child and Jean Fagan Yellin. Cambridge: Harvard University Press.

Jameson, Fredric. 1981. *The Political Unconscious: Narrative as a Socially Symbolic Act*. Ithaca: Cornell University Press.

———. 1992. *Signatures of the Visible*. New York: Routledge.

Keenan, Thomas. 1993. "The Point Is to (Ex)Change It: Reading *Capital*, Rhetorically." In *Fetishism as Cultural Discourse*, edited by Emily Apter and William Pietz. Ithaca: Cornell University Press.

Kipnis, Laura. 1996. *Bound and Gagged*. New York: Grove Press.

Krips, Henry. 1994a. "Ideology, Rhetoric and Boyle's *New Experiments*." *Science in Context* 7:18–29.

———. 1994b. "Interpellation, Antagonism and Repetition." *Rethinking Marxism* 7:59–71.

———. 1996. "Fetish and the Native Subject." *Boundary 2* 24:74–89.

Lacan, Jacques. 1977. *Écrits: A Selection*. Translated by Alan Sheridan. New York: Tavistock.

———. 1981. *The Four Fundamental Concepts of Psychoanalysis*. Edited by Jacques-Alain Miller. Translated by Alan Sheridan. New York: Norton.

Laclau, Ernesto, and Chantal Mouffe. 1985. *Hegemony and Socialist Strategy: Towards a Radical Democratic Politics*. London: Verso.

Laplanche, J., and J.-B. Pontalis. 1974. *The Language of Psychoanalysis*. Translated by Donald Nicholson Smith. New York: Norton.

Leach, Edmund. 1982. *Lévi-Strauss*. London: Fontana.

Lévi-Strauss, Claude. 1963. *Totemism*. Translated by Rodney Needham. New York: Beacon.

———. 1978. "The Story of Asdiwal." In *The Structural Study of Myth and Totemism*, edited by Edmund Leach, 1–47. London: Tavistock.

———. 1979. *Structural Anthropology*. Translated by Clair Jacobson and Brooke Grunfest Schoepf. London: Penguin.

———. 1981. *The Naked Man: Introduction to a Science of Mythology, Volume 4*. Translated by John Weightman and Doreen Weightman. London: Jonathan Cape.

Lukacs, Georg. 1983. *History and Class Consciousness: Studies in Marxist Dialectics*. Translated by Rodney Livingstone. Cambridge: MIT Press.

Lukes, Steven. 1975. *Émile Durkheim: His Life and Work*. London: Penguin.

MacKinnon, Catherine A. 1993. *Only Words*. Cambridge: Harvard University Press.

Mannoni, Oscar. 1964. "Je sais bien, mais quand même . . . ," *Les Temps Modernes* 2:212–236.

Mitchell, W. J. T. 1994. *Picture Theory*. Chicago: University of Chicago Press.

Morrison, Toni. 1987. *Beloved*. London: Picador.

Mulvey, Laura. 1995. "Visual Pleasure and Narrative Cinema." *Screen* 16:6–18.

———. 1996. *Fetishism and Curiosity*. Bloomington: Indiana University Press.

Petty, Sir William. 1927. *The Petty Papers. Some Unpublished Papers of Sir William Petty. Edited from the Bowood Papers by the Marquis of Lansdowne*. 2 vols. London: Constable.

Pfaller, Robert. 1999. "Das Kunstwerk, das sich selbst betrachtet, der Genuss und die Abwesenheit. Elemente einer Äesthetik der Interpassivität." In *Interpassivität Studien über delegiertes Geniessen*, edited by R. Pfaller. New York: Springer Verlag.

Rose, Jacqueline. 1986. *Sexuality in the Field of Vision*. London: Verso.

Shadwell, Thomas. 1966. *The Virtuoso*. Edited by M. H. Nicholson and D. S. Rhodes. London: Edward Arnold.

Shapin, Steven. 1994. *A Social History of Truth*. Chicago: University of Chicago Press.

Shapin, Steven, and Simon Schaffer. 1985. *Leviathan and the Air-Pump*. Princeton: Princeton University Press.

Sharp, Geoff. 1985. "Constitutive Abstraction and Social Practice." *Arena* 70:48–82.

Silverman, Kaja. 1992. *Male Subjectivity at the Margins*. New York: Routledge.

———. 1996. The Threshold of the Visible World. New York: Routledge.

Spillers, Hortense. 1987. "Mama's Baby, Papa's Maybe: An American Grammar Book." *Diacritics* 17:65–81.

Sprat, Thomas. 1667. *The History of the Royal Society of London*. London.

Stewart, Susan. 1993. *On Longing: Narratives of the Miniature, the Gigantic, the Souvenir, the Collection*. Durham: Duke University Press.

Taussig, Michael. 1993. *Mimesis and Alterity: A Particular History of the Senses*. New York: Routledge.

Taylor-Guthrie, Danielle. 1994. *Conversations with Toni Morrison*. Jackson: University of Mississippi Press.

Todorov, Tzvetan. 1984. *Mikhail Bakhtin: The Dialogical Principle*. Translated by Wlad Godzich. Manchester: Manchester University Press.

Ward, Beatrice. 1955. *The Crystal Goblet: Sixteen Essays on Typography*. London: Sylvan.

Weber, Samuel. 1991. *Return to Freud: Jacques Lacan's Dislocation of Psychoanalysis*. Translated by Michael Levine. Cambridge: Cambridge University Press.

Westfall, R. S. 1990. *Never at Rest*. Cambridge: Cambridge University Press.

Williamson, Judith. 1978. *Decoding Advertisements: Ideology and Meaning in Advertising*. London: Marion Boyars.

Wilson, Derek. 1996. *Hans Holbein: Portrait of an Unknown Man*. London: Weidenfeld and Nicholson.

Žižek, Slavoj. 1989. *The Sublime Object of Ideology*. London: Verso.

———. 1991. *Looking Awry*. Cambridge: MIT Press.

———. 1996. "'I Hear You with My Eyes'; or, The Invisible Master." In *Gaze and Voice as Love Objects*, edited by Renata Salecl and Slavoj Žižek. Durham: Duke University Press.

Index

Abstraction, 4, 182
Advertisements/ads, 76, 79, 106, 167–170,
181
Althusser, Louis, x, 9, 65, 73–95, 98, 149
Ambassadors, The, 6, 11–12, 100, 108–112, 147
Antagonism, 87, 89, 95
Anxiety, 7, 9, 18, 45, 47–48, 61, 66, 90, 93,
102–103, 112–113, 117, 141–145, 173,
177, 182–183
Arcimboldo, Guiseppe, 113
Auerbach, Eric, 121, 123, 134

Bacon, Francis, 123–124, 126
Baltrusaitis, Jurgis, 109–110
Barthes, Roland, 10–12, 98, 140, 148
Beloved, 46, 51–56
Benjamin, Walter, 11
Berger, John, 109, 166
Bhabha, Homi, 2, 10, 45–47, 56, 57
Boyle, Robert, 119–131, 135, 139–141,
145–148
Breast, 19, 21, 25, 28, 104
Brooks, Peter, 134, 136–137
Butcher's wife, 22
Butler, Judith, 74, 85, 87–88, 90–95

Canned laughter, 153, 157–161
Capitalism, 112–113, 116, 148, 166

Castration, 7–8, 45, 182–183
Catachresis, 21, 37
Cathexis, 23–25, 142–143, 157, 181
Chaperone, 9, 23, 28–30
Commodity, 21, 111, 166–167
Conscience, 90–91
Consciousness, 36–37
false, 80, 82
Copjec, Joan, 36
Cowie, Elizabeth, 101n
Crash, 4, 171–183
Cronenberg, David. *See Crash*
Cyborg, 171, 181–182
Cynicism, 166–170

Deception, 15–19, 25–28, 58–59, 63, 66
Demand, 19, 52
Denial (*Verneinung*), 145
Desire, 5, 9–10, 15, 22–24, 27–29, 31, 45–56,
64, 66, 75, 88–89
object of, 9, 27, 69
object-cause of, 9, 22
Ding, Das (the Freudian Thing), 60, 138
Disavowal (*Verleugnung*), 7, 10, 29, 31,
45–46, 51, 60–68, 176, 178
Dora, 5
Dream, 36–39
burning child, 36–37, 40–41

Drive (*Trieb*), 25, 27–28, 40–41, 66, 89,
    159–161, 178
  invocatory drive, 38, 41, 161
  object of the drive, 27, 70
  oral drive, 28
  partial drive, 39
  scopic drive, 25–26, 63, 104, 107–108,
    160–161, 166, 173, 175, 181–183
Durkheim, Émile, 61, 65, 74, 188

Ego-ideal, 79, 91
Eronemos, 10, 69
Exhibitionism, 25, 27, 107, 173–175

Father, 6, 39–40, 92
Feminism, ix, 2, 4, 183
Fetish, x, 7–10, 29–30
Fetishism, 2–4, 23, 28–32, 45–70, 135–136,
    176–178, 181–182. *See also* Perversion
Film, 4, 10, 97–98, 180
Flaubert, Gustave, 137, 141, 144. *See also*
    Madame Bovary
Fort-Da, 15–23, 27, 30–31, 40, 63, 104
Foucault, Michel, 5, 69, 74, 87, 91–95, 98

Gap, 20, 30, 35, 39, 64, 74, 174, 181
Gaze, x, 3, 10–12, 26–28, 63–65,
    97–117, 133, 138, 140, 148, 160,
    174–175, 183
God(s), 58, 61–62, 77
Goldman, Robert, 166–170

Heaven's Gate cult, 1–2
Hellenic Greeks, 68–70, 185
Hitchcock, Alfred, 172–175, 180
Holbein, Hans, 101–108. *See also*
    Ambassadors, The
Hopi, 10, 57–64, 67–68
Humanism, 22, 81
  Renaissance, 115–116

Idea (*Vorstellung*), 23, 25, 80
Ideal-ego, 75, 91
Identification, 5–6, 105–106, 176–177
Identity, 36, 87, 181
Ideology, 3, 6, 73–95, 99, 103, 105–107,
    112–114, 116–117, 149, 166–170, 178,
    180, 182–183, 189
  Christian, 77–82
Illusionism, 122, 147
Imaginary, 78–81, 92–94, 98, 107
Incidents in the Life of a Slave Girl, 47–51
Initiation, 58–62

Instinctual wish, 141–143
Interpassivity, 153–154, 157, 161, 163, 174,
    182
Interpellation, ix, 9, 65, 73, 95, 98, 117, 149

Jameson, Fredric, 137, 164, 166, 171–173,
    178–181
Joke, 157, 163–164
  Cracow and Lemberg, 17
  Hitchcock, 172, 180
  Petit-Jean, 16, 102–103
  the unconscious and, 155–156

Katcina, 10, 57–64, 67
Kipnis, Laura, 6

Lack, 3, 7–10, 18–21, 28, 30–31, 40, 48, 61,
    68–70, 89–90, 103, 112, 116, 177
Law, 39–40, 86, 88, 91, 94–95, 99
Leach, Edmund, 187–188
Lévi-Strauss, Claude, 64–68, 109,
    185–192
Libido, 25, 38, 160
Little Hans, 40, 142–145
Lure, 25–28, 51, 63–64, 66, 67, 70

MacKinnon, Catherine, 2, 5–6
Madame Bovary, 6, 12, 135–139, 141–144,
    146–148
Mannoni, Oscar, 57–64
Marx, Karl, x, 3, 86, 111, 113, 149
Mask, 26–28, 57–64, 67
Masson, Jeffrey, 1–3, 5–6
Materialism, 77, 79–80
Memory, 24, 60, 63, 103, 140, 148
Metaphor, 20, 21, 27, 34, 61, 65, 104, 134
Mimesis, 121, 123, 134
Mirror, 3
  thesis, 76–77, 81, 84, 88
  stage, 78–79, 91, 98, 106–107
  See also Specular
Misrecognition (*méconnaissance*), 74, 89,
    98, 107, 167, 178
Mitchell, W. J. T., 122, 147
Modernism, 134, 171, 180
Modernization, 4, 182
Morrison, Toni. *See Beloved*
Mother/M(Other), 7–9, 12, 19–22, 28, 31,
    68–70, 89, 91, 104, 176
Mulvey, Laura, 2, 182–183
Mystery Science Theatre 3000 (MST3K),
    12, 155, 161–170, 177–178, 181–183
Myth, 62, 67–68, 185–192

Narcissism, 91–93
Need, 19, 22, 27, 38–40

Objet a, 9–10, 18, 20–31, 50–53, 61, 63, 67,
    89, 104–106, 160
Obsession, 143, 144, 173
Oedipal stage, 92, 144
Oedipus myth, 7, 68–70, 185–192
Ojibwa, 10, 64–68
Other (*le grand Autre*), 8, 17–18, 48, 75, 82,
    177

Panopticon, 98, 105
Parapraxis. *See* slip
Penis, 2–3, 7–8, 29–30, 176
Pepys, Samuel, 119, 127, 131
Perversion, fetishism distinct from, 29n.
    See also Fetishism
Petit-Jean, 11, 102
Pfaller, Robert, 153
Phallus, 8–9, 177
Phantasy, 2, 8, 23, 142, 176–177
Photograph, 10–11, 148
Pleasure, 9–20, 22–28, 32, 38–39, 51, 87, 89,
    103, 107–108, 148, 157, 167, 173
Politics of the image, 98–99
Pornography, 3, 5–6
Postmodernism, 81, 154, 167, 171–173, 180,
    183
Poststructuralism, ix, 99
Primal scene, 9, 48, 103, 112–113, 116
Punctum, 10–11, 140, 146, 148

Real (*le Réel*), 37, 87, 93, 99, 101–102, 106,
    117
Realism, 109, 122–123, 134, 141, 144,
    146–148, 176, 178, 181
    Bazinian, 181
    Hollywood (or domestic), 4, 164–167,
        182
    hyper-, 110, 180
    subversive, 178–181
    See also Illusionism; Mimesis
Rear Window, 172–176
Religion, 4, 58, 126
Repetition (*Wiederholung*), 7, 9, 20, 89–90,
    95–103, 112, 144
Repression (*Verdrängung*), 7, 22–23, 30,
    39, 40, 60–62, 89, 142–143, 156, 177,
    181
Rhetoric, 122–124, 128–131, 140, 144, 147,
    168, 178
Rose, Jaqueline, 93, 97n

Sacred, 59, 68
Sardine can, 11, 100
Sartre, Jean-Paul, 65
Schaffer, Simon, 121, 128, 139
Science, 82–85, 124–127, 131, 144, 188
Screen theory, ix, 3, 10, 73, 78, 81, 92–95,
    97–100, 105–108
Sex, 4–5, 186–187
    the drive and, 38, 39
    the unconscious and, 33, 38–41
Shapin, Steve, 121–122, 124, 128, 139
Sharp, Geoff, 4, 182
Signifier, 8, 16–18, 20, 24, 34, 58, 98–99,
    154, 180
Silverman, Kaja, 98–100, 105
Simulacrum, 110–112, 148
Slave, 10, 45–56
    literature, 2, 46
    master-, 3, 46
Slip (Freudian), 23, 29, 34, 60
Specular, 76, 82, 105–106. *See also* Mirror
Speech, 16–18, 33–35, 37–38
Spillers, Hortense, 48–51
Splitting, 34–35, 38–39, 41, 46, 70, 90,
    175–178
Stereotypes, 3, 5, 45–46
Structuralism, ix, 33, 67
Subject, ix, 8–9, 35, 39–40, 64, 74–95,
    98–100
    the big, 76–78, 80, 88
    of *enoncé*, 34–35, 39, 41
    of *enonciation*, 34–35, 39, 41
Symbolic, 37–38, 58, 91–94, 99, 107, 112,
    174
Symptom, 1–5, 29, 34, 142–144, 176–177,
    181

Taleyseva, 57–64
Taussig, Michael, 58–59
Totem, 10, 64–68
    guardian spirit distinct from, 65n, 66
Trauma, 19, 24, 48, 62
Truth, 11, 17, 59, 81
Trompe l'oeil, 26–28, 110, 159, 165–166,
    177

Unconscious, 23, 38–41, 90, 158, 190
    structured like a language, 33–38
Unconscious associations, 3, 104, 106–107,
    113
Unconscious desire/wish, 18, 23, 142,
    145–146

Virtual witness, 121, 128, 130–131, 139
Vision as abstract category, 4, 182
Voice, 38, 160
Vorstellungsrepräsentanz, 16, 18, 20, 40–41, 58
Voyeurism, 25, 27, 65, 107, 173–175, 177, 180–181

Williamson, Judith, 78, 169

Zeuxis and Parrhasios, 26
Žižek, Slavoj, 111, 153, 159, 167